Sid Meier's
CIVILIZATION® II

The Official
Strategy Guide

NOW AVAILABLE FROM PRIMA

How to Order:

Sid Meier's
CIVILIZATION II

The Official
Strategy Guide

David Ellis

PRIMA PUBLISHING

Project Editor: Dallas Middaugh

ISBN: 0-7615-0106-1
Library of Congress Catalog Card Number: 95-68601

Printed in the United States of America
96 97 98 BB 10 9 8 7 6

CONTENTS

Contents

Contents

FOREWORD

"Our job is to make sure a person is having as much fun as possible." I said that in an interview about the original *Civilization,* way back in 1992. Since then, Civ has gone way past anything we expected—and it's all your fault. You bought it in ridiculous numbers. You gave it awards. You recommended it to all your friends. Best of all, you've continued to play it and have fun with it—but some of you weren't having as much fun as possible.

Every day for four years now, MicroProse has gotten suggestions from Civ players on how to make the game better. It doesn't bother me, because nobody's calling up to say, "Your game is no fun, so fix it!" They're saying, "This game is great! Here's a way to make it even better!" Of course, I wanted to design some new games. So we put Civ on the shelf for a while, but you wouldn't let up. You kept playing and playing and sending in suggestions. It was wonderful.

Finally, we couldn't stand it anymore. Here were all the people who made *Civilization* the phenomenon it is asking for more. How could I say no? Brian, Doug, Jeff, and I put our heads together, and the result is *Civilization II.* We tried to incorporate all of the reasonable suggestions we received *and* throw in a few ideas from our own thousands of hours of playing time. Now it's as much fun as possible.

Of course, if it turns out you still want more . . .

Sid Meier

Sid Meier

ACKNOWLEDGMENTS

*B*ecause *Civilization II* is one of those games where no two people can agree on one definitive strategy for success, it would be impossible to write a strategy guide for the game based on my perspective alone. So, I want to take just a little extra space to thank all those folks who took time out of their busy schedules to provide help and insight when I needed it.

Thanks to the people at MicroProse who provided some of the best strategies and hints in the book, especially Doug Kaufman and James King who gave me several pages of ideas (many of which I had never even considered!). Also, thanks to Mick Uhl and the members of MicroProse Q.A. for their input and suggestions, and to the lunch crew (you know who you are). Also, thanks to John Possidente (my de facto agent at MicroProse and fellow caffeine addict) who is always a great help in any of my writing projects.

The biggest thanks at MicroProse goes to Brian Reynolds, designer and programmer extraordinaire, who was always more than willing to put up with long discussions of game mechanics and formulae—even though he was still in the midst of writing the game. Brian, your patience was much appreciated. I hope this book is worthy of your excellent game.

I also want to thank Dallas Middaugh and the other folks at Prima for giving me yet another opportunity to work with them.

Finally, as always, thanks to Meghan, my wife. This time around she provided not only her patience and encouragement, but her ample *Civilization* insight as well. I couldn't do it without you.

Dave Ellis
December 27, 1995

I
CIVILIZATION II VERSUS CIVILIZATION: WHAT'S NEW

*I*n 1992, Sid Meier and MicroProse Software brought us a little game called *Civilization*. It was a game simple in execution but broad in scope. Within the technological confines of less than one megabyte of disk space, *Civilization* managed to convey the challenges and triumphs experienced over the last five thousand years of human evolution.

At first, there had been doubts as to how the gaming public would take to Sid's creation. Both Sid and *Civilization* co-creator, Bruce Shelley, were (and still are) history buffs, so of course the advance of mankind throughout the ages was interesting to them. But some members of the MircoProse management team at the time didn't quite "get" how this game could be fun. They feared that the broad concept of a game like *Civilization* would have a hard time finding a following in the general public. These fears, however, started to ebb as soon as the game went into play-testing. The testers were almost instantly hooked, and they were convinced that the public would be as well.

They were right. *Civilization* quickly became one of the most popular computer games on the market. Following the successful DOS version, the game was developed for the Amiga. After a couple of years, a Macintosh version—with updated, 256-color graphics—was released, and this Macintosh version was soon followed by a Windows version. Then, finally, after years of customer requests, a multiplayer version of *Civilization*, entitled *CivNet*, was released in November of 1995. Through all of these many versions, *Civilization* maintained its status as one of the most popular computer strategy games of all time.

And, as with so many good games, the next logical step was to create a sequel . . .

Welcome to *Civilization II*

After working with Sid Meier to create *Colonization* in 1994, designer and programmer Brian Reynolds went to work to create a follow-up to *Civilization*. Most gamers expected that the next *Civilization* product would begin on Alpha Centauri and that it would chronicle the evolution of the colonists sent there at the end of the original game. Brian, however, decided to go back to the original design and update it. In doing so, he created a richer, more detailed game, while avoiding the kind of complexity that would alienate new players.

Of course, in order to make the game interesting to veteran *Civilization* players, as well as newcomers too, a number of changes were made along the way. The next few sections give an overview of these changes and the new features added to the game.

The Object of the Game

The ultimate goal in *Civilization II* is the same as in its predecessors. You must develop your civilization more quickly and efficiently than those of your opponents, and you must do this through a combination of exploration, research, and the proper planning and development of cities. Along the way, you must effectively deal with neighboring civilizations, using either peaceful agreements or superior firepower to ensure your successes.

Three final situations result in victory. Two of these victory scenarios are absolute victories; the other is strictly a moral victory. The conditions of absolute victory are:

- ❖ **Victory through conquest,** in which you take over the entire world by destroying all of your opponents in battle.

and

- ❖ **Victory through technological achievement,** in which you are the first civilization to research, construct, and launch a spaceship that successfully builds a colony on Alpha Centauri.

The third victory condition is something that many *Civilization* players fail to regard as victory. If your civilization survives until the game is over (the year when you are automatically retired as ruler), this represents a victory of sorts. Certainly, this sort of victory isn't nearly as fulfilling or satisfying as either of the total victory scenarios, but think of what you have accomplished just by surviving! The fact that you have lasted so long means that you have managed to maintain the balance of power in the world without getting destroyed in the process and that you have kept your population content. This is really quite an achievement, especially at the higher difficulty levels.

Graphics and Interface Changes

One of the first things players who are familiar with *Civilization* will notice about *Civilization II* is the new look of the game. *Civilization II* utilizes what is known as a three-quarter perspective, rather than the two-dimensional view used in the earlier game (see Figure 1-1). As a result, the map takes on more of a three-dimensional look, and features of the terrain and cities stand out clearly. The overall look creates a more vivid experience, drawing you into the game with it's realism.

The unit icons have also taken on a new look. Rather than being simple, square counters, the *Civilization II* unit icons are now more detailed and better suited to the new three-dimensional look of the game. On the old-style icons, the controlling civilization was indicated by the icon's background color. Now

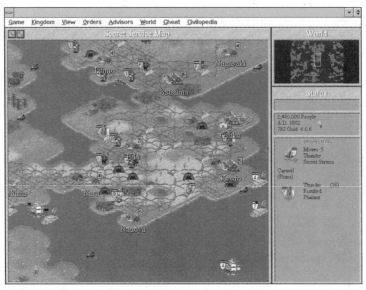

Figure 1-1 *The new look of* Civilization II.

however, ownership of *Civilization II* icons is indicated by a colored shield above the unit's picture (see Figure 1-2). The look of some of the new icons may take some getting used to, but most of them are either similar to the icons in the original game, or they are easily recognizable as to their function.

While the look of the game has changed significantly, the control interface has remained the same as that found in the Macintosh and Windows versions of *Civilization*. Units can be moved in any of eight directions by using the directional keys on your keyboard's numeric keypad (the 1, 2, 3, 4, 6, 7, 8, and 9 keys). You can also move units with the mouse, as described in the game manual, but using the keyboard for movement tends to be the better choice for more precise control.

Figure 1-2 *Example of a* Civilization II *unit icon.*

Chapter I: Civilization II vs. Civilization: What's New

Tip: The new three-quarter map view can be very confusing to players who are used to the two-dimensional map in *Civilization*. The terrain is still divided into individual squares just as it was in the earlier games, but until you get used to the new look of the game, it is very difficult to judge which terrain square a unit occupies. It might also be difficult for players to get the hang of using the keyboard directional keys for movement; the diagonal perspective makes it hard to tell which key should be pressed to move a unit in the direction you want it to move. This is illustrated in Figure 1-3, which shows a comparison of two-dimensional and three-dimensional movement using the keyboard controls. Note that movement directions have been shifted 45 degrees as a result of the new map perspective.

The easiest way to prevent incorrect moves and to get used to the new feel of the map is to turn on the map grid. This feature, activated by choosing "Show Map Grid" from the View menu (or by holding down the CTRL key and pressing G), superimposes a square grid over the map (see Figure 1-4). The grid clearly defines the Terrain squares, making it is easy to tell which square your unit currently occupies. The grid is also helpful for determining the extent of a city's City Radius (which is described in detail in Chapter 2).

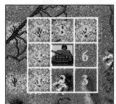

Figure 1-3 A comparison of movement between Civilization (left) *and* Civilization II (right).

Figure 1-4 Playing with the Map Grid option active.

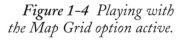

5

Updated Research Paths and New *Civilization* Advances

In *Civilization II*, just as in the original game, the research and acquisition of new technologies is vital to the survival and growth of your civilization. Almost every *Civilization* Advance that was in *Civilization* can still be found in *Civilization II*. In addition, 22 new Advances have been included, as shown in Table 1-1.

Advances were added to the game specifically to allow the construction of new Units, Improvements, and Wonders of the World. Some prerequisites for starting the research that leads to the acquisition of Advances have also been changed from the original game, and attempts were made to eliminate "dead end" research paths by adding benefits to Advances that formerly served little purpose. A complete discussion of *Civilization* Advances, research paths, and research strategies can be found in Chapter 6.

❖ **Table 1-1.** The New *Civilization* Advances

Amphibious Warfare	Combined Arms
Economics	Environmentalism
Espionage	Fundamentalism
Guerrilla Warfare	The Laser
Leadership	Machine Tools
Miniaturization	Mobile Warfare
Monotheism	Polytheism
Radio	Refrigeration
Seafaring	Sanitation
Stealth	Tactics
Theology	Warrior Code

Unit Updates and Additions

Many of the familiar units from the original game have been altered slightly or updated in *Civilization II*. These changes and updates generally increase the effectiveness of the units over their earlier counterparts. Details concerning all unit types can be found in Chapter 8.

In addition to the alteration of existing units, there are 23 brand-new units created specifically for the new game. These units are listed in Table 1-2.

✤ **Table 1-2.** The New Units in *Civilization II*

AEGIS Cruiser	Alpine Troops
Archers	Cruise Missile
Crusaders	Destroyer
Dragoons	Elephant
Engineers	Explorer
Fanatics	Freight
Galleon	Helicopter
Horsemen*	Howitzer**
Marines	Paratrooper
Partisans	Pikemen
Spy	Stealth Fighter
	Stealth Bomber

*The Horseman unit is the same as the Cavalry unit in *Civilization*. Cavalry units have been significantly upgraded in *Civilization II*.

**The Howitzer unit is similar to the Artillery unit in *Civilization*. The characteristics of *Civilization II*'s Artillery have been reworked from those in the original game.

New City Improvements

Civilization II also adds 14 new City Improvements, as shown in Table 1-3.

In addition to the new Improvements added to the game, many of the Improvements carried over from the original game have experienced changes in their function and cost. Complete descriptions of all the new City Improvements, and information regarding changes of old Improvements, can be found in Chapter 7.

New Wonders of the World

In keeping with the additions to other parts of the game, seven new Wonders of the World have been added to *Civilization II*. The new Wonders are listed in Table 1-4.

The addition of the seven new Wonders has caused a change in the time-period classification of the Wonders of the World. Instead of dividing them into three time periods (Antiquity, Middle Ages, and Modern Age), the Wonders are now split into four time periods: Ancient, Renaissance, Industrial, and Modern Age.

Several of the 21 Wonders carried over from *Civilization* have also been altered as to their function and expiration date. Effects once produced by certain original Wonders have been transferred to new Wonders in some cases and eliminated completely in others. The new Wonders, in turn, offer new and often powerful effects never before available. (For complete details on the effects of the Wonders of the World, see Chapter 7.)

Production Bonuses and Penalties

The production of units, Improvements, and Wonders of the World in *Civilization II* takes place in the same way as it did in *Civilization*. However, certain penalties and bonuses now apply. On all difficulty levels except for Chief, there is a penalty for switching the type of item being produced in a city in mid-production. On the other hand, there is a shield bonus accrued for disbanding a unit while it is inside one of your cities.

✤ **Table 1-3.** The New City Improvements

Airport	Capitalization
Coastal Fortress	Harbor
Offshore Platform	Police Station
Port Facility	Research Lab
SAM Missile Battery	Sewer System
Solar Plant	Stock Exchange
Supermarket	Superhighways

✤ **Table 1-4.** New Wonders of the World

Adam Smith's Trading Company
The Eiffel Tower
King Richard's Crusade
Leonardo's Workshop
Marco Polo's Embassy
The Statue of Liberty
Sun Tzu's War Academy

The New Combat System

One of the biggest frustrations expressed by players of the original *Civilization* was the resolution of combat between units. In the original game, combat was an all-or-nothing proposition: the winner's unit survived the battle unscathed, and the loser's unit was destroyed and removed from the game. This was especially frustrating when a clearly superior unit, like a Battleship, was destroyed when it attacked a simple Frigate.

    Civilization II improves the combat system of the game by adding two new factors to combat: Hit Points and Firepower. A unit's Hit Points determine the amount of damage it can take before it is destroyed. Firepower indicates the number of Hit Points of damage a unit inflicts in a successful attack. (The new combat system is discussed in detail in Chapter 8.)

Changes in Diplomacy

When you encountered another tribe in *Civilization*, you had the opportunity to participate in one of, or a combination of, the following:

- ✤ The exchange of *Civilization* Advances
- ✤ Bribing your neighbor or being paid off by them
- ✤ Signing peace treaties; or declaring war

These options are also available in *Civilization II*; however, there are now many more choices and decisions to be made when it comes to dealing with your neighbors. Among the new choices available during a negotiation are:

- ✤ Demanding the withdrawal of an opponent's units from your territory
- ✤ Signing a cease-fire agreement without actually declaring peace, and
- ✤ Entering an alliance

The artificial intelligence (or A.I.) has also been updated and modified with regards to negotiations and treaties. Your opponents in *Civilization II* remember your past transgressions and hold them against you. For example, if you are in the habit of making treaties with your neighbors and then attacking them when their guard is down, other leaders are less likely to enter a peace agreement with you. As a general rule, if you stick to your agreements, you are treated better by your opponents. For a complete discussion of diplomacy and interaction with other civilizations, see Chapter 9.

New Systems of Government

All of the systems of government available in *Civilization* are also available in *Civilization II*. However, the effects of the various government types are have been significantly updated and/or altered. Part of the reason for these changes is to make some of the earlier forms of government (Monarchy, for example) more appealing. In the original game, many players remained in Despotism until, through research of Wonders of the World, they could switch directly to Republic or Democracy. While such a jump in fundamental governing values is unlikely in a real-world situation, it was a perfectly viable possibility within the game. Under the new game system, a more logical progression in government is encouraged with changes in the benefits and penalties associated with the various types of government and Wonders.

Also, your choice of government now affects more aspects of the game than production and population happiness. The type of government in power now affects how you can divide your incoming Trade between Science, Taxes, and Luxuries. Early forms of government such as Despotism and Monarchy no longer allow you to dedicate one hundred percent of your Trade to scientific research. This factor alone can significantly affect the early game strategies of many veteran players.

In addition to changing the characteristics of the existing six governments, *Civilization II* adds a seventh system: Fundamentalism. Fundamentalism is a radical form of government that encourages the build up of military force at the expense of scientific advancement. For a complete description of the effects and conditions imposed by each system of government, see Chapter 9.

Changes in Trade

Whereas the value of a trade route in *Civilization* was based entirely on the trade produced by the source and destination city and the distance between the two cities, the new trade system is based on supply and demand; each city produces certain raw materials and finished goods that can be traded to cities requiring one or more of these items. Trade routes that are advantageous to the destination city generate more Trade than those established with cities not requiring the goods offered. Trade routes are discussed in detail in Chapter 9.

New Rules for Movement

Although most aspects of movement, including terrain effects, have remained the same as in *Civilization*, a few additions have been made. Some of the new units in *Civilization II* are able to treat all terrain types as roads, meaning they use only one-third of a movement point to travel in any type of terrain. Similarly, any unit moving along a River uses only one-third of a movement point per square moved. Movement bonuses and restrictions are discussed in Chapters 4 and 8, under the sections involving Terrain types and unit descriptions respectively.

General Changes in the A.I.

The artificial intelligence, the rules governing the actions and reactions of computer-controlled civilizations, has been updated and refined for *Civilization II*. Aside from the changes described under Diplomacy and Interaction earlier in this chapter, certain aspects of your opponents' behavior are significantly different than in the original game.

For example, in *Civilization*, Wonders of the World were "given" to computer players. Now, however, your opponents are forced to construct their Wonders just as you do. Computer opponents also have full command of all government types (based on their level of technology, of course). In the original game, computer civilizations never switched to Democracy, giving the human player a slight edge. This is no longer the case.

Additionally, computer players now make full use of their available technology with regards to the production and use of weapons. Nuclear attacks by computer civilizations are much more common than they once were. Another factor that has been enhanced, too, is the computer player's ability to bribe and subvert units and cities. This sort of event, which rarely took place in the original game, can become commonplace in *Civilization II*. More complete descriptions of common computer decisions and strategies concerning specific aspects of the game can be found in the appropriate chapters throughout this book.

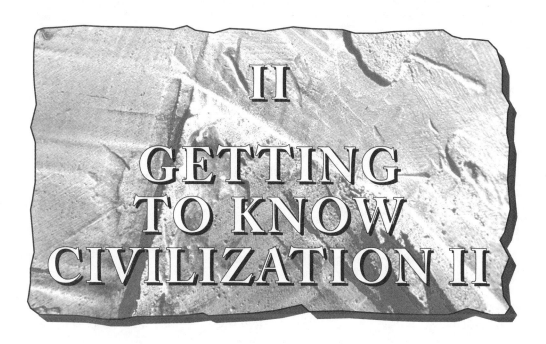

II
GETTING TO KNOW CIVILIZATION II

A Brief Tour of the Game and its Concepts

*A*lthough many readers of this book have played the original *Civilization* in one of its many incarnations, it is unfair to assume that everyone has. There are references to certain game screens, icons, and concepts throughout the book that must be understood in order to comprehend the information and advice presented.

The purpose of this chapter is to allow those unfamiliar with the game to get accustomed to the screens and terminology used in the following chapters. If you are a *Civilization* veteran, you may want to skip ahead to the next chapter. For those of you who are new to the game, this chapter should bring you up to speed and prepare you for the rest of the book.

The Main Screen

When you start the game, the first view that greets you is the Main Screen. The Main Screen is the view from which most of the game is played. It consists of three separate windows: the Map Window, the World Map, and the Status Window. Although the size and arrangement of the three windows can be altered to suit personal taste, the default arrangement is the one shown in Figure 2-1.

The function of each section of the Main Screen is described in the following sections.

THE MAP WINDOW

The Map Window is the large window that dominates most of the Main Screen display (see Figure 2-2). This window shows a close-up view of one section of the game world. It is here that you can examine the Terrain, control the actions and movement of your units, and observe the movements and cities of rival civilizations.

Figure 2-1 The Main Screen

As described in the game manual, the view displayed in the Map Window can be zoomed in for a more detailed view of one section of the map or zoomed out to provide a wider view of the world. You can also open additional Map Windows if you want to view several areas simultaneously. Sections of the world which have not been explored by your civilization appear as areas of black. These areas are revealed as you move units into them.

Figure 2-2 The Map Window

When a unit becomes active, the Map Window automatically centers on that unit. The Map Window also automatically centers on cities when some activity takes place there (the construction of a unit, Improvement, or Wonder; civil disorder; Food shortages; etc.). During the computer's turn, the Map Window continually re-centers itself on the activities of rival civilizations within the parts of the world you have explored. The Map Window can also be re-centered manually by clicking anywhere within the window or by clicking on any section of the Window Map.

THE WORLD MAP

In the default arrangement of the Main Screen, the World Map appears in the upper-right corner. This window, generally the smallest of the three, displays a miniature view of the entire game world (see Figure 2-3).

Figure 2-3 The World Map

Sections of the world that you have explored appear as green (land) or blue (water) areas on the World Map. Black areas represent sections of the world you have not yet visited. Inside the window is a small square. The area inside this square represents the portion of the world currently displayed in the Map Window. The square moves and changes size to match the movements and zoom changes of the Map Window. You can re-center the view in both windows by clicking anywhere in the World Map. This is the easiest and fastest way to re-center the Map Window on a distant section of the world.

THE STATUS WINDOW

The last of the three windows that compose the Main Screen is the Status Window (see Figure 2-4). In the default window arrangement, the Status Window appears directly below the Window Map.

The Status Window conveys a great deal of information about the overall status of the game as a whole, as well as the status of individual units. The window is actually composed of three separate sections, each of which gives information on a different aspect of the game.

Figure 2-4 The Status Window

The Status Report Section

The largest portion of the Status Window is the Status Report Section. This portion of the Status Window includes information on several vital aspects of your civilization (see Figure 2-5).

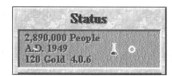

The following information is shown in the Status Report (from top to bottom):

Figure 2-5 The Status Report Section of the Status Window

- ♣ **Population**—Your civilization's current population
- ♣ **Date**—The current game date, preceded by BC or AD (example: BC 3200)
- ♣ **Treasury**—The amount of money currently in your treasury

Next to the treasury report are three numbers separated by periods. These numbers indicate the division of Trade between Taxes, Luxuries, and Science. For example, if the numbers read "3.1.6", this indicates that 30% of your Trade is being converted to Taxes, 10% is being used to generate Luxuries, and 60% is being used for Science. This division can be changed by selecting the Tax Rate option from the Kingdom menu. (Trade is discussed in detail in Chapter 4.)

In addition to text information, the Status Report is also home to two indicators: a research indicator and a "sun" indicator. These are icons which are interpreted as follows:

The Science icon in the Status Report indicates your scientists' progress toward the discovery of a new Civilization Advance. When research on a new topic is begun, the beeker is blue. As progress is made toward discovery, the Science icon gets progressively brighter, and turns bright yellow on the turn when the Advance is finally discovered. This cycle repeats for every Civilization Advance throughout the game. (The research of Civilization Advances is discussed fully in Chapter 6.)

The second icon, which represents the sun, indicates the current danger of global warming. This indicator doesn't appear until pollution is present somewhere in the world. When it first appears, the indicator is dark brown. As the number of polluted squares in the world increases, the icon gets progressively lighter. This continues until worldwide pollution reaches critical levels and global warming occurs. At this point, the indicator once again goes dark, and the cycle begins again until the pollution problem is addressed. (The subjects of pollution and global warming are discussed in Chapter 5.)

Also found in the Status Report section is the Peace Bar. This white line indicates how long a state of peace has existed amongst all the nations of the world. The more turns that pass with no battles taking place, not just between your civilization and its neighbors but between all the civilizations of the world, the longer the Peace Bar grows. Although it doesn't specifically show how many turns or years the state of peace has existed, the length of the Peace Bar gives you a general idea of how things are going.

The Units Section

The bottom section of the Status Window is known as the Units Section. This portion of the window monitors the progress of each of your units during their turn and the actions of rival units during the computer's turn (see Figure 2-6).

When a unit is active, its icon appears in the upper left. To the right of the icon, the following information is listed:

- ❧ The top line lists the number of movement points the unit has available in the current turn.

- ❧ The next line shows the name of the unit's home city.

- ❧ Below the unit's home city is the unit's nationality (the name of the civilization to whom the unit belongs).

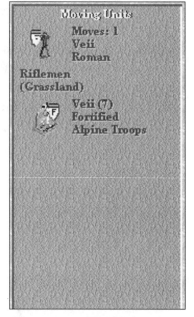

Figure 2-6 The Units Section of the Status Window

Below the unit icon, several other pieces of data are presented:

- ❧ Directly below the icon is the name of the active unit. If the unit has achieved Veteran status, this is indicated to the right of the unit name.

- ❧ Below the unit name is the type of Terrain the unit currently occupies.

- ❧ If there are any Special Resources—such as Buffalo, Silk, or Gold—in the Terrain square the unit currently occupies, this is indicated below the Terrain type.

- ❧ If there are any Terrain improvements—such as roads, irrigation, or mines—in the Terrain square the unit currently occupies, this is indicated below the Special Resources indicator. (If there are no Special Resources, the terrain improvements appear directly below the Terrain type.)

The area below this information displays a number of different things depending on the situation. If any other units occupy the same Terrain square as the active

Note: The number of movement points remaining may appear odd in certain circumstances. For instance, if the unit is moving along a road or a River, or has moved through such Terrain at any time during its turn, the number of movement points remaining might be a fraction. A unit with two movement points per turn that has, for example, moved across one Grassland square (one movement point) and two road squares (two-thirds of a movement point) would have a remaining movement of 0 1/3 listed in the Units Section of the Status Window. This indicates that the unit has one third of a movement point remaining in the current turn.

Air units that must return to a friendly carrier, base, or city at the end of their second turn, such as Bombers and Stealth Bombers, use a different notation for remaining movement. For example, at the start of its first turn of movement, the moves remaining for a Bomber reads 8 (16). The number outside the parentheses indicates the number of movement points available in the current turn. The number inside the parentheses indicates the number of movement points remaining until the unit must return to a friendly carrier, base, or city.

unit, their icons are displayed along with their nationality, current status (fortified, sentry, etc.), the unit type, and Veteran status (if applicable).

If the currently active unit is a ship that is transporting ground or air units, the information concerning the units being transported appears in the area below the active unit information. If there are too many units to fit in the Units Section, a notation appears at the bottom of the window indicating the number of units that could not be displayed. To see the hidden units, click inside the Units Section of the window. If there are still units that do not fit inside the display, you must expand the window to see all the units.

At the bottom of the Units Section is the end of turn indicator. This flashes when all your units have been moved or have been given orders and it is time to begin the next turn.

The City Display

The other screen where you spend a great deal of time is the City Display (see Figure 2-7). This screen shows you detailed information concerning a city's population and production, and the status of units supported by the city. The City Display is accessed by clicking on a city in the Map Window. Each city has its own City Display.

The City Display is divided into a several different sections, each of which presents you with information specific to a particular aspect of the city's operation. Each portion of the display is described in the following sections.

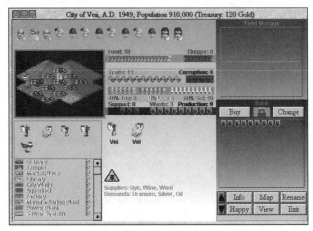

Figure 2-7 The City Display

THE TITLE BAR

The title bar at the top of the City Display window provides several pieces of general information. From left to right, it lists the name of the city, the current game date, the city's population, and the amount of money currently available in your treasury.

THE POPULATION ROSTER

In the upper left portion of the City Display, just below the title bar, is a box containing citizen icons. This is the Population Roster (see Figure 2-8). Each represents part of the city's population. The number of citizen icons in the Population Roster is equal to the size number appearing beside the city in the Map Window.

These icons also represent members of the city's production force: the people who work the land surrounding the city to produce Food, Shields (raw materials), and Trade. Each citizen icon, with the exception of Specialists (explained later in this section), works one Terrain square within the City

Figure 2-8 The Population Roster

Radius. The City Radius is shown in the Resource Map, which is described later in this chapter.

The citizen icons in the Population Roster serve as an indicator of the mood of the city's inhabitants as well. Your citizens can be happy, content, or unhappy. Happy citizens appear at the left end of the line of the Population Roster. Content citizens appear to the right of the happy citizens. Unhappy citizens appear to the right of the content citizens. When unhappy citizens outnumber happy citizens, the city enters a state of Civil Disorder. (Population happiness and Civil disorder are described in detail in Chapter 5.)

Citizens can, in time of need, be removed from their production roles on the Resource Map and assigned to perform other tasks to benefit the city. These citizens are known as Specialists. Specialists come in three varieties: Entertainers, Tax Men, and Scientists. Specialists appear to the right of the other citizen icons, slightly removed from the others. Each type of Specialist serves a different purpose. (The various Specialists are described in detail in Chapters 5 and 6.)

THE RESOURCE MAP

Just below the Population Roster on the left side of the City Display is the Resource Map. This shows a small section of the Map Window, centered on the city whose display is active. (See Figure 2-9).

The Resource Map shows the territory that can be developed by the city. This area, known as the City Radius, consists of 21 Terrain squares, including the center square which is occupied by the city itself (see Figure 2-10). Each of the Terrain squares within

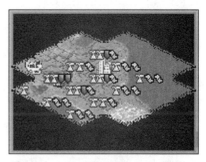

Figure 2-9 The Resource Map

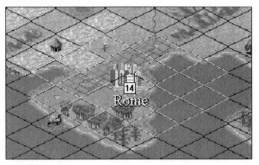

Figure 2-10   Diagram Illustrating the City Radius

the City Radius is known as a production square.

Production symbols for Food, Shields, and Trade appear on the squares where citizens are working the land. As new citizens are added to the Population Roster, they are automatically put to work in one of the squares on the Resource Map. If the need arises, citizens can be moved from one production square to another to produce different types of resources. Citizens can also be removed from production entirely and converted into Specialists.

THE RESOURCES CHART

In the center of the City Display are several lines of information concerning the various resources generated by the city. This section of the display is known as the Resources Chart (see Figure 2-11). The Resources Chart shows a detailed breakdown of incoming resources and how they are being distributed and utilized.

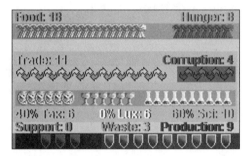

Figure 2-11   The Resources Chart

The Resources Chart consists of four sections, each corresponding to a single resource type. (All resource types are explained in full in Chapter 4.)

The Food Chart

The top line of the Resources Chart shows the amount of Food being produced by the city. The Food line is divided into two sections. The left section shows the amount of Food that is consumed by the city's population each turn. This is shown as a row of food icons. For clarity the amount of Food produced is also displayed as a number above the icons. Each person in the Population Roster requires two units of Food per turn in order to survive.

Any Food produced in excess of the amount needed to support the city's population is displayed in the right section of the Food Chart, as both a row of icons and a number. If the city is producing insufficient Food to support its population, the amount of the Food deficit is displayed in the right portion of the Food Chart in place of the surplus display. A Food deficit is represented by a row of black Food icons.

The Trade Chart

Below the Food Chart is the Trade Chart. The Trade Chart consists of two separate lines, each conveying different aspects of the city's Trade status.

The first line of the Trade Chart is divided into two sections. The left portion of the chart shows the total amount of Trade available to the city, displayed as a row of trade icons and, for clarity, as a number above the icons. The right portion of the line shows the amount of the city's generated Trade that is being lost to corruption. Corruption is represented by black icons.

Line two of the Trade Chart reflects the current division of Trade. As described earlier in this chapter, incoming Trade is divided between Taxes, Luxuries, and Science. This line of the Trade Chart shows how much of each commodity is being generated by the city.

The left-hand portion of this line shows the amount of Trade that is being used to generate Taxes. The Taxes collected by the city are shown as gold coins. The amount is also shown numerically below the icons, along with the current percentage of Trade allocated to Taxes.

The center portion of the line shows the amount of Trade that is being used to generate Luxuries. The Luxuries generated are represented by goblets. The amount is also shown numerically below the icons, along with the current percentage of incoming Trade allocated to Luxuries.

The right portion of the line shows the amount of Trade allocated to Science. Scientific research is represented by beakers. The amount is also shown numerically below the icons, along with the percentage of incoming Trade allocated to Science.

Although the second line of the Trade Chart primarily deals with the division of incoming Trade, this line also takes into account the Taxes, Luxuries, and Science generated by Specialists, City Improvements, and Wonders of the World.

The Shields Chart

The bottom line of the Resources Chart shows the amount of raw materials generated by the city. Raw materials are commonly referred to as "Shields" because of the icon that is used to represent them. Shields are used to support units controlled by the city and to build new units, City Improvements, and Wonders of the World.

The Shields Chart consists of as many as three separate sections. The left portion of the chart shows the number of Shields utilized to support units owned and controlled by the city. If no unit support is being paid by the city, this section is omitted.

The center portion of the Shields Chart shows the number of Shields lost to waste. This concept is similar to that of Trade corruption. Waste is represented by a row of black Shield icons. If the city is experiencing no waste, this section is omitted.

The right-hand portion of the Shields Chart shows the amount of surplus Shields produced by the city. These Shields, which are not used to support units, are utilized in all types of city production. Surplus Shields are shown as a row of Shield icons.

THE FOOD STORAGE BOX

In the upper-right corner of the City Display is the Food Storage Box. Any Food produced by the city, but which is not used to feed the population, is placed in this area. Stored Food appears as rows of food icons. As long as surplus Food is produced, it accumulates in the Food Storage Box. When the box is filled, all the Food icons disappear, and a new citizen is added to the city's population. Surplus

Food then begins to accumulate once again, re-starting the growth process.

If the city has a Granary, a line appears halfway down the Food Storage

Box. In this situation, only half of the Food in the Food Storage Box disappears when population is added to the city. This effectively doubles the city's rate of population growth. (Granaries are described in Chapter 7.)

If the city is experiencing a Food shortage and there is Food available in the Food Storage Box, the population continues to survive. Once the Food stores have been exhausted, one citizen "dies", and is removed from the Population Roster, decreasing the city size by one. The population continues to shrink at a rate of one per turn until the Food shortage has been corrected. (Food shortages are discussed in Chapter 5.)

THE UNITS ROSTER

Directly below the City Map is the Units Roster. This box displays the icons of all units belonging to the city. Below these are a series of smaller icons that provide additional information about each unit. A Shield icon appearing below the unit indicates that the unit charges the city one Shield per turn for support. Each food icon appearing below a Settler or Engineer icon indicates that the unit requires the city to expend a unit of Food each turn to support the unit.

Two other icons might also appear in the Units Roster. Under the Republic and the Democracy, military units away from their home cities cause unhappiness amongst the population. Each black "frowning face" icon appearing below a unit indicates that one citizen is unhappy due to the unit's absence from the city.

Under the Republic, one military unit can be away from the city without causing social unrest. A gray face icon that is neither smiling nor frowning indicates that the unit is away from the city, but that it is not at present causing unhappiness.

THE IMPROVEMENTS ROSTER

Directly below the Units Roster is the Improvements Roster, a scrolling list containing the names and icons of the City Improvements and Wonders of the World in the city.

Appearing next to most City Improvements is a gold coin icon. This icon indicates that the Improvement can be sold for cash. You can sell one Improvement per turn simply by clicking its name in the list. Palaces and Wonders of the World cannot be sold.

THE INFORMATION BOX

In the bottom-center of the City Display, directly below the Resources Chart, is the Information Box. This multi-purpose display shows a wide variety of information and can be set to three separate display modes: Info, the Support Map, and the Happiness Roster.

Info Display

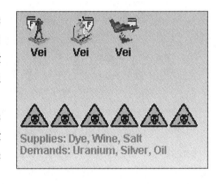

When the City Display is first opened, the Information Box defaults to the Info Display. This display is divided into several different sections, each providing specific information on one aspect of city operations.

The top section of the Info Display shows all the units currently inside the city. The first three letters of each unit's home city are printed below their icons.

Directly below the unit icons is the city's Pollution Indicator, a series of pollution icons that appears when the city runs the risk of generating pollution. The more Pollution icons, the higher the probability of pollution in that city. (Pollution is discussed in detail in Chapter 5.)

Below the Pollution Display are two lines listing the city's supplies and demands with regards to trade routes. Supply and demand play an important role in establishing successful trade routes.

The last three lines of the Info Display show information regarding the city's trade routes. Listed for each trade route is the name of the destination city, the type of goods Traded, and the amount of additional Trade generated each turn as a result of each trade route. Each city can have up to three active trade routes. (Trade routes are discussed in Chapter 9.)

The Support Map

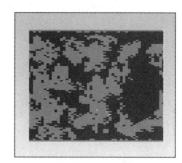

The Support Map is accessed by clicking the "Map" button in the City Display controls. This map shows a slightly larger world map than the one displayed in the Window Map. Like the maps in both the World Map and Map Windows, unexplored territory is black.

The Support Map shows the city whose display is currently active in white. Cities belonging to other civilizations are shown as colored dots. The active city's trade routes are traced on the map, appearing as lines linking the origin city with the destination city. All units belonging to the active city are shown on the map as dots, coded to match your civilization's color.

This map view is useful not only to trace your active trade routes, but to locate units abroad that might be causing civil unrest.

The Happiness Roster

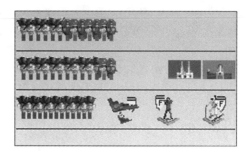

The Happiness Roster is accessed by clicking the "Happy" button in the City Display controls. This display allows you to monitor the factors that contribute to the happiness of the city's population.

The Happiness Roster consists of up to five separate lines of information. Each line shows a row of citizen icons like those in the Population Roster, and illustrates one of the factors that influence the attitude of your citizens. The five lines display the following information:

❧ The first line shows the attitude of your citizens before any modifications are applied.

❧ The second line shows the effect of Luxuries on the population. This includes your civilization's overall Luxury rate, as well as the effects of Entertainers.

❧ The third line shows the effect of City Improvements on population happiness.

* The fourth line shows the effects of martial law and military service on the happiness of the population.

* The fifth line shows the effects of Wonders of the World on the population's happiness.

The combined effects of all the factors affecting the happiness of your citizens is reflected in the Population Roster. (Population happiness is discussed in detail in Chapter 5.)

THE PRODUCTION BOX

Just below the Food Storage Box is the Production Box. It is here that you control your city's production of units, City Improvements, and Wonders of the World. The top section of the Production Box shows what is being produced and provides controls for production. The bottom section shows the number of Shields that have been allocated to the production of the item.

The "Buy" button gives you the opportunity to purchase the item currently under production rather than waiting for its completion. Clicking the Buy button displays a message indicating the cost (in coins) to complete production of the item. Provided you have sufficient funds available in your treasury, you can have the item completed at the start of the next turn.

The bottom section of the Production Box shows multiple lines of Shield icons. At the start of each turn, all the surplus Shields produced by the city are allocated toward the production of whatever item is currently under construction. These excess Shields continue to accumulate in the Production Box until the number of Shields in the Production box is equal to the cost of the item. You may then select a new item for the city to produce.

THE CITY DISPLAY CONTROLS

The final section of the City Display houses the controls for a number of city functions. The

City Display Controls, located below the Production Box, consist of the following buttons:

- ✤ **Info**—Switches the Information Box to Info Display mode
- ✤ **Map**—Displays the Support Map in the Information Box
- ✤ **Rename**—Allows you to change the name of the city
- ✤ **Happy**—Displays the Happiness Roster in the Information Box
- ✤ **View**—Shows a 3-D view of the city from a tourist's perspective
- ✤ **Exit**—Closes the City Display

To the left of these six buttons are up- and down-arrows. These controls allow you to scroll through the City Displays for each of your cities, eliminating the need to click the city icons in the Map Display.

The Turn-Based Game System

Civilization II is a turn-based game. Each turn can be sub-divided into three distinct phases of activity: the Production Phase, the Human Movement Phase, and the Computer Movement Phase.

THE PRODUCTION PHASE

At the start of each turn, the game examines the status of each of your cities and of your civilization as a whole, and performs a number of tasks and calculations that affect your activities for the current turn.

The first task for the computer each turn is to tally up the resources produced by each of your cities. The amount of Food produced by each city is counted, and any Food not used for support in each city is placed in the Food Storage Box of each city. The number of Shields produced by each city is counted, and any Shields not used for the support of military units are placed in each city's Production Box and used for production of units, Improvements, or Wonders in the city. The amount of Trade generated in each city is counted, and the incoming Trade is subdivided into Taxes, Luxuries, and Science according to the percentages specified by the Tax Rate setting. Any Taxes not used to pay maintenance for City Improvements are added to your treasury. Luxuries are applied to each city, and the happiness of the cities' populations are adjusted accordingly. All Science is added to the Civilization Advance research currently in progress.

After all resource production has been applied, the game checks on your current research and production status. If enough Science icons have been accumulated to allow the discovery of the Civilization Advance you are researching, the discovery is announced and you are given the opportunity to select the next Advance you want to research.

The production of each city is also checked at this time. If enough Shields have accumulated in a city's Production Box to complete the unit, Improvement, or Wonder currently under construction, you are notified of its completion and given the opportunity to change production to a new item.

Finally, the size and attitude of each city's population is adjusted. If enough Food has accumulated to fill a city's Food Storage Box, the population of the city is increased. The population of all cities is then checked for unhappiness. If the number of unhappy citizens in a city outnumbers the number of happy citizens, that city goes into a state of Civil Disorder. (Civil Disorder is discussed in detail in Chapter 5.)

THE HUMAN MOVEMENT PHASE

Once all the activities of the Production Phase are complete, you have the opportunity to give orders to and move your units. The Human Movement phase is also the portion of your turn where you are able to initiate contact with the leaders of other civilizations and engage in combat.

Moving Your Units

Units receive orders and move one at a time. During the Human Movement Phase, each available unit becomes "active" one at a time. When a unit becomes active, the Map Window centers on it, and the unit blinks. After each unit receives its orders or completes its movement, the the next available unit becomes active.

Not all units move each turn. Settlers and Engineers who are engaged in tasks that take more than one turn, such as building roads or mines, continue with their tasks until they have completed their duties or until they are ordered to stop. Likewise, any unit that is fortified or on sentry duty must be reactivated before it is included in the movement rotation.

THE COMPUTER MOVEMENT PHASE

After the Human Movement Phase, it is the computer's turn to play. During the Computer Movement Phase, all computer-controlled units receive orders or complete their movement. Any attacks initiated by rival civilizations take place at this time.

THE PASSAGE OF GAME TIME

Each turn signifies the passage of a certain amount of time. The amount of time that passes each turn varies depending on the game difficulty level. On each difficulty level, a different number of turns is spent at each of several turn durations. Every game, regardless of difficulty level, lasts from 4000 BC to 2020 AD. However, the variance in the number of turns at each turn duration effectively makes games at the harder levels shorter. The various years-per-turn combinations are shown in Table 2-1.

✤ **Table 2-1.** Number of Turns at Each Rate of Time Passage (Based on Difficulty Level)

YEARS PER TURN PER TURN	NUMBER OF TURNS			
	CHIEFTAIN WARLORD	PRINCE	KING	EMPEROR DEITY
50	250	60	60	60
25	—	40	40	40
20	—	—	50	75
10	50	150	50	25
5	50	50	50	—
2	50	50	50	50
1	150	150	150	150

III
GAME SETUP AND OPTIONS

*A*mong the first issues affecting your game strategy are the settings and options you choose at the start of each new game. *Civilization II* has a wide variety of gameplay choices, including customization of the world and selection of difficulty level. Depending on the combination of options chosen, one game can be radically different from the next. This chapter describes the game's opening menus, and explains the benefits and consequences of the options and difficulty levels you choose.

The Main Menu

After the opening animation sequence, the Main Menu appears (see Figure 3-1). The following options are presented on the Main Menu:

❧ **Start a New Game**—Set up the standard game options and begin a new game.

Figure 3-1 *The Main Menu*

- **Start on Premade World**—Start a new game, but play on a world map created in the map editor included with *Civilization II*. (Building a customized map with the map editor is discussed in Chapter 10.)
- **Customize World**—Start a new game, but customize certain features of the random world generated by the game.
- **Begin Scenario**—Load and play a stored Civilization II Scenario (.scn) File.
- **Load a Game**—Continue playing a game that was previously saved to disk.
- **View Hall of Fame**—Display a list of the top five rulers and their Civilization Scores.

Customizing the World

When you choose "Start a New Game" from the Main Menu, a map is randomly generated for your game. As you learn the ways in which different Terrain types affect gameplay, you might want to ensure that certain Terrain types are common in your game world. Choosing "Customize World" rather than "Start a New Game" increases your chances of playing on an optimal map by giving you control over the size, climate, and age of the world.

WORLD SIZE

The first aspect of the world that you can change is the size of the map. Map size, obviously, determines the amount of Terrain available for exploration. The

> Note: While customizing the world can provide variety and challenge to experienced players, it is best to choose the default options if you are new to the game. The default options create a planet with just the right mixture of elements to allow a novice player to experience varied Terrain conditions while helping to prevent undue frustration over a lack of suitable city sites.

World Map is divided into individual "squares," each of which represents one space of movement (see Figure 3-2).

Three pre-determined world-size options are available:

- ✤ 40 x 50 squares
- ✤ 50 x 80 squares
- ✤ 75 x 120 squares

The default world size is 50 x 80 squares. The "Custom" button, located on the World Size menu, allows you to enter custom dimensions for the map.

The amount of Terrain available for exploration affects the length of the game. When playing on a small world, the entire map

Figure 3-2 The Movement Grid of the World Map

can be explored in a relatively short amount of time. This means that other civilizations are encountered more quickly, which ultimately leads to a shorter game. When playing on a large map games tend to take longer, since civilizations tend to be more spread out. On large worlds, centuries of exploration may be required in order to locate even one rival civilization. In addition certain factors of gameplay, including the amount of time required to research Civilization Advances, are subtly altered based on the size of the map so that the larger the map, the longer the game.

Unlike the other customize world options, you have the opportunity to change the size of the world at the start of the game even if you don't choose "Customize World" from the Main Menu.

CHOOSING LAND MASS SIZE

After choosing the size of the map, you are given the opportunity to select the land/water ratio of the world. The three choices available and their characteristics are as follows:

* **Small**—More water than land
* **Normal**—About an even mix of water and land
* **Large**—More land than water

The default land mass size is "Normal." Clicking the "Random" button on the Customize Land Mass menu randomly chooses one of the three available options.

Land mass controls the actual number of land squares that appear on the map. A map with small land mass has proportionally more Ocean than land, while a map with large land mass has proportionally more land than Ocean.

CHOOSING THE TYPE OF LAND FORM

In addition to controlling the amount of land mass, *Civilization II* allows you to choose the dominant type of land form found on the map. The three choices available are:

* **Archipelago**—A world which is predominantly water, interspersed with individual islands and chains of islands (see Figure 3-3)
* **Varied**—A random distribution of land, ranging from small islands to large continents (see Figure 3-4)

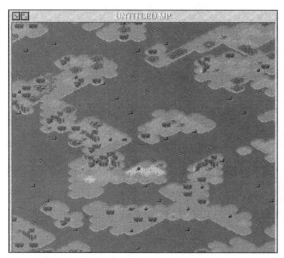

Figure 3-3 Example of an archipelago world

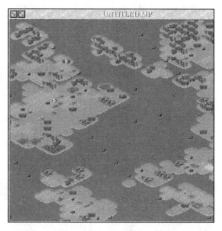

Figure 3-4 Example of a varied world

❧ **Continents**—A world predominated by several large, contiguous land forms (see Figure 3-5)

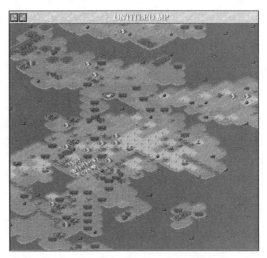

Figure 3-5 Example of a world with large continents

The default choice is "Varied." Clicking the "Random" button on the Customize Land Form menu randomly selects one of the three options.

Land form size affects several aspects of the game. A world predominantly composed of islands and small continents leaves less room on each continent to explore and establish cities. In order to continue expanding your civilization, you are forced to acquire the ability to build Triremes early in the game so that you can take to the seas and continue your exploration. Of course, if you are forced to follow this course of action, your opponents must do likewise, possibly leading to early "visits" to your territory by neighbors and would-be conquerors. You might, in fact, find that you are sharing a relatively small continent with another civilization at the start of the game. This usually results in one of you being destroyed in a fight over the limited resources of the island you share.

Large continents do not guarantee that you won't meet other civilizations early in the game. Depending on the number of civilizations in the game and the size of the map, it is fairly likely that you aren't the only one that starts the game on a large continent, but often you are left alone for a longer period of time if there are plenty of good city sites to go around.

Customize Land Form works in tandem with Customize Land Mass to create the overall layout of a custom world. By experimenting with different combinations you can create anything from a world composed of dozens of small island-continents, to a world with all the land concentrated into one or two large masses with very little in the way of separating Oceans. The best way to get an idea of the type of map produced by different combinations of land mass and land form is by using the Map Editor to create a number of custom worlds. Then, try playing on each of the worlds you create to see which layout best suits your playing style.

SELECTING THE WORLD'S CLIMATE

Once the details of land mass and land form have been decided, it's time to customize the climate. The following climatic choices are available:

+ **Arid**—A dry climate, with higher-than-normal occurrence of dry Terrain types such as Deserts and Plains

+ **Normal**—An average mixture of all Terrain types

+ **Wet**—A rainy climate, with higher-than-normal occurrence of wet Terrain types (such as Jungles and Swamps) and Rivers

The default climate is "Normal." Clicking the "Random" button on the Customize Climate menu randomly chooses one of the three options.

The amount of moisture present in the world affects the prosperity of your cities. Primarily, climate affects the amount of potential Food, Trade, and water available. The predominance of Deserts and Plains in arid climates limits the potential for Food production. Even with the addition of irrigation, Desert and Plains Terrain do not produce as much Food as Grasslands. Rivers also occur less frequently when the Arid climate option is chosen. The upside to both Deserts and Plains is that they produce more Shields than most Grasslands squares.

On the opposite end of the spectrum, the numerous Jungles and Swamps found in Wet climates also tend to be very poor Food producers. Trade in these Terrain types is nonexistent, and cannot be increased with the addition of roads. Although Rivers are fairly commonplace in wet climates, they often run through one of these undesirable Terrain types.

In both Arid and Wet climates, massive terraforming is often necessary to create suitable city sites. Normal climates, with their variety of Terrain types, make the best overall choice for worlds in which cities tend to flourish. (For a complete discussion of Terrain and resources, see Chapter 4.)

SETTING THE WORLD'S TEMPERATURE

Another aspect of climate control is the ability to customize the average temperature of the world. The following temperature choices are available:

✤ **Cool**—A climate where world-wide average temperatures are below Earth's norm, resulting in more widespread occurrences of Tundra and Glaciers but fewer Deserts

✤ **Temperate**—A climate very similar to Earth's, with a good mixture of all Terrain types

✤ **Warm**—A climate with very a limited amount of Tundra and Glaciers, but a higher than normal concentration of Deserts

The default temperature is "Temperate". Clicking the "Random" button on the Customize Temperature menu randomly selects one of the three options.

The planet's temperature specifically controls the occurrence of the inhospitable Terrain types (Desert, Tundra, and Glacier). Temperate worlds are very much like the climate on Earth. Deserts are scattered throughout the world, mostly occurring in the central latitudes, while Tundra and Glacier Terrain are concentrated in the northern and southern polar regions. On cool worlds, a percentage of the Terrain that would normally be Desert appears as either Tundra or Glacier Terrain. On warm planets, the Tundra and Glaciers found near the poles are even more localized, giving way to more Desert Terrain in the north and south. (For a complete discussion of Terrain, see Chapter 4.)

SELECTING THE WORLD'S AGE

The final Customize World option is the age of the world. The following choices are available:

✤ **3 Billion Years**—A relatively "young" world, with large tracts of similar Terrain types

✤ **4 Billion Years**—A world approximately the age of Earth, having occasional areas of contiguous similar Terrain

✤ **5 Billion Years**—An old planet, where Terrain types tend to vary greatly over relatively short distances

The default age is "4 Billion Years". The "Random" button on the Age menu randomly chooses one of the three options.

The age of the planet determines the distribution of Terrain types throughout the world. Young worlds, having been spared the ravages of time, tend to have large areas of similar Terrain. For instance, large concentrations of Jungle growth, large tracts of Grasslands, and long, continuous Mountain ranges are common. Old worlds, on the other hand, show the effects of erosion and climate change that accompany geological age. Mountain ranges have been worn down in some places to mere foothills. Grasslands have given way to scattered patches of Forest growth, and Plains have dried up in places to form small Deserts. The middle-aged planet is caught somewhere in the midst of this process, showing evidence of both large tracts of similar Terrain and areas of scattered, varied Terrain.

The effects of planetary age can be profound when it comes to city construction. Cities usually work best in an area where the Terrain is varied, so that they can generate a good mix of Trade, Shields, and Food. Young planets, with their dense concentrations of identical Terrain, tend to provide an abundance of one or two resources, while giving no option for the production of the others. Old planets often have an abundant number of potentially good city sites. However, the unpredictability of the Terrain distribution often creates production situations even less hospitable than those on a young world. The default, four billion-year-old world is the best choice overall, since it offers a limited opportunity to experience both extremes, while still offering the potential for lots of good city sites. (For a complete discussion of Terrain and city placement, see Chapter 4.)

Difficulty Level

After you customize the world (or choose the size of the map, if you are using a random world), you must choose a difficulty level. The difficulty level you choose determines the aggressiveness of the computer opponents, the speed at which Civilization Advances are discovered, the initial happiness of your citizens, city production, and a myriad of other details. Many of these items may be unfamiliar to new players, but they are explained in later chapters. Six difficulty levels are available in *Civilization II* (as opposed to the five in *Civilization*). They are (in order from least to most difficult):

- Chieftain
- Warlord
- Prince
- King
- Emperor
- Deity

❖ **Table 3-1.** Gameplay factors affected by difficulty level

GAME FEATURES	CHIEF	WARLORD	PRINCE	KING	EMPEROR	DEITY
Starting Funds	50	0	0	0	0	0
Content Citizens	6	5	4	3	2	1
Rows in Food Storage Box	15	13	12	10	9	8
Rows in Shield Box	15	13	12	10	9	8
Science Increment (Human)	6	8	10	12	14	14*
Science Increment (Computer)	14	13	12	11	10	10*
Barbarian Attack Strength	25%	50%	75%	100%	125%	150%

*On Deity level, this number may be adjusted + or - 1, depending how far ahead or behind you are in research.

Table 3-1 shows the effects of difficulty level on various aspects of gameplay. The following game features are listed in the table:

- ❖ **Starting Funds**—The amount of money you have in your treasury at the start of the game

- ❖ **Content Citizens**—The number of citizens in each city that are "born" content. All citizens added to the population after this number are automatically unhappy (see Chapter 5 for details).

- ❖ **Rows in Food Storage Box**—The number of Food icons it takes to fill a single row in the Food Storage Box of a computer-controlled city. The higher the number, the slower the city's population grows. (By default, this number is 10 for human players on any difficulty level.)

- ❖ **Rows in Shield Box**—The number of Shield icons it takes to fill a single row in the Production Box of a computer-controlled city. The higher the number, the longer it takes for cities to produce units, Improvements, and Wonders. (By default, this number is 10 for human players on any difficulty level.)

- ❖ **Science Increment (Human)**—The modifier used to help determine how many Science light bulbs are required to discover the next Civilization Advance for the player. The smaller the number, the more quickly Advances are discovered.

❦ **Science Increment (Computer)**—The modifier used to help determine how many Science light bulbs are required to discover the next Civilization Advance for computer-controlled civilizations. The smaller the number, the more quickly Advances are discovered.

❦ **Barbarian Attack Strength**—The percentage by which the base attack strength of Barbarian units is multiplied when attacking your units. (On Deity level, for example, a Barbarian unit with an Attack Factor of 2 would attack with a strength of 3.)

The number of years that pass during each turn and the overall progression of game time are also affected by difficulty level. The differences in time passage are shown in Chapter 2 in Table 2-1.

Besides the items listed in Table 3-1, there are several other miscellaneous modifications based on the level of difficulty you choose:

❦ **Chief Level**—The Attack Factor of your units is doubled. Also, you are not charged the 50% Shield penalty normally incurred when you change the type of item being built in a city in mid- production (see Chapter 7 for details).

❦ **Prince Level (and higher)**—The A.I.-controlled civilizations may be "assisted" by the computer if you are significantly ahead of them in technology. This is especially true in the case of Civilization Advance research. Also, the higher the difficulty level, the more likely alliances will be formed against you. At the higher difficulty levels, A.I. civilizations try harder to build spaceships; and if you are the first to launch a spaceship, the computer-controlled civilizations often team up to achieve your destruction before the spaceship reaches Alpha Centauri (regardless of treaty status).

❦ **King Level (and higher)**—Your Spies can be expelled from enemy cities.

❦ **Emperor and Deity Level**—At the two highest difficulty levels, computer-controlled civilizations have the ability to bribe your cities to join their empire through the use of Diplomats and Spies. Also, at these difficulty levels, A.I. civilizations won't trade you any technology that allows you to build a Wonder of the World that they are already building.

As you can see, as the difficulty level increases, the computer players acquire more abilities and intelligence. In many respects, at both Emperor and Deity level the computer players have a number of significant advantages over you. If you desire an "even" game, choose King level; this is the level of difficulty where the modifiers and abilities of the computer players most closely match your own.

Level of Competition

The next choice you have is the number of computer-controlled civilizations you want to play against. Note that the number you choose *includes your civilization*. In other words, if you choose "7" from the menu, that means your civilization is facing six opponents. You can choose from three to seven civilizations, or allow the computer to choose the number randomly.

The number of civilizations, like the size and layout of the world, affects the amount of time that usually passes before you are forced to interact with your opponents. If you are just learning the game, or if you are a devout isolationist, choose a small number of civilizations. In addition to allowing you to expand farther without opposition, you have less competition with regards to building Wonders of the World. On the other hand, a small number of opponents also limits your opportunities for establishing trade routes and exchanging Advances. If you are a war monger who likes to conquer his or her opponents, or if you seek the greatest possible challenge, choose a higher number of civilizations. A large number of opponents allows for more intense competition as well as diverse trading opportunities.

Select Level of Barbarian Activity

This is an option that wasn't available in the original *Civilization*. In that game, the Barbarians were everywhere. For some players, this added to the excitement of the game, while others felt that they shouldn't be forced to deal with Barbarian activity—especially after the player's civilization had advanced well into the modern era.

Barbarians still can't be "turned off" entirely, but their level of activity can be severely curtailed. You can choose from the following levels of Barbarian activity:

- ✦ **Villages Only**
- ✦ **Roving Bands**
- ✦ **Restless Tribes**
- ✦ **Raging Hordes**

These options are listed in order from least to most in terms of Barbarian Activity. "Villages Only" means that no Barbarians are randomly roaming the map; they are only found in villages (also known as "Goodie Huts"—see Chapter 4). On the opposite end of the spectrum, "Raging Hordes" means that Barbarian encounters are fairly common. This is the level that most closely approximates (and perhaps exceeds) Barbarian activity in the original *Civilization*. If you like barbaric surprises, choose "Random" to have the computer pick the level of Barbarian activity.

Select Tribe

After choosing the level of Barbarian activity, and selecting your gender (you have a 50-50 shot at that one, and you should get it right on the first try), you are prompted to select your tribe. You can choose from one of the 21 existing tribes, or you can click the "Custom" button to create your own tribe. (Creating custom tribes is discussed in the game manual.)

Select City Style

One of the many graphical nuances added to *Civilization II* are the new city icons that appear on the map. As your cities grow, the icons reflect that growth by adding newer, taller buildings that spread out to fill the city square. You can choose from four different architectural styles for your cities.

Enhanced Features and Options

Civilization II gives you several additional options that allow you to further customize the game to suit your tastes. These options are as follows:

- ❧ **Simplified Combat**—This option allows you to choose the combat resolution system from the original *Civilization* (see Chapter 8 for details).

- ❧ **Accelerated Start**—Gets your game off to a flying start by automatically giving you (and every other civilization in the game) one or two cities, several free units, many squares of pre-improved Terrain, and a number of Civilization Advances. You can choose to start in three different time periods; the later in time you start, the more cities, Advances, units, and Improvements you start with. This option eliminates the many turns of limited activity associated with starting a game normally.

- ❧ **Flat World**—Eliminates the ability to "circumnavigate" the map. In other words, units can normally exit the east or west edge of the map and end up on the opposite end (like sailing around the world). With the "Flat World" option selected, units cannot move past the east and west map borders, making it far more difficult and time-consuming to interact with civilizations and cities existing on the other side of the world.

- ❧ **Select Computer Opponents**—Allows you to choose the A. I. civilizations you want to play against. You select each opponent from a list of three choices. (A fourth choice, "Random", which randomly chooses from the other three, is also available.) Choosing your opponents is an excellent opportunity to assume some control over the way you are treated throughout the game. Opponents can be chosen on the basis of their leaders' personality traits to create the best possible conditions to suit your mood. (Leader personalities are discussed in Chapter 9.)

- ❧ **Bloodlust (No Spaceships Allowed)**—This final Enhanced Features option is for warmongers only. There are two ways to win at *Civilization II*—be the first civilization to land a spaceship on Alpha Centauri or take over the world by destroying all other civilizations. In a "Blood-lust" game, you are forced to conquer the world in order to win.

The Game Menu Options

Once you have chosen or set all the pre-game options, the game begins. Once the game starts, none of the pre-game options can be altered. There are a number of other features that you *can* customize once the game starts. These are accessed by selecting "Game Options", "Graphics Options", and "City Report Options" from the Game menu. Although none of these options affect the course of the game, they do allow you to set certain aspects of the game to your personal preferences and specifications. Details on the Game menu options can be found in the game manual.

IV
RESOURCE PRODUCTION AND CITY CONSTRUCTION

*O*nce you have set up the game, it's time to start building your empire. The first step in creating your civilization is to build a city. But where should you build it? How can you be sure that the site you select will provide adequate resources to allow the city to grow quickly and prosper?

That's what this chapter is all about. The first section explains Food, Shields, and Trade—the three resources that are vital to the success and growth of your cities. You are then taken on a brief tour of the game map, as each type of Terrain and Special Resource is discussed. The second section discusses how to choose the best possible city site and how to improve the surrounding Terrain to maximize city growth and prosperity.

Resources and Terrain

Before you build your first city, it is important to understand the factors that define a certain area as a "good city site." In order to make an informed decision about where a city should be built, you need to know the way in which each resource type affects the city, and which Terrain types produce the best mix of resources for city growth.

THE THREE RESOURCES

There are three basic resource types in *Civilization II*, each of which is necessary to some aspect of a city's growth and well-being. These three resources—Food, Shields, and Trade—are generated in various quantities by different types of Terrain (as detailed in the "Terrain Types" section later in this chapter). The following sections explain the role and importance of each resource type.

Food

In *Civilization II*, Food is represented by the icon illustrated to the right. Every city is capable of generating a certain amount of Food each turn. The amount is dependent on the type of Terrain surrounding the city and the improvements that have been made to increase Food production.

Food serves three roles in the game. First, every citizen in each city must eat in order to survive. Every turn, each citizen consumes two units of Food. If the city's Food production is inadequate to meet the needs of the population and no Food reserves are available in the city's Food Storage Box, one citizen "dies" each turn until the Food deficit is corrected.

Like the citizens living in the city, Settlers and Engineers must also consume Food every turn in order to survive. The amount of Food necessary to support these units is one or two units of Food per turn, depending on your form of government. If the home city of the Settlers/Engineers is not producing enough Food to feed them, the Settler/Engineer unit is eliminated. (Settlers and Engineers are discussed in Chapter 8.)

Finally, the accumulation of surplus Food controls the growth of a city's population. When enough surplus Food accumulates to fill the Food Storage

Box, the city's population increases by one. The faster surplus Food is accumulated, the faster a city grows. (See Chapter 2 or the game manual for more information.) Therefore, cities with abundant Food supplies have the potential to grow more quickly.

Shields

Raw materials, such as lumber and metals, are represented by Shield icons. Each city is capable of producing a different number of Shields each turn. The actual number produced depends on the type of Terrain surrounding the city.

Shields serve two basic functions in the game. First, they are used by cities to support units. Whether or not a unit requires support each turn depends on your government type; but as a general rule, most units require that support in the amount of one Shield per turn be paid by their home city. If the city cannot pay support for a unit, the unit is removed from the game.

Any Shields not used for the support of units are accumulated in the city's Production Box. These surplus Shields are used to pay for the construction of new units, City Improvements, and Wonders of the World. Each unit, Improvement, and Wonder has a set cost, which is expressed in the number of Shields required to build it. Once enough Shields accumulate in the Production Box to meet the cost of the item currently under construction, the item is completed. Surplus Shields then begin accumulating toward the completion of the next item.

Cities generating an abundance of Shields can support more units and are able to produce units, Improvements, and Wonders more quickly than cities generating few Shields.

Trade

Trade is represented by the icon illustrated on the right. Unlike Food and Shields, Trade is broken down into three component parts. The breakdown of Trade can be seen in the Resource Chart of the City Display (see Figure 4-1). You can control the percentage of Trade allocated to each of

Figure 4-1 The Breakdown of Trade Components in the City Display

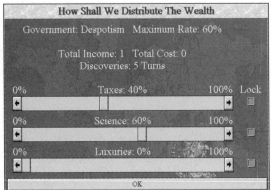

Figure 4-2 Allocating Trade Income.

its three facets by accessing the "Tax Rate" command from the Kingdom menu (see Figure 4-2). Trade is broken down into the following three components:

TAXES

Taxes represent the cash income obtained from Trade. This includes such things as tariffs, income and sales tax, and profits from trade goods. Taxes acquired from each city are pooled together into a single lump sum and disbursed to all friendly cities as needed each turn.

Taxes are necessary to the ongoing operation of a city. Many City Improvements require that a fee be paid each turn in order to maintain them. This maintenance fee is deducted from your Tax income. If insufficient funds exist to maintain the Improvements in all your cities, an Improvement is randomly sold from one of your cities to cover the deficit. Improvements continue to be sold at the rate of one per turn until the deficit is corrected.

Any Tax income not used for the maintenance of Improvements is placed in your treasury for later use. Funds in the treasury can be used to temporarily cover maintenance costs during a Tax deficit. Treasury funds can also be used to pay for the completion of units, Improvements, and Wonders; to bribe enemy units and cities; or to appease greedy enemy leaders.

SCIENCE

The second component of Trade is Science. The Science portion of Trade represents the ideas and concepts that are learned through dealings with other cultures whose representatives travel to your cities (and vice-versa).

Perhaps the most important component of Trade, the amount of Science collectively produced by your cities determines the speed at which you discover new Civilization Advances. Like Taxes, Science produced by each city is pooled together. The total amount of Science produced is applied to the Civilization Advance research currently in progress. When sufficient Science has accumulated, the Advance is discovered, and research on a new topic begins. The more Trade you allocate to Science, the faster you discover new Advances.

LUXURIES

The third component of Trade is Luxuries. Luxuries represent the portion of Trade that deals with the import of luxury items and commodities that make the lives of your citizens more pleasant and enjoyable.

The purpose of Luxuries is to keep your citizens happy: every two Luxuries make one unhappy citizen content or one content citizen happy. The higher you set the Luxuries rate, the happier they are. This component of Trade is less important than the others early in the game and on lower difficulty levels. The effects produced by a high Luxuries rate can be reproduced in other ways, such as the construction of certain Improvements and Wonders and the creation of Entertainers (see "Improving Resource Production" later in this chapter for details).

Further along in the game, when populations are high and you are (probably) using an advanced form of government such as Republic or Democracy, raising the Luxuries rate becomes indispensable when dealing with the increasing unhappiness of your citizens.

SURVEYING THE TERRAIN

Now that you have an understanding of the three resources required for survival, it's time to take a look at the Terrain types in the game and see where these resources can be found. The Terrain survey consists of two separate sections. The first section examines the basic Terrain types, and second looks at the various Special Resources that can add value to the basic Terrain types.

Terrain Types

There are 11 basic types of Terrain in *Civilization II*, each of which produces different proportions of Food, Shields, and Trade, as well as affecting several other aspects of gameplay. Statistics for all Terrain types are consolidated in Table 4-1. And, in addition to the raw Terrain statistics, commentary on overall usability of the Terrain in terms of resource production and city construction is provided after Table 4-1. The following information is listed for each Terrain type:

- ✤ **Food**—The amount of Food produced by the Terrain
- ✤ **Shields**—The number of Shields produced by the Terrain
- ✤ **Trade**—The amount of Trade produced by the Terrain
- ✤ **Movement Cost**—The number of movement points a unit must expend to move into this type of Terrain
- ✤ **Defensive Bonus**—The bonus multiplier to a unit's Defense Factor when the unit occupies the Terrain type (expressed as a percentage of the unit's normal Defense Factor). "Normal" indicates that the unit's Defense Factor is not modified. (Unit Defense Factors are discussed in Chapter 8.)
- ✤ **Results of Irrigation**—The resource bonus or Terrain change resulting from irrigation of the Terrain. An entry of "N/A" indicates that the Terrain cannot be irrigated.
- ✤ **Results of Mining**—The resource bonus or Terrain change resulting from the construction of a mine on the Terrain. An entry of "N/A" indicates that the Terrain cannot be mined.
- ✤ **Results of Roads**—The bonuses received for building a road in this type of Terrain

✣ Table 4-1. Resource Statistics for Terrain Types

Terrain Type	Food	Shield	Trade	Move Cost	Defensive Bonus	Results of Irrigation	Results of Mining	Effects of Roads*	Engineering Transformation	Possible Special Resources
Deserts	0	1	0	1	Normal	+1 Food	+1 Shield	+1 Trade	Plains	Pheasant, Oil
Forests	1	2	0	2	+50%	Plains	N/A	none	Grasslands	Game, Silk
Glaciers	0	0	0	2	Normal	N/A	+1 Shield	none	Tundra	Ivory, Oil
Grasslands	2	0	0	1	Normal	+1 Food	Forest	+1 Trade	Hills	Grassland (shield)
Hills	1	0	0	2	+100%	+1 Food	+3 Shields	none	Plains	Coal, Wine
Jungles	1	0	0	2	+50%	Grassland	Forest	none	Plains	Gems, Fruit
Mountains	0	1	0	3	+200%	N/A	+1 Shield	none	Hills	Gold, Iron
Oceans	1	0	2	1	Normal	N/A	N/A	N/A	N/A	Fish, Whales
Plains	1	1	0	1	Normal	+1 Food	Forest	+1 Trade	Grasslands	Buffalo, Wheat
Swamps	1	0	0	2	+50%	Grasslands	Forest	none	Plains	Peat, Spice
Tundra	1	0	0	1	Normal	+1 Food	N/A	none	Desert	Musk Ox, Furs

* Roads reduce the movement cost of ANY Terrain type to 1/3 of a movement point.

+ **Results of Transformation**—The Terrain type that results when Engineers are utilized to transform this type of Terrain.
+ **Possible Special Resources**—The Special Resource types that can possibly exist on the Terrain type.

DESERTS

Food:	0
Shields:	1
Trade:	0
Movement Cost:	1
Defensive Bonus:	Normal
Results of Irrigation:	+1 Food
Results of Mining:	+1 Shield
Results of Roads:	+1 Trade; Movement Cost = 1/3
Results of Transformation:	Plains
Possible Special Resources:	Oasis or Oil

Deserts, and areas surrounded by Deserts, make poor city sites due to their lack of Food. Shield production in Deserts can be increased through mining, and Trade can be produced through the construction of roads; but even with proper development of the land, Deserts are still one of the least hospitable types of Terrain for city development.

FORESTS

Food:	1
Shields:	2
Trade:	0
Movement Cost:	1
Defensive Bonus:	+ 50%
Results of Irrigation:	Plains
Results of Mining:	N/A
Results of Roads:	Movement Cost = 1/3
Results of Transformation:	Grasslands
Possible Special Resources:	Pheasant or Silk

Chapter IV: Resource Production and City Construction

Forests are wonderful assets to a city due to the number of Shields they produce. One or two Forests within the City Radius can greatly increase city production and act as a defensive perimeter to slow down attacking forces. Forests also provide a minimal amount of Food and a defensive bonus for defending units. Forests are not, however, recommended as actual sites for city construction, since the low amount of Food produced leads to slow growth early in the city's existence. Barring the presence of Special Resources, Forests cannot produce Trade.

GLACIERS

Food:	0	
Shields:	0	
Trade:	0	
Movement Cost:	2	
Defensive Bonus:	Normal	
Results of Irrigation:	N/A	
Results of Mining:	+1 Shield	
Results of Roads:	Movement Cost = 1/3	
Results of Transformation:	Tundra	
Possible Special Resources:	Ivory or Oil	

Glaciers are evil places. Unless a Special Resource is present, Glaciers produce nothing: no Food, no Shields, and no Trade. Although mining provides a meager increase in Shield production, it takes so long to mine a Glacier that the effort is hardly worth it. Barring the presence of Special Resources, Glaciers cannot produce Trade. If no Special Resources are present, Glaciers should not be allowed inside a City Radius; and, Special Resources or no, they should NEVER be used as a city site.

Note: Note to Veteran Civilization Players: The Glacier Terrain type replaces the "Arctic" Terrain type found in the original game.

GRASSLANDS

Food:	2
Shields:	0
Trade:	0
Movement Cost:	1
Defensive Bonus:	Normal
Results of Irrigation:	+1 Food
Results of Mining:	Forest
Results of Roads:	+1 Trade; Movement Cost = 1/3
Results of Transformation:	Hills
Possible Special Resources:	Grassland (Shield)

Grasslands are an important addition to any City Radius, and make good city sites. The high Food production (which can be further increased through irrigation) provides the opportunity for rapid city growth, and the production of Shields is adequate when augmented by the presence of a resource Shield and/or nearby Hills or Forests. Grasslands can be made to produce Trade through the construction of roads.

HILLS

Food:	1
Shields:	0
Trade:	0
Movement Cost:	2
Defensive Bonus:	+ 100%
Results of Irrigation:	+1 Food
Results of Mining:	+3 Shields
Results of Roads:	Movement Cost = 1/3
Results of Transformation:	Plains
Possible Special Resources:	Coal or Wine

Hills provide an invaluable source of Shields for a city when mined. It is a good idea to include at least one Hills square within the City Radius for this purpose. Due to their low Food production, their inability to produce Trade (barring the presence of Special Resources), and nonexistent Shield production (prior to mining), Hills are not a good choice for city sites per se.

JUNGLES

Food:	1
Shields:	0
Trade:	0
Movement Cost:	2
Defensive Bonus:	+ 50%
Results of Irrigation:	Grassland
Results of Mining:	Forest
Results of Roads:	Movement Cost = 1/3
Results of Transformation:	Plains
Possible Special Resources:	Gems or Fruit

Generally, jungles serve only limited usefulness in the game. Although they posses the same basic resources as Hills, the useful development of Jungles cannot take place short of converting the Jungle to a different Terrain type through irrigation, mining, or transformation. However, jungles containing a Special Resource are a different story because they can produce Trade, and the presence of a Special Resource can make a Jungle square a welcome addition within the City Radius (see the Special Resources entries for Gems and Fruit for details). Remember though, Jungles should *never* be used as city sites.

MOUNTAINS

Food:	0
Shields:	1
Trade:	0
Movement Cost:	3
Defensive Bonus:	+ 200%
Results of Irrigation:	N/A
Results of Mining:	+1 Shield
Results of Roads:	Movement Cost = 1/3

Results of Transformation:	Hills
Possible Special Resources:	Gold or Iron

Mountains represent another Terrain type that is entirely unsuitable for use as a city site. Like Glaciers, Mountains cannot be made to produce Food unless transformed into another Terrain type. Mountains are less profitable than Hills in terms of Shield production. However, they become infinitely more useful when they contain Special Resources (see the Special Resources entries for Gold and Iron for details). Barring the presence of Special Resources, Mountains cannot produce Trade.

OCEANS

Food:	1
Shields:	0
Trade:	2
Movement Cost:	1
Defensive Bonus:	Normal
Results of Irrigation:	N/A
Results of Mining:	N/A
Results of Roads:	N/A
Results of Transformation:	N/A
Possible Special Resources:	Fish or Whales

Obviously, Ocean squares cannot be city sites. However, it was no accident that most civilizations of the ancient world established cities in coastal regions. You will note that Oceans are the only type of Terrain that produce Trade on their own. The Trade gained from cities established near the Ocean can make all the difference in the world early in the game when it comes to getting a head-start on Civilization Advance research. For this reason, along with the opportunity for increased mobility offered

Note: The "lakes" that are often scattered about the game map are actually inland seas. They have all the same characteristics and statistics as normal Ocean squares.

by sea travel, you should seriously consider establishing your first city near an Ocean square, even if it means exploring for a few turns to find one.

PLAINS

Food:	1
Shields:	1
Trade:	0
Movement Cost:	1
Defensive Bonus:	Normal
Results of Irrigation:	+1 Food
Results of Mining:	Forest
Results of Roads:	+1 Trade; Movement Cost = 1/3
Results of Transformation:	Grasslands
Possible Special Resources:	Buffalo or Wheat

Plains are valuable because they can potentially provide a mix of all three resources. Because of the addition of Shield production to cities built on non-Shield producing Terrain, however, non-Shield Grasslands are better choices as city sites. Still, in spite of being slightly less productive than Grasslands in terms of Food, Plains remain an extremely versatile Terrain type. Plains can be made to produce Trade through the construction of roads.

SWAMPS

Food:	1
Shields:	0
Trade:	0
Movement Cost:	2
Defensive Bonus:	+ 50%
Results of Irrigation:	Grasslands
Results of Mining:	Forest
Results of Roads:	Movement Cost = 1/3
Results of Transformation:	Plains
Possible Special Resources:	Peat or Spice

Swamps in their base form are identical to Jungles (compare the stats). So, like Jungles, it is best to avoid including them within the City Radius unless they possesses Special Resources (or you are willing to spend the time and effort to convert them to another Terrain type). Barring the presence of Special Resources, Swamps cannot produce Trade.

TUNDRA

Food:	1
Shields:	0
Trade:	0
Movement Cost:	1
Defensive Bonus:	Normal
Results of Irrigation:	+1 Food
Results of Mining:	N/A
Results of Roads:	Movement Cost = 1/3
Results of Transformation:	Desert
Possible Special Resources:	Game or Furs

Unless it contains Special Resources, Tundra squares are almost as inhospitable as Glaciers. Although it can produce some Food, Tundra produces neither Shields nor Trade unless it is converted to another type of Terrain or contains Special Resources. Tundra should never be used as a city site.

What About Rivers?

Players of the original *Civilization* have probably noted that Rivers were not mentioned among the Terrain types described in the previous section. The reason for this is that *Civilization II* doesn't treat Rivers as separate and distinct Terrain types.

In *Civilization II*, Rivers can flow through any type of Terrain except for Mountains and Hills. When a River flows through any Terrain square, the Terrain type retains its own production characteristics, but gains a number of bonuses from the River. The presence of a River in any type of Terrain adds the following:

- One unit of Trade is added to the Terrain's production.
- Movement cost along the River is 1/3 point per square (treated as moving along a road).
- Rivers are a source of water for irrigation of adjacent squares.
- Rivers provide a 50% Defensive Bonus.

In addition to retaining the normal production characteristics of the Terrain, Special Resources may also be present. For example, a Grassland square with a River might also have a Special Resource Shield. The production value of such a square is two Food, one Shield, and one Trade.

> **Note:** Although Rivers are not randomly generated in Mountains and Hills, they can be added to these Terrain types on maps you design using the Map Editor.

> **Tip:** Grassland-River squares make very good city sites because of their high Trade and Food production, and their Defensive Bonus.

Special Resources

As noted in the statistics for each Terrain type, there is a possibility that Special Resources could exist. Special Resources are items that enhance the value of a Terrain square by adding some combination of additional resources (Food, Shields, and/or Trade) to the resources already produced by the Terrain. Special Resources are randomly distributed when the map is generated.

The statistics for all Special Resources are consolidated in Table 4-2. The following information is provided for each of the 22 Special Resources:

- **Terrain Type**—The type of Terrain where the Special Resource is found
- **Food**—The amount of Food produced by the Terrain when the Special Resource is present
- **Shields**—The number of Shields produced by the Terrain when the Special Resource is present

✦ Table 4-2. Special Resource Statistics

Special Resources	Terrain Type	Food	Shield	Trade	Result of Irrigation	Results of Mining	Engineering Transformation
Buffalo	Plains	1	3	0	Normal	Pheasant	Grassland (Shield)*
Coal	Hills	1	2	0	Normal	Normal	Buffalo
Fish	Oceans	3	0	2	N/A	N/A	N/A
Fruit	Jungles	4	0	1	Grassland (Shield)*	Silk	Wheat
Furs	Tundra	2	0	3	Normal	N/A	Oil (D)
Pheasant	Forest	3	2	0	Buffalo	N/A	Grassland (Shield)*
Musk Ox	Tundra	3	1	0	Normal	N/A	Oasis
Gems	Jungle	1	0	4	Grassland (Shield)*	Pheasant	Buffalo
Gold	Mountains	0	1	6	N/A	Normal	Coal
Grassland (Shield)	Grasslands	2	1	0	Normal	Pheasant/Silk	Coal/Wine
Iron	Mountains	0	4	0	N/A	Normal	Wine
Ivory	Glaciers	1	1	4	N/A	Normal	Game (T)
Oasis	Deserts	3	1	0	Normal	Normal	Buffalo
Oil (D)	Deserts	0	4	0	Normal	Normal	Wheat
Oil (G)	Glaciers	0	4	0	N/A	Normal	Furs
Peat	Swamps	1	4	0	Grassland (Shield)*	Pheasant	Buffalo
Silk	Forest	1	2	3	Wheat	N/A	Grassland (Shield)*
Spice	Swamps	3	0	4	Grassland (Shield)*	Silk	Wheat
Whales	Oceans	2	2	3	N/A	N/A	N/A
Wheat	Plains	3	1	0	Normal	Silk	Grassland (Shield)*
Wine	Hills	1	0	4	Normal	Normal	Wheat

Note: Where it appears as the result of a Terrain transformation of some sort, Grassland (Shield) is marked with an asterisk (*). The reason is that, about 50 percent of the time, such a transformation results in a normal Grassland square. However, a subsequent transformation or mining of that same square produces Special Resources according to the rules for the Grassland (Shield) Terrain.

✦ **Trade**—The amount of Trade produced by the Terrain when the Special Resource is present

✦ **Results of Irrigation**—The resource bonus or Terrain change resulting from irrigation of the Terrain. An entry of "N/A" indicates that the Terrain cannot be irrigated. "Normal" means that the result is the same as irrigating the Terrain type without the Special Resource present.

✦ **Results of Mining**—The resource bonus or Terrain change resulting from the construction of a mine on the Terrain. An entry of "N/A" indicates that the Terrain cannot be mined. "Normal" means that the result is the same as mining the Terrain type without the Special Resource present.

✦ **Results of Transformation**—The Terrain type that results when Engineers are utilized to transform this type of Terrain. "Normal" means that the result is the same as transforming the Terrain type without the Special Resource present.

BUFFALO

Terrain Type:	Plains	
Food:	1	
Shields:	3	
Trade:	0	

Results of Irrigation:	Normal
Results of Mining:	Game (F)
Results of Transformation:	Grassland (Shield)*

The presence of Buffalo increases the Shield production of a Plains square by two, making Plains much more valuable when included in the City Radius. Buffalo squares also make good city sites, providing excellent Shield production, as well as an adequate supply of Food and Trade.

COAL

Terrain Type:	Hills
Food:	1
Shields:	2
Trade:	0
Results of Irrigation:	Normal
Results of Mining:	Normal
Results of Transformation:	Buffalo

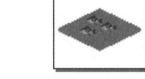

Coal can do wonders for city production. When mined, a Coal square produces a total of 5 Shields every turn. When Coal deposits are found, you should make an effort to build a city close enough to utilize this valuable resource. Never use Coal squares as city sites: the irrigation automatically built in the city square eliminates the opportunity to mine the Coal.

FISH

Terrain Type:	Ocean
Food:	3
Shields:	0
Trade:	2
Results of Irrigation:	N/A
Results of Mining:	N/A
Results of Transformation:	N/A

Fish provide even more incentive to establish cities in coastal regions. In addition to the Trade normally provided by Ocean squares, city growth can benefit significantly from the two additional units of Food obtained from the presence of Fish. In terms of the overall mix of resources, Whales are the better choice if any are nearby. (see Special Resource "Whales").

Fruit

Terrain Type:	Jungles	
Food:	4	
Shields:	0	
Trade:	1	
Results of Irrigation:	Grassland (Shield)*	
Results of Mining:	Silk	
Results of Transformation:	Wheat	

Fruit converts the Jungle, a virtually worthless Terrain type, into a viable source of Food. This, plus the added bonus of one unit of Trade, makes the Fruit square a welcome addition to any city's production environment. A city built in a Fruit square can be fairly prosperous, provided the surrounding Terrain produces a good resource mix. Not only does such a city have a fairly good mix of resources, its units gain the defensive bonus provided by the Jungle.

Furs

Terrain Type:	Tundra	
Food:	2	
Shields:	0	
Trade:	3	
Results of Irrigation:	Normal	
Results of Mining:	N/A	
Results of Transformation:	Oil (D)	

Tundra squares are much more desirable from a production standpoint than normal Tundra squares. They provide double the Food and a handsome amount of Trade. Although you should never go out of your way to build cities in Tundra regions, the presence of Fur within the City Radius can mean the difference between survival and death in such an area. Although you could do worse than a Furs square in terms of city sites, the abundance of other Tundra and Glacier Terrain nearby usually makes such a site impractical and unproductive without considerable Terrain modifications.

PHEASANT

Terrain Type:	Forest
Food:	3
Shields:	2
Trade:	0
Results of Irrigation:	Buffalo
Results of Mining:	N/A
Results of Transformation:	Grassland (Shield)*

Forests, which are already valuable commodities due to their high Shield production, become even more valuable with the presence of Game. The additional Food generated by the Game helps cities to grow more quickly. The one factor that makes the Game (F) square impractical as a city site is its lack of Trade.

MUSK OX

Terrain Type:	Tundra
Food:	3
Shields:	1
Trade:	0
Results of Irrigation:	Normal
Results of Mining:	N/A
Results of Transformation:	Oasis

If you must build a city that includes Tundra within the City Radius, Game (T) squares are certainly better than plain Tundra. They produce a viable amount of Food and offer a small increase in Shields ("1" certainly beats "0"). With the addition of irrigation, Game (T) squares actually produce more Food than Game (F) squares. Their lack of Trade production makes Game (T) squares poor city sites.

GEMS

Terrain Type:	Jungle
Food:	1
Shields:	0
Trade:	4
Results of Irrigation:	Grassland (Shield)*
Results of Mining:	Pheasant
Results of Transformation:	Buffalo

Gems are to Jungles what Furs are to Tundra: they provide a tremendous amount of Trade in a Terrain type that normally has none. The four units of Trade provided by this Special Resource make a Jungle so endowed a viable addition to a city's production, provided that alternate sources of Food and Shields are readily available. In such a situation, Gem squares can make decent city sites as well.

GOLD

Terrain Type:	Mountains
Food:	0
Shields:	1
Trade:	6
Results of Irrigation:	N/A
Results of Mining:	Normal
Results of Transformation:	Coal

If you're having trouble producing Trade, Gold could definitely be your answer. Its presence turns a Mountain into, well, a gold mine of Trade, generating a whopping six Trade icons each turn. The downside is that Food production is still nonexistent, and Shield production is still negligible. If other production squares can provide sufficient Food and Shields, the Trade from a Gold Mountain can be a great asset. Their lack of Food, though, makes Gold squares untenable as city sites per se.

GRASSLAND (SHIELD)

Terrain Type:	Grasslands
Food:	2
Shields:	1
Trade:	0
Results of Irrigation:	Normal
Results of Mining:	Pheasant / Silk
Results of Transformation:	Coal / Wine

The presence of a Shield in the already valuable Grassland square makes this Terrain more popular than normal. When fully developed, Grassland (Shield) squares are among the best Terrain squares in the game, providing a nice balance of Food, Shields, and Trade. (See the section on "Terrain Improvements" later in this chapter for information on Terrain development.) Grassland (Shield) squares are best avoided as city sites, even though they would work just fine as such. Since you get a free Shield when you build on Terrain that normally produces no Shields, the net result of building a city on a Grassland (Shield) square is the same as building on an unendowed Grassland square. It is better to simply include the Grassland (Shield) square within the city radius and take advantage of the extra Shield.

IRON

Terrain Type:	Mountains
Food:	0
Shields:	4
Trade:	0
Results of Irrigation:	N/A
Results of Mining:	Normal
Results of Transformation:	Wine

Mountain squares containing Iron provide a definite Shield production improvement over Mountains alone. When mined, the Iron square produces a total of 5 Shields each turn. Although this is a significant amount, Iron-Mountain squares are still less productive overall than Coal squares, which (when mined) produce the same number of Shields and a unit of Food as well. Unless Food production in other nearby squares is abundant, it is better to avoid Iron in favor of Coal when looking for a Shield-rich environment. Because of the lack of Food and Trade production in Iron squares, it goes without saying the this Terrain makes a poor city site.

IVORY

Terrain Type:	Glaciers
Food:	1
Shields:	1
Trade:	4
Results of Irrigation:	N/A
Results of Mining:	Normal
Results of Transformation:	Musk Ox

Normally, Glaciers are best avoided at all costs. The presence of Ivory, however, makes a Glacier much more attractive. Ivory produces a significant amount of Trade and also manages to create one unit each of Food and Shields. Still, due to the difficulty involved in developing this Terrain type, even Glaciers with Ivory are best avoided if more flexible environments are available.

OASIS

Terrain Type:	Deserts
Food:	3
Shields:	1
Trade:	0
Results of Irrigation:	Normal
Results of Mining:	Normal
Results of Transformation:	Buffalo

Since they can be made to produce Trade (through the construction of roads), and they do produce Shields, the main difficulty with Deserts is the lack of Food. The presence of an Oasis actually allows a Desert square to produce more Food than Grasslands! Provided that you don't have to build your city in the midst of several Desert squares to take advantage of it, the inclusion of an Oasis within the City Radius can be a tremendous asset to Food production. An Oasis also makes a good city site.

OIL

Terrain Type:	Deserts and Glaciers
Food:	0
Shields:	4
Trade:	0
Results of Irrigation: (Glaciers)	Normal (Deserts); N/A
Results of Mining:	Normal (Deserts and Glaciers)
Results of Transformation:	Wheat (Deserts); Furs (Glaciers)

Oil deposits found in Desert squares, while not as productive as a mined Coal square, can nevertheless significantly increase Shield production for a city. While the same is true for a Glacier-Oil square, Glacier-Oil squares are less valuable overall due to the Glacier's lack of adaptability to Food and Trade production. A Desert-Oil square could conceivably be used as a city site, but the lack of Trade in a Glacier-Oil square makes it unsuitable for this purpose.

PEAT

Terrain Type:	Swamps
Food:	1
Shields:	4
Trade:	0
Results of Irrigation:	Grassland (Shield)*
Results of Mining:	Pheasant
Results of Transformation:	Buffalo

Swamps are much more valuable when Peat is present. However, despite the sizable increase in Shield production, Peat doesn't alter the Swamp's inability to produce Trade. As with several other Special Resources, you should include a Peat-Swamp square inside the City Radius only if the other Terrain surrounding the city offers a good supply of the resources this Terrain type lacks. Because of the inherent adaptability problems of Swamps in terms of Trade, Peat squares make poor city sites.

SILK

Terrain Type:	Forests
Food:	1
Shields:	2
Trade:	3
Results of Irrigation:	Wheat
Results of Mining:	N/A
Results of Transformation:	Grassland (Shield) *

The presence of Silk adds the one resource that is missing from the already useful Forest square: Trade. As mentioned earlier, Forests are valuable additions to a city's production; the three units of Trade offered by Silk make it even more desirable. If you can find a Forest-Silk square, you should definitely consider its inclusion within the City Radius. However, the inability to increase the Food production of this Terrain makes it a poor choice for a city site.

SPICE

Terrain Type:	Swamps
Food:	3
Shields:	0
Trade:	4
Results of Irrigation:	Grassland (Shield) *
Results of Mining:	Silk
Results of Transformation:	Wheat

The presence of Spice in a Swamp square not only provides four units of Trade, it triples the Food production of the Terrain. Despite the lack of Shield production, these factors make the Swamp-Spice square extremely tempting for inclusion in the City Radius. Just make sure that adequate Shield production is provided by other Terrain squares surrounding the city. Provided that the city is properly supported by nearby Shield-producing squares, Spice squares make surprisingly good city sites. They provide resources galore *plus* a defensive bonus for units stationed inside the city.

WHALES

Terrain Type:	Oceans
Food:	2
Shields:	2
Trade:	3
Results of Irrigation:	N/A
Results of Mining:	N/A
Results of Transformation:	N/A

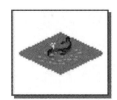

No other Terrain type or Special Resource offers such a wonderful balance of Food, Shield, and Trade production. If cities could be built on Ocean squares, a Whales square would be an excellent choice for a city site. Even though that isn't possible, the inclusion of an Ocean-Whales square within the City Radius offers a terrific boost to the generation of every resource type in that city. Whale squares should be actively sought out and exploited.

WHEAT

Terrain Type:	Plains
Food:	3
Shields:	1
Trade:	0
Results of Irrigation:	Normal
Results of Mining:	Silk
Results of Transformation:	Grassland (Shield) *

The presence of Wheat in a Plains square actually raises Food production to a higher level than that of Grasslands. In fact, irrigated Plains-Wheat squares produce more Food than irrigated Grasslands. For this reason, a Plains-Wheat square makes an excellent city site. The high Food production in the city square itself provides for faster city growth early in the city's development cycle.

WINE

Terrain Type:	Hills
Food:	1
Shields:	0
Trade:	4
Results of Irrigation:	Normal
Results of Mining:	Normal
Results of Transformation:	Wheat

When Wine is present in Hills Terrain, Hills become a significant source of Trade. Irrigation can also be added to increase the Food supply. The only downside is the lack of Shields available. If the Hills-Wine square is mined, the Wine resource disappears.

Tip: If you want to really speed up research early in the game, try building a city on a Wine square. Under any form of government except Despotism, the city square itself produces a good balance of resources with an emphasis on Trade (two Food, one Shield, and five Trade).

Villages

During your exploration, you might, from time to time, come across small, brown huts. These villages, also referred to as "minor tribes" and "goodie huts," belong to no one; they are, rather, a type of Special Resource that is not linked to Terrain type. Often, when you enter a village, the inhabitants of the village randomly treat you to some sort of reward. Although the reward may be an attack by a horde of Barbarians, more often than not the result of visiting villages is a pleasant one.

The following events can result from entering a village:

❧ **The village is empty**—You receive nothing for entering.

❧ **You are attacked by Barbarians**—Upon entering the village, several Barbarian units attack you.

❧ **You receive a gift of cash**—The minor tribe inhabiting the village gives you from 25 to 100 coins, which are added to your treasury.

> **Tip:** It seems that finding a mercenary unit is one of the most common occurrences when visiting a village. Unfortunately, if you continue to pick up mercenary units from villages near one of your own cities, the cumulative maintenance cost for these units can bring the city's production to a grinding halt, and eventually result in the loss of units when maintenance costs can no longer be paid. If you pick up too many mercenaries, move the ones you don't need into their home city and disband them. Not only does this eliminate the unit's maintenance from consideration, it also applies half the unit's Shield cost to the city's current production project.

- **You receive a "Scroll of Ancient Wisdom"**—The elders of the minor tribe give you one free Civilization Advance.
- **A mercenary unit joins your army**—the people of the minor tribe unite to form a military unit in your army. This unit's home city is the closest city to the location of the village where the unit is discovered. If the closest city is a rival city, or if you have yet to build a city, the mercenary unit has *no* home city and therefore requires no support.
- **A band of nomads joins your civilization**—the village is converted into a Settler unit which joins your civilization. Nomad Settlers have no home city, and never require any support.
- **You discover an advanced tribe**—The inhabitants of the village are so awed by your presence that they form a new city, for free, on the site of the village and join your civilization.

As you can see, the positive results of visiting a village definitely outnumber the negative. You should make it a point to visit every village you come across. If you are lucky enough to start the game on a continent with lots of villages, you can get a significant head start in the game depending on the results of your visits. The money, knowledge, and units that can result from your village visits far outweigh the dangers of the occasional Barbarian surprise. And the possibility of a free city alone should send you rushing toward any village that you see.

USING VILLAGES TO YOUR ADVANTAGE

There are a couple of things to keep in mind when dealing with villages. First, if you see a village before you build your first city, it is worth sacrificing a few turns to enter it. Sure, there is a possibility that Barbarians might appear and end your game several turns after it starts, but that risk is minimal when weighed against the possible benefits. At worst, you could have 25 coins added to your treasury. At best you could end up with a second Settler or a free military unit (remember, if you find a Settler or unit before you build a city, they cost nothing to maintain). If you're lucky, you might even get your first city without even having to build it. This leaves your initial Settler free to found a second city, or to develop the Terrain around the first one.

Also, remember that yours is not the only civilization in the game. If one of the opposing civilizations notices a village, they may make a run for it in order to beat you to it and keep you from reaping its benefits. Civilization veterans may be surprised by this, as computer-controlled opponents never moved into villages in the original game. When you see a village, visit it quickly to prevent this situation.

Tip: An interesting fact about "goodie huts" is that they *never* contain Barbarians if they are inside the City Radius of one of your cities. An alternative to exploring villages with your first Settler is to build a city next to the village and then check out the village's contents. Unless it is empty, the village is guaranteed to contain something good.

Tip: The contents of villages are randomly generated at the moment your unit enters the village's Terrain square. This provides you with the perfect opportunity to manipulate the results of your village encounter to suit your needs.

Save the game just before you enter the square, and then move in. If you don't like the results, load the saved game and try again. Repeat this as many times as necessary to achieve the desired results.

Building Cities and Optimizing Terrain

Your civilization is nothing more than a collection of individual cities. While each city must be self-sufficient and provide for the needs of its citizens, all the cities must also work together to support the civilization as a whole. Therefore, two of the most important concepts in *Civilization II* are choosing the proper locations for your cities and learning how to optimize each city's environment to allow for growth of both the city and the civilization as a whole.

CHOOSING A CITY SITE

Now that you are able to recognize the Terrain types on the map, and you have some idea of the resources they produce, you are ready to build a city. The proper selection of city sites can mean the difference between a prosperous civilization and one that must constantly struggle to survive.

Obviously, Terrain type is the most important deciding factor when choosing a city site. As noted earlier in this chapter, the type of Terrain chosen determines how much of each resource type your city can potentially produce.

Each city generates resources by putting its citizens to work in the Terrain squares surrounding the city. As described in Chapter 2, cities control a total of 21 Terrain squares (the city square and 20 surrounding squares) known collectively as the City Radius. When a city is first built, it has a population of one. That citizen is automatically put to work producing resources in one of the city's production squares. The resources produced by your citizens are represented on the Resource Map by the same icons used to represent them in the City Resources Chart of the City Display (see Figure 4-3).

You will note that the city square itself is also generating resources. This is the case no matter how many citizens inhabit the city. The city square itself actually generates more resources than normal for the Terrain type it occupies. The reason for this is that the city square automatically receives all possible Terrain Improvements. For example, a city built on Plains receives the normal one Food and one Shield provided by that Terrain type plus an additional unit of Food (for irrigation) and one unit of Trade (for a road). After

Chapter IV: Resource Production and City Construction

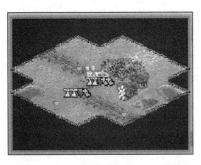

Figure 4-3 The Resource Map of a newly-founded city

the discovery of the Railroad Civilization Advance, the road in the city square is automatically upgraded to a railroad, increasing the production of Food, Shields, and Trade by 50%, regardless of Terrain type. And, after the discovery of Refrigeration, double-irrigation of eligible Terrain squares produces 50% more Food if the city has a Supermarket. (Detailed information on Terrain Improvements can be found later in this chapter.)

Table 4-3 shows the total amount of resources produced by the city square itself when cities are built on each type of Terrain and Special Resource square.

In addition to choosing the proper Terrain type for the city site itself, it is very important to study the Terrain surrounding the potential site. Even if the city square itself is an optimum site, the resources produced therein won't do much to support the city if the surrounding Terrain types don't provide the proper mix of Food, Shields, and Trade for the city to survive. Any Terrain can be changed to a better type through irrigation, mining, or transformation, but all of these actions take time. There is no substitute for choosing a good city site that is surrounded by Terrain that provides an adequate variety of resources for the city.

Note: *Civilization II* gives you a nice bonus that you didn't receive in the original *Civilization*. Terrain types that normally produce no Shields produce one Shield when a city is built in that Terrain square. Keep this extra Shield in mind when choosing a city site, since it can mean potentially more production for the city. For instance, if you have the choice of building on a Grasslands square (which produces no Shields) or an adjacent Grassland (Shield) square (which produces one Shield), build your city on the normal Grasslands square. That way, you'll get the free Shield for the city, and you'll still be able to exploit the Shield in the Grassland (Shield) square.

✤ **Table 4-3.** Resources Produced by City Squares in
Each Terrain/Special Resource Type

TERRAIN/RESOURCE TYPE	FOOD	SHIELDS	TRADE
Deserts	1	1	1
Forests	1	2	0
Glaciers	0	1	0
Grasslands	3	1	1
Hills	2	1	0
Jungles	1	1	0
Mountains	1	1	0
Oceans	N/A	N/A	N/A
Plains	2	1	1
Swamps	1	1	0
Tundra	2	1	0
Buffalo	2	3	1
Coal	2	2	0
Fish	N/A	N/A	N/A
Fruit	4	1	1
Furs	3	1	3
Pheasant	3	2	0
Musk Ox	4	1	0
Gems	1	1	4
Gold	1	1	6
Grassland (Shield)	3	1	1
Iron	1	4	0
Ivory	1	1	4
Oasis	4	1	1
Oil (D)	1	4	1
Oil (G)	0	4	0
Peat	1	4	0
Silk	1	2	3
Spice	3	1	4
Whales	N/A	N/A	N/A
Wheat	4	1	1
Wine	2	1	4

The site chosen for your first city can truly make or break your game. A good resource mix is important throughout the game, but never more so than at the start. The amount of Food produced affects the growth of the city. The amount of Shields produced affects the speed at which a city can build units, Improvements, and Wonders. And the amount of Trade produced affects the speed at which Civilization Advances can be discovered.

It is a mistake to concentrate too heavily on any one resource early in the game. A city that produces tons of Shields is ultimately useless if research and population growth is stunted by lack of Food and Trade. A city that produces massive amounts of Trade is great for advancing your knowledge, but you can't take advantage of all the new units, Improvements and Wonders made possible by that knowledge unless you have the Shields to build them. And although a Food-rich environment will make the city grow quickly, the quick population growth will cause massive unhappiness unless you have Trade to spend on Luxuries and Shields to build Improvements and Wonders to make the people happy.

The best strategy is to build the first city on a Terrain type that produces at least two Food, one Shield, and one Trade. (Don't forget the automatic modifications received by the city—use Table 4-4 as a guide.) Make sure that the site you choose is surrounded by Terrain types that complement one another: strong Shield-producers like Hills and Forests should be offset by strong Food-producers like Grasslands, for instance. When possible, find a site that includes one or more Special Resources within the City Radius. Rivers, too, should be sought out, since they greatly aid movement and contribute to Trade. Finally, if you are near the coast, build a city adjacent to one or more Ocean squares. Not only does this aid in the exploration of the world by allowing sea travel (when the appropriate Advances are discovered), it also provides an excellent source of Trade.

Finally, it is very important that you explore all of the Terrain that is to be included within the City Radius *before* you build your city. Unexplored areas (black squares) cannot be used to produce resources for the city, and are therefore useless to the city until they are revealed. The one exception to the "explore before you build" rule applies to building cities on the coastline of a continent. It is usually impossible to reveal the Ocean squares off the coast until you can build sea units. In these cases, make sure you explore the hidden Ocean squares as soon as you are able to build a Trireme.

Tip: Some players hold to the practice of building a city right away, no matter where they are when the game starts. Their argument is that the sooner the first city is built, the faster you can begin researching Civilization Advances. This is true, of course, but I've always found this practice to be a bit reckless. I've found that it often pays to take a couple of turns to explore the immediate area, and pick-and-choose between potential city sites in the vicinity. It's possible that this strategy might put you a little behind in your initial research, but the lost time can be made up quickly if you find a city site with particularly good Trade generation potential. Wouldn't you be upset to find that, just outside your City Radius, is a Special Resource you could have been exploiting if you had just explored a bit first?

These principles hold true for every city you establish. If you follow these guidelines, all your cities will be prosperous. There is more leeway as the game progresses, however, since strong, well-established cities can help to support a newly-founded city that might not be built in the best of locations.

INCREASING RESOURCE PRODUCTION

You can only get so far on the resources produced in the city square and one other production square. Luckily, as your population grows, each new citizen is automatically put to work in one of the empty production squares on the Resource Map. Therefore, as the population continues to increase, so do the resources generated.

Eventually, the naturally occurring resources just aren't enough to sustain the needs of the city itself or the civilization as a whole. Fortunately, there are ways of increasing the production of each resource type. This can be accomplished in a number of different ways.

Terrain Improvements

One of the easiest and least costly methods of increasing resource production is by making improvements to the Terrain surrounding the city. From the start of the game, Settlers are capable of modifications that, under the proper conditions, can increase the production of Food, Shields, and Trade of certain types of Terrain. As Civilization Advances are discovered Settlers (and, eventually, Engineers) gain even more Terrain improvement capabilities.

The types of terrain improvement possible are as follows:

* **Irrigation**—In Deserts, Grasslands, Hills, Plains, and Tundra, irrigation can be used to increase Food production by one unit per turn. After the discovery of Refrigeration, Food production in cities with the Supermarket Improvement can be increased by an additional 50 percent by building Farmland (irrigating twice) in these types of Terrain.

* **Mining**—Shield production in Deserts, Glaciers, Hills, and Mountains can be increased through mining. Shield production is increased by one per turn when a mine is built in each of these Terrain types, with the exception of Hills where Shield production is increased by three.

* **Roads**—Aside from Oceans, no Terrain type naturally produces Trade unless there is a Special Resource or River present. One unit of Trade per turn can be generated in Deserts, Grasslands, and Plains, however, if they contain a road. (Roads also reduce the movement cost of any Terrain type to 1/3 of a movement point.)

* **Railroads**—Railroads can be constructed by Settlers and Engineers after the discovery of the Railroad Civilization Advance. A railroad passing through any type of Terrain square increases the Shield and Trade production of that square by 50 percent. (Railroads also eliminate movement cost in all types of Terrain.)

* **Transformation**—With the exception of Oceans, any type of Terrain can be changed into another through the process of Engineer transformation. Additionally, irrigation and mining have similar transformation effects on certain types of Terrain. This is a time-consuming procedure, but it is often the only way to make a useless Terrain square productive.

The results of each type of terrain improvement are noted in Table 4-1.

Adjusting the Work Force

As noted earlier, as new citizens are added to the city's work force, each is automatically put to work in one of the city's production squares. When this occurs, the game attempts to anticipate your needs and place the citizen in the production square where it can produce what the computer feels that the city requires the most. Sometimes a situation may arise where you need more of one particular resource for a short period of time. You might, for instance, need extra Shields to produce a unit quickly.

In times like these, the best way to increase the resource you need the most is to move one or more citizens to Terrain squares that produce more of the resource you need. See Figures 4-4 and 4-5.

Figure 4-4 shows the automatic distribution of the city's Work Force as chosen by the computer. Note that the city is exhibiting reasonable overall resource production, though Shield production is somewhat low, slowing the construction of the unit, Improvement, or Wonder the city is currently building.

By removing citizens from the two Ocean-Fish squares and placing them in the Forest squares (as shown in Figure 4-5), Food production is reduced to bare minimum and Trade production is significantly reduced. Shield production, however, is tripled as a result of the change. This makes it possible to complete the item currently under production in the city three times faster than with the original Work Force distribution shown in Figure 4-4. Once the item has been produced, the work force can be returned to its former configuration.

Production is moved from one production square to another by clicking once on the original production square, then clicking on the empty square to which you want the production relocated.

It is a good idea to check the distribution of each city's work force from time to time to make sure that their resource produc-

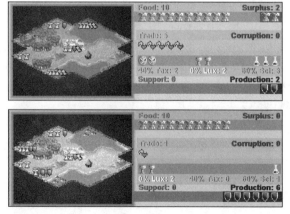

Figures 4-4 and 4-5 Increasing Shield Production by Adjusting the Work Force

tion is meeting the needs of the city and your civilization as a whole. Although the computer's automatic distribution usually works fairly well, minor adjustments here and there can sometimes vastly improve your overall production.

Construction of Improvements and Wonders

Another factor that can greatly affect the resource production of a city are the City Improvements and Wonders of the World you choose to build there. Certain Improvements and Wonders greatly increase the production of a given resource type. The following sections provide a brief summary of how each resource type can be enhanced through city construction. Full information on the effects of each Improvement and Wonder mentioned here can be found in Chapter 6.

FOOD

Both the Supermarket and Granary Improvements affect the Food supply of a city. The presence of a Supermarket increases the Food production of double-irrigated (farmland) squares by 50%. While the Granary doesn't actually increase Food production, it cuts by half the amount of accumulated Food required for an increase in a city's population.

The only Wonder that affects Food in any way is the Pyramids. The Pyramids act as a granary in every one of your cities.

SHIELDS

Shield production is increased through the construction of Factories, Manufacturing Plants, Power Plants, Hydro Plants, Nuclear Plants, Solar Plants, and Offshore Platforms. The effects of Shield production increase for each of these Improvements is discussed fully in Chapter 6.

Two Wonders also affect Shield production: King Richard's Crusade and the Hoover Dam. King Richard's Crusade increases Shield production by one in every square within the City Radius. Hoover Dam acts as a Hydro Plant Improvement in every friendly city.

TRADE

Because Trade is, for the most part, dealt with on the basis of its component parts (Taxes, Luxuries, and Science), Improvements and Wonders usually affect a single aspect of Trade. Details on the effects produced can be found in Chapter 6.

- ❧ **Capitalization** converts all Shield production into cash, effectively increasing income from Taxes.

- ❧ **Marketplaces, Banks, and Stock Exchanges** increase both Taxes and Luxuries in the city.

- ❧ **Libraries, Universities, and Research Labs** increase Science output, as do the Copernicus' Observatory, Isaac Newton's College, and SETI Program Wonders.

There are exceptions to this rule, however. The Superhighway Improvement increases overall Trade in production squares containing roads or railroads by 50%, and the Colossus Wonder adds one unit of Trade to every square that is already producing some Trade.

Trade Routes

By using Caravans and Freight units to establish trade routes, a city's Trade can be increased. A trade route can be established with any friendly or opposing city that is at least ten squares distant from the home city of the unit establishing the route.

When a trade route is established, you receive an immediate cash reward that is added to your treasury. Then, each turn, the city that initiated the trade route receives a set amount of Trade as long as the route operates. The profitability of the trade route depends on a number of factors, including the distance between the origin and destination cities and the destination city's demand for the items traded.

More information about trade routes can be found in Chapter 7.

Increasing Production by Changing Governments

The varying levels of personal and economic freedom allowed by different forms of government affect the level of resource production enjoyed by a civilization. The specific details concerning production advantages and limitations under various ruling systems are discussed in Chapter 9. However, the general rule is the more advanced the government, the more lucrative the production.

V

CITY MANAGEMENT

*Y*our job with respect to city management isn't over even when you get the knack of surveying the Terrain. On the contrary, it has only begun. Although your cities can manage most turn-to-turn tasks on their own, there are some functions that demand your attention from time to time in order to keep the cities running at peak efficiency.

In this chapter, we'll look at solutions to some of the most common problems faced in the management of cities.

Population Growth

As discussed in previous chapters, population growth of cities results from the accumulation of surplus Food in the city's Food Storage Box. Each time the Food Storage Box is completely filled, another citizen is added to the city's population.

The following formula is used to determine how much Food must be accumulated in order for a city's population to increase:

$$Food\ Rows \times (city\ size + 1) = full\ Food\ Storage\ Box$$

where:

Food Rows = the number of rows of Food icons in the Food Storage box, and the default value for Food Rows = 10

Based on the default value for Food Rows, a city with a size of "1" requires the accumulation of 20 units of Food in order to grow to size "2" ($10 \times (1 + 1) = 20$). As the size of the city increases, so does the amount of accumulated Food required for the city to grow. For a size "2" city to grow to size "3," it requires the accumulation of 30 Food. For a size "3" to grow to a size "4," it requires 40 Food, and so on (see Figure 5-1).

If the city is generating only enough Food to support its citizens and Settlers, no surplus Food is generated, and the city experiences no growth. If the Food demands of the city exceed the amount of Food generated by the city each turn, Food is taken from the Food Storage Box to cover the amount of the deficit. If no Food is available to cover the deficit, one Settler/Engineer is destroyed or one point of population is lost each turn until the Food supply can once again cover the city's needs.

It is important to make sure that the Food demand does not exceed the city's supply. Ideally, a city should enjoy a steady growth at all times. If this is not the case, you might have chosen a poor city site. Use the Terrain improvement methods discussed in Chapter 4 to increase the Food supply as needed. Also, keep in

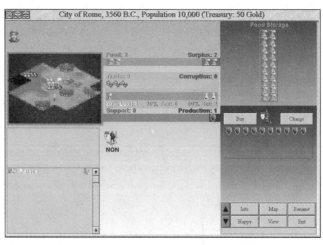

Figure 5-1 A city on the verge of population growth

>
>
> **Tip:** It is equally import to remember that some Food production is lost if you happen to change from an advanced form of government to a more primitive form (Republic to Despotism, for example). If this change lasts for a long period of time, cities that were growing steadily under the more advanced form of government begin to experience population loss due to lower Food production.

mind that resource production of all types, including Food production, is increased under the more modern systems of government (see Chapter 9 for details). You can also establish Food trade routes between a Food rich city and one that is experiencing a Food shortage. Each Food trade route increases the destination city's Food production (and decreases the source city's Food production) by one unit of Food per turn.

Population Unhappiness

One side effect of city growth is growing unrest among your population. Although unhappy citizens are not usually a problem early in the game (except at higher difficulty levels), the larger your cities grow, the more frequently you have to deal with this problem

Average citizens exist in three states: happy, content, and unhappy. Happy citizens appear on the left end of the Population Roster. Content citizens appear to the right of the happy citizens. Unhappy citizens appear to the right of the content citizens (see Figure 5-2).

When a city is first established, each citizen added to the population is automatically content. The number of citizens in each city who are "born" con-

Figure 5-2 The Population Roster, showing happy, content, and unhappy citizens

tent varies according to difficulty level (see Table 3-1 for details). After the population reaches this number, every new citizen is automatically unhappy when he/she is added to the city's population.

In Republics and Democracies, citizens also become unhappy as a result of military units that are away from their home cities. Any ground or sea units (aside from Settlers, Engineers, Diplomats, Spies, Caravans, Transport, and Freight units) not inside a friendly city or inside a fortress within three squares of a friendly city (in the case of ground units) has the possibility of causing one or more citizens to become unhappy. Air units and missiles cause unhappiness regardless of their location. (Specific details on unhappiness caused by units in Republics and Democracies can be found in Chapter 9.)

Another factor that contributes to population unhappiness is the size of your empire. The more cities you have, the more uneasy your citizens become. Once you have more than a certain number of cities under your control, additional unhappy citizens start to appear. The number of cities you can control without experiencing additional unhappiness is based on a number of factors, including the game difficulty level and the type of government you are using. The equation used to determine this number is as follows:

Max. Cities = Riot Factor −((difficulty level × 2) × ((government ÷ 2) + 2))/2)

where:

the default value of *Riot Factor* = 14

difficulty level = a range from 0 (Chieftain) through 5 (Deity)

government = 0 (Anarchy) 1 (Despotism) 2 (Monarchy) 3 (Communism) 4 (Fundamentalism) 5 (Republic) 6 (Democracy)

The effects caused by this rather daunting equation can be easily explained. High difficulty levels and/or lower forms of government lessen the number of cities you can control before additional unhappiness occurs. Low difficulty levels and/or more sophisticated forms of government allow for the effective control of more cities.

Note: Riot Factor is read in from RULES.TXT.

CIVIL DISORDER

The ultimate result of population unhappiness is Civil Disorder. When unhappy citizens outnumber happy citizens, the city enters a state of Civil Disorder (see Figure 5-3).

Civil Disorder is a state of affairs to be avoided at all costs. When a city is in Civil Disorder, no Taxes are collected, no Science is generated, and the production of units, Improvements, and Wonders is halted.

The effects of Civil Disorder can be far-reaching. The loss of Tax revenues from the

Figure 5-3 A city in Civil Disorder

cities in disorder puts a financial burden on your other cities, since the Upkeep costs for Improvements in the disrupted cities must still be paid. The loss of Science normally generated by these cities slows down your research of new Advances. Under a Democracy, if one or more cities remain in Civil Disorder for two consecutive turns, the government collapses into Anarchy.

PREVENTING UNHAPPINESS

Luckily, citizens can be swayed from their natural tendency to become unhappy. If proper steps are taken, you should be able to keep your population content, and Civil Disorder, if it occurs, should last no more than one turn. The following steps can be taken to keep your citizens from becoming unhappy or to diffuse a state of Civil Disorder (should one occur). The effects of each of these cures for unhappiness can be monitored on the Happiness Chart of the City Display. (Details on how to read the Happiness Chart can be found in Chapter 2.)

Adjust the Luxuries Rate

One potential solution that increases citizen happiness in all your cities is increasing the percentage of your Trade that is converted to Luxuries. This percentage can be adjusted by selecting the "Tax Rate" option from the Kingdom menu. By moving the appropriate slider, the Luxuries rate can be increased or decreased. (see Figure 5-4).

Luxuries are represented by Luxury icons in the Resources Chart of the city display. Every two Luxury icons make one unhappy citizen content, or one content citizen happy. So, for example, at a Luxuries rate of 20%, a city producing 10 units of Trade each turn generates two Luxury icons, enough to appease one citizen.

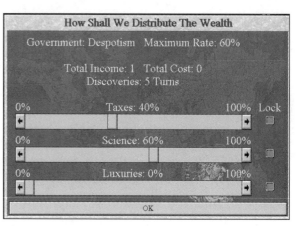

Figure 5-4 Adjusting the Luxuries rate

Although this solution is one of the most effective in slowing the growth of unhappiness in your cities, remember that every time you increase the Luxuries percentage, either the Taxes or Science percentage is decreased proportionally to compensate. A lower Science rate means that Civilization Advance research takes longer. A lower Tax rate means that less money is available for the maintenance of City Improvements each turn. Fortunately, the Tax Rate adjustment window has a section at the top that monitors the number of turns required to discover new Advances and the amount of Tax income versus the maintenance cost of Improvements. If either of these values becomes unacceptable as a result of increasing the Luxuries rate, you must seek another solution to your unhappiness problem.

Declare Martial Law

Under any form of government except Fundamentalism, Republic and Democracy, it is possible to suppress unhappy citizens by maintaining a strong military presence in the city. Up to three military units can be used to impose martial law. Each unit makes two unhappy citizens content.

Although this is an excellent way to keep order in a city in the short term, dependence on this method to ensure happiness limits you to the more basic forms of government. If your citizens are happy only because martial law makes them so, switching to a Republic or Democracy under these circumstances could be disastrous in terms of widespread Civil Disorder. Also, the maintenance costs of the units imposing martial law can eventually become quite a strain if the city is supporting a large number of units.

Convert to Fundamentalism

Fundamentalism is a form of government that did not exist in the original *Civilization*. This ruling system has a number of unique characteristics that are discussed in detail in Chapter 9.

The feature of Fundamentalism that applies specifically to the subject at hand is that, under this form of government, *no citizen is ever unhappy!* And, furthermore, any Improvement or Wonder that would normally make citizens happy instead produces money. Choosing to rule your civilization through Fundamentalism completely eliminates the headaches and strife that usually accompany the effort to keep your people happy.

Of course, there are several drawbacks to Fundamentalism. Foremost among these is that Science production is halved, significantly slowing your research of Civilization Advances. For this reason, Fundamentalism should not be adopted solely as a solution to unhappiness.

Convert Citizens to Entertainers

Unhappiness can be offset on a local basis by converting one or more of a city's citizens to Entertainers. Entertainers belong to a special class of citizens known as "Specialists." Specialists are citizens who have been removed from their normal jobs of generating resources for the city to perform specialized functions.

To convert a citizen into an Entertainer, click on any Terrain square on the Resource Map that is generating resources. The resource icons disappear, and one citizen icon in the Population Roster disappears. Simultaneously, the Entertainer's icon appears to the right of the normal population icons (see Figure 5-5). When the Entertainer's services are no longer needed, he can be returned to his resource-production role by clicking on any empty production square on the Resource Map.

Figure 5-5 The Population Roster showing Entertainers

Each Entertainer generates two Luxury icons, which has the effect of making one content citizen happy. Each happy citizen offsets the effects of one unhappy citizen. As mentioned earlier, as long as unhappy citizens don't outnumber happy citizens, Civil Disorder is averted.

You can create as many Entertainers as necessary to appease the city's population. The unfortunate side effect of creating Entertainers, however, is the resulting loss of resource generation. Each Entertainer created is one less citizen working to produce resources. Creating too many Entertainers, therefore, could result in deficits in Food and Shields, and/or a significant reduction in Trade. For this reason, Entertainers should be considered a short-term solution to unhappiness rather than a permanent fix. If you need more than one Entertainer in a single city, it is usually a pretty good sign that you are doing something wrong.

Build City Improvements and Wonders of the World

The most permanent, and therefore the best, solution to unhappiness is the construction of Improvements and Wonders that improve the mood of your citizens by offsetting the cause of their unrest. Table 5-1 lists the Improvements and Wonders that affect the happiness of your citizens.

> Tip: Production of units, Improvements, and Wonders in a city ceases when the city enters a state of Civil Disorder. In most cases, this means that the item currently under production cannot be completed, either through allocation of Shields or through purchase, until the unhappiness problem has been eliminated. This is not the case, however, when the item under production is an Improvement or Wonder that makes your people happy, such as a Cathedral or Michelangelo's Chapel. Although no Shields are allocated to their production until the city is no longer in Disorder, you *can* pay to have such items completed. If you have sufficient funds, buying a happiness-inducing Improvement or Wonder is an excellent way to end Civil Disorder quickly.

✤ **Table 5-1.** Improvements and Wonders that
Affect Population Happiness

IMPROVEMENTS	EFFECT
Bank	Increases Luxuries by 50% (cumulative with Marketplace)
Cathedral	Makes 4 unhappy citizens content (3 with Communism)
Colosseum	Makes 3 unhappy citizens content (4 with Electronics)
Courthouse	Makes 1 content citizen happy (only under a Democracy)
Marketplace	Increases Luxuries by 50%
Police Station	Decreases unhappiness caused by units away from the city by one per unit
Stock Exchange	Increases Luxuries by 50% (cumulative with Marketplace and Bank)
Temple	Makes up to 2 unhappy citizens content

WONDERS	
Cure for Cancer	Makes one content citizen happy in every friendly city
Hanging Gardens	Makes one content citizen happy in every friendly city
J. S. Bach's Cathedral	Reduces unhappy citizens by two in every friendly city
Michelangelo's Chapel	Counts as a Cathedral in each of your cities
Oracle	Doubles the effectiveness of all Temples
Shakespeare's Theatre	All unhappy citizens in the city where Wonder is built are made content
Women's Suffrage	Acts as a Police Station in every friendly city

Note: While the effects of some of the Improvements and Wonders listed in Table 5-1 are cumulative, some of them expire or cancel the effects of one another. Consult Chapter 7 for complete information on each item listed.

In addition to the Improvements and Wonders that directly affect the happiness of your citizens, you should also consider building the Improvements and Wonders that increase Trade as a whole. Remember, an increase in Trade also means an increase in Luxuries. The more Luxuries a city generates, the more citizens remain happy. (Complete information on the effects of Improvements and Wonders can be found in Chapter 7.)

"WE LOVE THE (LEADER) DAY!"

One sure sign that you are doing a more than adequate job of keeping your citizens happy is the celebration of "We Love the King (Despot, President, etc.) Day" in one or more of your cities. This cele-bration in your honor is held in

Figure 5-6 We Love the King Day

a city whenever 50% or more of the city's population is happy (see Figure 5-6).

A city celebrating We Love the (Leader) Day receives a resource produc-tion bonus: its resource production is treated as if the city were ruled by the next highest form of government. For example, a city celebrating We Love the (Leader) Day under a Despotic government is treated as if it were ruled by a Monarchy. In other words, the resource production penalties experienced under Despotism are alleviated (see Chapter 9 for details). Additionally, under both Republic and Democracy, one new citizen is added to the celebrating city each turn until the celebration ends. These bonuses significantly improve both the growth of the city, and the production of units, Improvements, and Wonders.

The celebration and its accompanying benefits continue as long as 50% or more of the population remains happy. As soon as the number of happy citizens drops below 50% of the city's population, the celebration ends.

Shield Shortages

Just as it is possible to experience a shortage of Food, there is also a possibility that a city might not generate enough Shields to operate effectively. When a city is built in an area where the Terrain has low Shield output, or when the number of units supported by the city is particularly high, production can quickly grind to a halt due to a lack of surplus Shields. Units might also start to disappear if the city can no longer support them.

The best solution to this problem is to choose your city sites wisely, making sure that there are plenty of Shield-generating Terrain squares within the City Radius. If you happen to run into a Shield deficit, there are a number of solutions available to ease the problem.

IMPROVE THE TERRAIN

Terrain improvements made by Settlers or Engineers are the least costly way to increase the number of Shields generated by the city. By building a mine in Deserts, Hills, and Mountains, you can significantly increase the city's potential Shield supply.

MOVE YOUR CITIZENS TO DIFFERENT PRODUCTION SQUARES

You can increase the number of Shields produced in the city by moving your citizens to production squares that generate a high number of Shields. For example, the number of Shields produced can be dramatically increased by moving production from a Grassland square to a mined Hills square.

When using this technique, it is important to monitor the effect of the production change on the other two resources, especially Food. If moving production to generate more Shields causes a Food deficit, you should seek another solution to your problem rather than risk a population loss due to lack of food.

DISBAND OR REASSIGN UNITS

Under most forms of government, units require that their home city pay a maintenance cost of one Shield per turn to support the unit. When a single city is supporting a number of units, the cumulative maintenance costs add up quickly and choke the city's production capabilities.

Tip: If you are forced to disband a unit, always disband the unit inside one of your cities when possible. When you disband a unit inside a city, 50% of the unit's original Shield cost is applied to whatever is currently being built in that city.

Make sure that all the units supported by each city are being used to their fullest potential. Units that are not being used should be disbanded at once. If all the units are playing a vital role, consider assigning them to another city. Find a city that is supporting few units, move the unit into that city, and press the "H" key, or choose the "Home City" option from the Orders menu. The unit now treats this city as its home city: maintenance costs are paid by the new city, freeing up resources in the unit's former home.

BUILD IMPROVEMENTS AND WONDERS

As with Food and Trade shortages, a Shield deficit can be alleviated by building certain City Improvements and Wonders of the World. The increase in Shield generation gained in this way is usually permanent, making Improvements and Wonders is one of the two best long-term solutions to a Shield shortage (the other being Terrain Improvements). Table 5-2 lists the Improvements and Wonders that enhance Shield production.

Interference From Opposing Units and Nearby Cities

Even though you might have the hang of controlling the resource production of your cities, there are outside forces, often beyond your control, that can interfere with their well-being. Primary among these are opposing units and nearby cities.

Units belonging to another civilization need not attack in order to have a detrimental effect on your cities. Terrain squares occupied by non-allied units cannot produce any resources (see Figure 5-7). See Chapter 9 for details on alliances.

When an opposing unit moves into any square within the City Radius that is generating resources, the production is automatically moved to a different Terrain square (if one is available). The square occupied by the enemy unit

Figure 5-7 An enemy unit blocking resource production

✤ **Table 5-2.** Improvements and Wonders that Enhance Shield Production

IMPROVEMENTS	EFFECT
Factory	Increases the city's Shield output by 50%.
Hydro Plant *	Increases Factory output by 50%.
Manufacturing Plant	Increases the city's Shield output by 50% (cumulative with Factory).
Nuclear Plant *	Increases Factory output by 50%.
Offshore Platform	All Ocean squares in the City Radius produce one Shield.
Power Plant *	Increases Factory output by 50%.
Solar Plant *	Increases Factory output by 50%.
WONDERS	
Hoover Dam†	Acts as a Hydro Plant in all friendly cities.
King Richard's Crusade	Every square in the City Radius of the city where this Wonder is built produces one extra Shield.

* Only one type of power plant can exist in any one city.
† The effects of Hoover Dam are not cumulative with existing power plants.

remains incapable of production until such a time as an alliance is formed with the owner of the unit, the unit is voluntarily withdrawn, or the unit is destroyed. The latter solution is usually the most expedient, but you must be prepared for the consequences of war if you choose this course of action.

The other outside force that can reduce a city's resource production is the presence of another city nearby. If the second city is close enough to allow the City Radii of the two cities to overlap, one or both cities experiences a loss of resource production. The reason for this is that a production square cannot be developed by two cities simultaneously. This is true whether the interfering city is one of your own cities or one belonging to an opposing civilization.

In this situation, production squares under development by the interfering city are outlined in white on the Resource Map (see Figure 5-8). These squares remain off-limits as long as they are in use by the other city.

The only good solution to this problem is to avoid allowing cities to be built in such a way that their City Radii overlap. This is easily done with regards to cities you build yourself, but a little trickier when it comes to preventing the enemy from doing so. Keep your eyes open, and quickly eliminate any enemy cities that are built too close to your own. If you attack early enough, you might be able to destroy the city completely as opposed to capturing it (which wouldn't solve the problem). If you aren't lucky enough to destroy the city, you must make the best of the situation. The only thing you can do is adjust production and Terrain in such a way as to give both cities enough resources to survive.

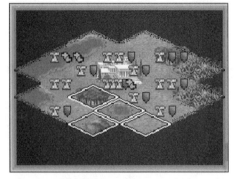

Figure 5-8 The effects of a nearby city on resource production

Pollution

One of the negative byproducts of a rapidly growing civilization is pollution. Although you seldom have to deal with this problem early in the game, you are forced to deal with it more and more frequently as time progresses. Knowing the causes, effects, and solutions to the growing pollution problem are important to your success in the game.

CAUSES OF POLLUTION

Pollution can be caused by a number of different things. However, the primary sources of pollution are the Shield production and population of your cities.

Pollution caused by the production of Shields is known as Resource Pollution. The following equation is used to calculate each city's Resource Pollution:

Resource Pollution = (# of Shields Produced ÷ divisor) − 20

The "divisor" in the Resource Pollution equation is usually "1". However, the construction of certain City Improvements can increase the "divisor," thus reducing the total amount of Resource Pollution. These Improvements and their divisors are listed in Table 5-3.

The other factor that contributes to city-produced pollution is the size of a city's population. Population size doesn't become a problem until you discover

Industrialization. After this point, the size of the city's population and the continued advance of technology combine to generate increasing levels of Population Pollution. The formula used to calculate Population Pollution is as follows:

$$Population\ Pollution = (City\ Population \times Tech.\ Multiplier) \div 4$$

The "Tech. Multiplier" is a numerical value used to represent the level of your technology. The multiplier is "0" until the discovery of Industrialization, when it becomes "1". From this point, the multiplier is modified based on the discovery of certain Civilization Advances and by the construction of certain City Improvements, as shown in Table 5-4. These modifiers are cumulative.

✤ **Table 5-3.** City Improvements that Reduce Resource Pollution

IMPROVEMENT	DIVISOR
Hydro Plant	2
Nuclear Plant	2
Recycling	3
Solar Plant	0*

* Solar Plants completely eliminate the city's Resource Pollution

✤ **Table 5-4.** Modifiers to the Tech. Multiplier
Used to Calculate Population Pollution

TECHNOLOGY/IMPROVEMENT	MODIFIER
Automobile	+1
Mass Production	+1
Plastics	+1
Environmentalism	-1
Sanitation not yet discovered	+1
Mass Transit	0*
Solar Planet	-1

* Mass Transit completely eliminates the city's Population Pollution.

Figure 5-9 Pollution icons.

The pollution potential of a city is represented in the City Display by pollution icons in the Information Box (see Figure 5-9). The number of pollution icons produced by a city is calculated in the following manner:

$$Pollution\ icons = Resource\ Pollution + Population\ Pollution$$

POLLUTION EXAMPLE: A city with a population of 19 is producing a total of 49 shields per turn, and has no Improvements that reduce Resource Pollution. The civilization has discovered both Mass Production and Sanitation. The city's pollution icons are calculated as follows:

$$Resource\ Pollution = (49 \div 1) - 20$$
$$Population\ Pollution = (19 \times 1) \div 4$$
$$Pollution\ icons = 29 + 4\ (rounded\ down\ from\ 4.75)$$
$$Pollution\ icons = 33$$

Once the number of pollution icons has been calculated, the game uses this number as part of the following complex formula every turn to determine whether the city pollutes one of the squares within its City Radius:

$$Pollute = difficulty\ level \times (\#\ of\ Advances \div 2)$$
$$Random = a\ random\ number\ between\ 0\ and\ (256 - Pollute)$$
$$If\ Random < (Total\ Pollution\ icons \times 2)$$
$$Then\ Pollution\ occurs\ in\ one\ Terrain\ square\ within\ the\ City\ Radius$$

where:

difficulty level = 0 (Chieftain) or 1 (Warlord) or 2 (Prince) or 3 (King) or 4 (Emperor) or 5 (Deity)

# of Advances = the total number of Civilization Advances that you have discovered EXCLUDING the ones you are given at the start of the game

Although cities are the most common polluters in the game, pollution can also be produced in two other ways: nuclear accidents and nuclear incidents. The meltdown of a Nuclear Plant in a city causes severe pollution within the City Radius. The detonation of a Nuclear Missile also causes massive pollution to appear in the Terrain squares surrounding its target.

Note: After you have discovered a certain number of Future Technologies, the "Pollute" number in the above equation becomes larger than 256. In other words, the city always produces pollution. Fortunately, building a Solar Plant in the city eliminates this problem.

THE EFFECTS OF POLLUTION

When pollution appears on the map, it is represented by a wicked-looking skull icon (see Figure 5-10). The symbol used is very appropriate: pollution is a serious problem that, if left unchecked, can cause many difficulties as the game progresses. The presence of pollution instantly causes a localized drop in resource production and can eventually lead to the more far-reaching crisis of global warming.

Figure 5-10 Pollution rears its ugly head.

Production Loss

The immediate effect of pollution is a loss of productivity. Resource generation in a polluted Terrain square is reduced by 50%. For example, a mined Hills-Wine square that normally produces one Food, three Shields, and four Trade produces only one Food, two Shields, and two Trade when polluted. If a city is allowed to continue polluting the surrounding Terrain, resource production for that city could quickly drop to critical levels.

Global Warming

If pollution continues to spread unchecked, it can eventually reach levels high enough to affect not only local resource production, but the ecology of the entire world. When critical levels of pollution are reached, there is a chance that the planet will experience global warming.

Global warming is a worldwide rise in temperature caused by the buildup of pollutants in the atmosphere. When the average temperature of the planet rises sufficiently, the polar ice caps melt, raising the level of the oceans. In game terms, this means the widespread transformation of Terrain adjacent to Ocean squares into Jungles and Swamps. In areas not adjacent to coastlines, many Grasslands and Plains squares are transformed into Desert.

The chance for global warming is based on the number of polluted squares under your control. Once eight polluted squares exist, there is a chance for global warming. If world pollution continues to grow, global warming can reoccur over and over again. For each successive occurrence, the amount of pollution that potentially triggers the crisis increases by two. (The second global warming occurs when ten squares are polluted, the third occurs at twelve, and so on.)

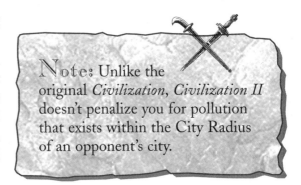

Note: Unlike the original *Civilization*, *Civilization II* doesn't penalize you for pollution that exists within the City Radius of an opponent's city.

Monitoring Global Warming

As soon as pollution appears in one map square, a "sun" icon appears in the Status Report Section of the Status Window (see Figure 5-11). The color of this icon serves as a gauge of the imminent threat of global warming by indicating the number of map squares currently polluted. The colors are interpreted as follows:

> **Dark Red**—1 square polluted
> **Light Red**—2–3 squares polluted
> **Yellow**—4–5 squares polluted
> **White**—6 or more squares polluted

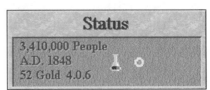

Figure 5-11 The Status Report, indicating the presence of pollution

> **Tip:** Every Solar Plant you build negates one-half of one polluted square. In other words, if there are six polluted squares in your territory, and four of your cities have Solar Plants, the game counts only four squares of pollution toward the global warming total.

POLLUTION SOLUTIONS

Because of its effects on resource production, and the prospect of losing massive amounts of productive Terrain as a result of global warming, pollution is a problem that is best dealt with before it reaches crisis levels. There are a number of methods available that allow you to clean up pollution when it occurs and prevent it from occurring in the future.

Use Settlers/Engineers to Remove Pollution

Settler and Engineer units have the ability to clean up pollution. Simply move them into the polluted Terrain square and press the "P" key, or select "Clean Up Pollution" from the Orders menu. It takes four turns for a single Settlers unit to clean up pollution, and two for a single Engineers unit.

Build Improvements and Wonders

A number of Improvements and Wonders are specifically designed to reduce or eliminate pollution. These are listed in Table 5-5. Complete information on the Improvements listed here can be found in Chapter 7.

> **Note:** The Hydro, Nuclear, and Solar Plants each produce two effects: they increase Factory Shield production by 50%, and they decrease Resource Pollution. If there is no Factory present, the city still receives the pollution benefits of these three Improvements. Also note that the benefits of these effects are NOT cumulative with one another, since only one of the three can exist in a city at any given time.

✤ **Table 5-5.** Improvements and Wonders that Reduce Pollution

IMPROVEMENTS	EFFECT
Hydro Plant	Reduces a city's Resource Pollution by 50%.
Mass Transit	Eliminates a city's Population Pollution entirely.
Nuclear Plant	Reduces a city's Resource Pollution by 50%.
Recycling Center	Reduces a city's Resource Pollution by 66% (2/3).
Solar Plant	Eliminates a city's Resource Pollution entirely.

WONDERS	
Hoover Dam *	Acts as a Hydro Plant in all friendly cities.

* The effects of Hoover Dam are not cumulative with existing power plants.

Decrease Shield Production

If a city is constantly polluting the surrounding Terrain, and you haven't the technology to build the Improvements that decrease pollution, you might have to take a radical step and slow the city's production of Shields. By moving citizens into Terrain squares that generate less Shields, you can eliminate some of the city's Resource Pollution. Another option is to sell Shield-enhancing Improvements such as Factories and Manufacturing Plants. By doing so, you can decrease the number of Shields produced by the city (thus reducing overall pollution) until you have the technology to eliminate pollution problems.

Corruption and Waste

As your civilization grows, spreading out over the continent where you start the game and eventually establishing new cities overseas, the problems of corruption and waste become increasingly severe.

Corruption is Trade that is lost, presumably through shady business practices, embezzling and the like. Trade lost to corruption is represented by dark-colored Trade symbols on the Resource Chart of the City Display. Waste is a loss of Shields due to inefficient production. Shields lost to waste are represented by dark-colored Shield icons on the Resource Chart (see Figure 5-12). Under most systems of government, the corruption and waste experienced by a city increase with distance from your capital.

Figure 5-12 A city experiencing corruption and waste.

The formula used to calculate a city's corruption is as follows:

$$Corruption = ((Trade \times Distance) \times 3) \div (20 \times (4 + government))$$

where:

government = 1 (Despotism) 2 (Monarchy) 3 (Fundamentalism) 4 (Republic) 0 (Communism and Democracy)*

Distance = the city's distance from your captial (diagonal squares count as 1.5 squares when figuring the *Distance*)

the maximum value of *Distance* = 36

government = *government* +1, if the city is celebrating "We Love the King Day"

Distance = (*Distance* × 2) + *difficulty level* (possible values = 0 through 5), if the government is Despotism

The formula used to calculate a city's waste is as follows:

$$Waste = ((Shields \times Distance) \times 3) \div (20 \times (4 + government))$$

Here the waste modifiers are the same as the corruption modifiers, except that the maximum value of *Distance* = 16.

Note: Waste is calculated based on the city's surplus Shields. It does not take into account the Shields utilized to support the city's units.

*Communism and Democracy do not experience corruption.

As you can see, both waste and corruption rob your cities of valuable resources. Luckily there are some steps you can take to reduce, or even eliminate, corruption and waste:

❧ **Build Roads and Railroads.** Cities connected to the capital by roads or railroads experience slightly less corruption and waste.

❧ **Build a Courthouse.** The Courthouse Improvement reduces corruption and waste in a city by 50%.

❧ **Switch to a more advanced form of government.** As demonstrated by the government modifiers in the corruption and waste equations, more advanced forms of government experience lest corruption and waste than their primitive counterparts.

❧ **Govern Through Communism or Democracy.** Neither of these systems of government experience any corruption or waste whatsoever.

Financial Difficulties

One frequently recurring problem experienced by players is the tendency to run low on cash. This is most common toward the middle of the game, when your civilization is in the midst of rapid growth, establishing new cities and building new City Improvements at breakneck speed. With all the information and situations that require your attention, it is easy to lose track of the fact that your treasury is slowly dwindling each turn because your expenses have exceeded your monetary income. Sometimes it's not until your Domestic Advisor reports that funds are low that you sit up and take notice of what's happening. And at that point, quite an effort is required in order to recover.

Although money comes from a variety of sources including tithes from other civilizations and plunder earned as a result of conquering enemy cities, it is mostly generated by Trade in the form of Taxes. The funds generated each turn are pooled together and used to pay the maintenance costs of City Improvements in all your cities. Funds generated above and beyond maintenance costs are placed in your treasury for later use.

If insufficient funds are generated to pay the maintenance costs of all your Improvements, money is drawn from the treasury to cover the deficit. This continues each turn until the treasury is depleted. At this point, an Improvement in one of your cities is automatically sold, and the profit from the sale is placed in the treasury and used to cover expenses. This process continues until the deficit is corrected.

You should frequently monitor the status of your income to make sure that you are making a profit or, at least, breaking even. The easiest way to monitor your funds at a glance is to watch the Status Report section of the Status Window at the end of each turn. The treasury changes to indicate the financial results of the prior turn. If the amount increases, you're making a profit. If the amount decreases, your treasury is being tapped to cover a financial deficit. If the amount remains the same, your expenses and income are equal.

You can obtain a clearer picture of your financial status by accessing the Trade Advisor from the Advisors menu. The Trade Advisor's report gives you a detailed breakdown of all Improvements in every city and their per-turn maintenance costs. It also shows the total maintenance paid each turn contrasted with your total income (see Figure 5-13). Maintenance versus income information is also displayed at the top of the Change Taxes window.

If, by chance or neglect, you should fall into financial difficulties, there are a number of methods you can use to solve this problem.

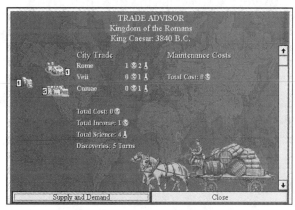

Figure 5-13 The Trade Advisor's Report

Note: If your income and expenses are equal to one another, you are not in immediate financial trouble. Remember, however, that unless your financial situation changes, the addition of even one new Improvement requiring maintenance in any city is enough to create a financial deficit.

Increase the Tax Rate

An obvious solution to a financial deficit is to increase the amount of Trade dedicated to Taxes. You can adjust the Tax rate by selecting "Change Taxes" from the Kingdom menu.

The major drawback to this solution is that in order to raise Taxes, you are forced to lower either the Science rate or the Luxuries rate, resulting in a slowdown in research or possible civil unrest. Another problem with raising Taxes is that it only works the first few times. In a rapidly growing civilization, rising maintenance costs inevitably exceed Tax revenues. Without taking other precautions, even setting your Trade income to 100% Taxes cannot cover your expenses.

Because of these drawbacks, it is best to raise Taxes only as temporary stopgap measure while seeking a more permanent solution to your money problem.

Convert Citizens to Tax Collectors

Tax revenue can be increased on a city-by-city basis by converting citizens into Tax Collectors. Tax Collectors (like Entertainers, which are described earlier in this chapter) are Specialists: citizens removed from resource generation to perform a specialized task. Tax Collectors are created by first creating an Entertainer, then clicking the Entertainer's icon in the Population Roster of the City Display. The Tax Collector icon is shown in Figure 5-14.

Each Tax Collector increases the number of Tax units generated in the city by two. The Tax Collector bonus for a city is increased by the presence of Marketplaces, Banks, and Stock Exchanges.

Tax Collectors provide an excellent source of additional income. They have two drawbacks, however. First, in order to have a Tax Collector, the city must have a population of five or greater. This means that if you run into a money crisis while your city populations are relatively small, you don't have the option of creating Tax Collectors.

Figure 5-14 The Population Roster, showing a Tax Collector

The second drawback is obvious. In order to create Tax Collectors, you must remove citizens from their jobs of generating resources for the city. In certain situations, the resulting loss in resources can become a bigger problem than the financial crisis you are trying to resolve.

Sell City Improvements

In times of dire financial emergency, quick cash can be raised by selling City Improvements. Improvements can be sold by clicking their icon in the Improvements Roster. Your Palace and Wonders of the World cannot be sold. You can sell one Improvement each turn.

If selling an Improvement is your only way out, do it before the game forces you to. If you sell a City Improvement before one is forcibly sold, you can choose which Improvement is sold from which city. If you wait until you go bankrupt, the game chooses the city and Improvement and performs the sale automatically. Obviously, the sale of Improvements is a last-ditch, temporary fix to your financial woes, and cannot be relied upon as a long-term solution.

Build Improvements and Wonders

Just as there are City Improvements and Wonders of the World whose purpose is to make citizens happy, there are also Improvements and Wonders geared to increase the financial well-being of your civilization. These are listed in Table 5-6, along with a brief description of their effects.

> Tip: If you decide that you need to sell an Improvement to make ends meet, take a moment to examine each of your cities before deciding what to sell. The best choices for sale are Improvements that have a high per-turn maintenance cost and/or Improvements that you aren't really using. Finally, NEVER sell an Improvement that is increasing your Tax revenues or your Trade production in general. That's just plain counterproductive.

✦ **Table 5-6.** Improvements and Wonders that Increase Cash Flow

IMPROVEMENTS	EFFECT
Bank	Increases city Tax revenues by 50% (cumulative with Marketplace)
Marketplace	Increases city Tax revenues by 50%
Stock Exchange	Increases city Tax revenues by 50% (cumulative with Marketplace and Bank)

WONDERS	
Adam Smith's Trading Co.	Pays the Upkeep on all Improvements with an Upkeep of 1

In addition to the Improvements and Wonders that directly affect Taxes, you should also consider building the Improvements and Wonders that increase Trade in general. Remember, an increase in Trade also means an increase in Tax revenues. (Complete information on the effects of Improvements and Wonders can be found in Chapter 7.)

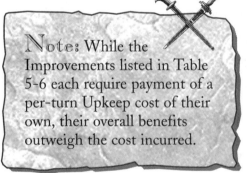

Note: While the Improvements listed in Table 5-6 each require payment of a per-turn Upkeep cost of their own, their overall benefits outweigh the cost incurred.

Capitalization

Although officially listed as a "City Improvement," Capitalization is neither an Improvement nor a Wonder. It is actually more of an activity.

After the discovery of the Corporation, Capitalization appears as one of the options on the Production Menu for each city. When you order a city to "build" Capitalization, all the surplus Shields that are normally used to build a unit, Improvement, or Wonder are transformed into Tax revenues. In other words, a city that would normally produce ten surplus Shields each turn instead produces ten units of Tax revenue.

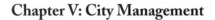

> Tip: Capitalization is also a terrific option for cities that have been "maxed out" (have produced all Improvements and Wonders possible). If you have no need to produce a steady stream of units from a maxed out city, convert its surplus Shields into cash through Capitalization.

Capitalization is a wonderful option. Although it halts the production of units, Improvements, and Wonders in the city while it is utilized, the extra money generated by setting one or two cities to this option can be just the thing you need to solve a financial crisis.

Switch to a New Government

Advanced systems of government generally increase Trade, and therefore increase the amount of Tax revenue collected by your civilization. As explained earlier in this chapter, more advanced systems of government also enjoy lower rates of corruption. In addition, Republics and Democracies produce an additional unit of Trade in every existing Trade-producing square, thus increasing the overall money supply.

There is also one form of government that is particularly adept at raising money. Due to the fact that no citizen is ever unhappy under Fundamentalism, the Improvements and Wonders that normally make citizens happy (see Table 5-1) instead produce "tithes" equal to the number of people they would normally make happy. For example, Temples, which normally make two citizens happy, instead produce two units of Tax Revenue under Fundamentalism. As stated earlier, however, there are major drawbacks to Fundamentalist rule (see Chapter 9 for details on Fundamentalism and other systems of government).

Changing to an advanced form of government is, by far, the most reliable way to assure a constant cash flow.

Other Ways to Increase Income

Basically, anything that increases Trade provides a potential increase in Tax revenue. Trade routes are one good example. While the income from a single trade route might be negligible, operating the maximum of three trade routes per city can provide a significant boost in Taxes. In addition, you also receive a cash advance when each route is initially established. (For more information on trade routes, see Chapter 9.)

VI
THE ADVANCE
OF KNOWLEDGE

One thing that Sid Meier took great pains to illustrate in the original *Civilization* was that, in spite of mankind's long history of philosophical and territorial struggles, the most challenging struggle of all was the never-ending quest for knowledge. The need to grow technologically is the driving force behind every civilization—in life as well as in the game.

The advance of knowledge plays just as large a role in *Civilization II* as it did in the original game. The victorious civilization is usually the one that manages to acquire knowledge the fastest. This is true even if you choose to attempt military victory rather than technological achievement, since the more Advances you achieve, the better your weapons. So, if you outdistance your opponents in technology, you are usually capable of out-gunning them as well.

This chapter is designed to help you choose your research path wisely. The first section describes the pursuit of knowledge, explaining the acquisition of new Civilization Advances and exploring ways to accelerate the research process. The second section describes the benefits of each Advance and provides you with an easy-to-reference guide to the discovery of each technology. The last portion of the chapter attempts to answer the question "what should I research next?" by presenting a variety of research strategies.

The Science of *Civilization II*

At the start of each new game, your civilization is automatically endowed with some level of knowledge. Every civilization starts with the basic abilities of road construction, irrigation, and mining. These basic skills allow your Settlers to perform all their basic functions. In addition, you can build Warrior units, the Barracks Improvement, and additional Settlers. Besides the basic skills mentioned above, the game might randomly select one or more low-level Civilization Advances with which to endow your culture. When this happens, you gain the additional research and production privileges allowed by these Advances. When you choose the "Accelerated Start" option, you automatically receive a number of additional Advances at the start of the game.

You are stuck with the abilities you start with until you start accumulating Trade. Ideally, this begins when you build a city. Provided the city is producing at least one Trade, you are prompted to select the first Civilization Advance you want to research within a turn or two of building your first city. Once you have chosen an Advance, all the Science you generate each turn is allocated to the research effort.

The accumulation of scientific knowledge is treated like the accumulation of any other resource in the game. As explained in Chapter 4, Trade is the primary source of Science. The Trade income of all your cities is totaled at the

Tip: The number of additional Civilization Advances given to you at the start of a normal (non-accelerated) game is partly based on the proximity of your opponents, the size of your starting continent, and the proximity of favorable Terrain. If you get an extraordinary number of bonus Advances in the beginning, it is a good bet that another civilization is starting the game fairly close to you. (This is also the reason that you occasionally start the game with two Settlers instead of one.)

beginning of each turn and applied to each of the three Trade components (Taxes, Science, and Luxuries) according to the percentages you choose using the Tax Rate option on the Kingdom menu.

All the Science icons generated are applied to research each turn. When enough icons have accumulated, the Advance is discovered, and you are prompted to choose the next topic of research. This process repeats continuously throughout the game. The number of icons required for the discovery of each Advance varies based on several factors, including difficulty level, the number of Advances you have already discovered, and the difference in technology levels between you and your opponents. At high levels of difficulty, the computer might assist your research effort if you are considerably behind your A.I. opponents. The computer also lends a helping hand to your computer rivals if *you* are considerably ahead of *them*.

With each successive discovery, the number of Science icons required for the completion of the next research project increases. This, of course, increases the number of turns required to acquire each successive Advance. Table 3-1 in Chapter 3 shows the amount of increase per Advance, for both your civilization and those of your computer opponents, on each level of difficulty.

IMPROVING YOUR RESEARCH ABILITY

Like other game resources, it is possible to fall behind in the production of Science. In fact, because the amount of Science you produce is directly affected by both Taxes and Luxuries, it is very easy to neglect Civilization Advance research in the scramble to balance your game budget and keep your citizens happy. Luckily, there are a number of ways that you can enhance the amount of Science produced by your civilization.

Adjust the Tax Rate

Using the Tax Rate option to adjust the percentage of Trade allocated to Science is the most obvious way to increase your rate of technological advancement. The higher the Science percentage, the more Science icons your cities produce. At the start of the game, when there are no City Improvements that require money for maintenance and there is little danger of population unhappiness (except at the highest difficulty levels), allocating as much Trade as possible to Science is an excellent strategy. As soon as the game starts, adjust your Tax Rate to maximize Science output. Leave the percentages set this way as long as possible, and your early research moves along at a brisk pace.

Unfortunately, you are eventually unable to avoid raising Taxes and/or Luxuries to support and appease your civilization. When you are forced to increase these Trade factors, Science must suffer. By the time this occurs, however, you should have other Science-enhancing options available to you.

> **Note:** One of the favorite tactics of veteran *Civilization* players, setting Science to 100% and setting Taxes and Luxuries to zero at the beginning of the game, is no longer possible due to the changes in government characteristics. Aside from Democracy, no government allows all of your Trade to be allocated to scientific research.

Increase Trade Income

Trade is an important resource. It is also the least common resource type; you have to work to increase a city's Trade income. Depending on the Terrain surrounding the city, this can be a time consuming task.

The only Terrain type that provides Trade, other than Special Resource squares, is Ocean. Rivers also provide Trade in the Terrain squares through which they pass. It is very possible for a newly built landlocked city that has no Rivers nearby to produce as little as one unit of Trade per turn (from the city square itself) or no Trade at all if it is built in a particularly bad spot. If this is the case, an immediate effort should be made to build roads in any Desert, Grassland, or Plains squares within the City Radius as soon as possible. The addition of roads to these Terrain types adds one unit of Trade to the Terrain square's normal resources. Once the Railroad is discovered, roads can be converted into railroads, increasing the production of all resources (including Trade) in any Terrain square by 50%. If there are Trade-rich Special Resources within the City Radius, such as Gold or Spice, they should be exploited. As soon as it is possible to move a citizen into one of these squares without causing a serious disruption of Food or Shield production, do it.

Besides exploiting the Terrain, there are other ways to increase Trade. The Superhighway City Improvement increases the Trade output of Terrain containing roads and railroads by 50%. The Colossus, one of the Ancient Wonders of the World, adds one unit of Trade production to every Terrain square that is already producing Trade in the city where the Wonder is built. You can also increase a city's Trade production by building Improvements and Wonders that prevent or lessen corruption and by switching to a more advanced form of government.

Build Improvements and Wonders that Enhance Research

Like Taxes and Luxuries, the other two facets of Trade, Science production and your research effort in general can be enhanced by a number of City Improvements and Wonders of the World designed specifically for this purpose. These Improvements and Wonders and their effects are listed in Table 6-1. The construction of Improvements and Wonders is the most concrete and permanent way to augment your research effort.

Convert Citizens to Scientists

Another way to increase the Science output of a city is to remove one or more of the city's residents from their resource production roles and turn them into Scientists. Scientists are a type of Specialist, like Entertainers and Tax Collectors (see Chapter 5 for details).

Just as Entertainers increase Luxuries and Tax Collectors increase Taxes, Scientists increase the amount of Science generated by the city. Every Scientist generates a minimum of three additional Science icons. This amount is increased if the city has any of the Improvements and Wonders listed in Table 6-1. In order to support a Scientist, the city must have a population of at least five.

Scientists, like other Specialists, have some drawbacks. Every citizen you remove from production and turn into a Scientist reduces the amount of resources generated for the city. Unless the other production squares are generating sufficient Food and Shields to cover the city's needs, you can quickly end

✤ **Table 6-1.** Improvements and Wonders that Affect Research

IMPROVEMENTS	EFFECT
Library	Increases a city's Science output by 50% in the city where built
Research Lab	Increases a city's Science output by 50% (cumulative with Library and University)
University	Increases a city's Science output by 50% (cumulative with Library)

WONDERS	
Copernicus' Observatory	Increases Science output by 50% in the city were built
Darwin's Voyage	Grants two automatic Civilization Advances
Great Library	Automatically gives you any Advance already discovered by two other civilizations
Isaac Newton's College	Increases Science output by 100% in the city where built
SETI Program	Counts as a Research Lab in every city

up with a serious resource shortage. Scientists should only be used as a temporary solution to a Science shortage.

Switch to a New Form of Government

As with all other types of resource production, more advanced forms of government tend to greatly increase the amount of Science your civilization produces. Actually, systems of government affect the amount of *Trade* generated, but the effect is the same. The more Trade you generate, the more Science you generate.

There is one exception to the usual government rule in the case of Science, and that is Fundamentalism. While considered an "advanced" form of government (higher on the scale than both Despotism and Monarchy), Fundamentalism has several drawbacks. Primary among these is its Science production. The lack of population unhappiness and the ease of military and financial buildup under a Fundamentalist system are offset by the fact that this form of govern-

> **Tip:** Removing citizens from Trade-producing squares to create Scientists can be counterproductive. Remember, Science is a component of Trade, and in most cases, Science makes up the largest percentage of your overall Trade income. The Trade you lose from the city's overall production by removing a citizen from production can reduce the overall amount of Science generated. Make sure that the amount of Science generated by the Scientist is going to be greater than the amount of Science generated by the Trade income of the vacated production square. Scientists are most helpful when the city's population has exceeded the number of Terrain squares available for that city's development.

ment produces only 50% of the normal amount of Science. If Scientific advancement is your main goal, Fundamentalism should be avoided at all costs. (For more details on Fundamentalism and other systems of government, see Chapter 9.)

The Civilization Advances

One of the first things you have to do after building your initial city is decide which Civilization Advance to research. In fact, this is a question that recurs frequently over the course of the game. You can, of course, choose your research projects at random, but that usually leads to trouble. Your research effort produces much better results if you set a research goal and work toward it.

Each Civilization Advance discovered can have a number of effects. It might give you the technology necessary to build new types of units, City Improvements, and/or Wonders of the World. It might also lead to the ability to research more advanced technologies. In fact, many Advances allow all of the above. In order to set meaningful goals it is necessary to know what each Advance offers and what its discovery can do to improve your civilization.

This section describes all 89 Civilization Advances in the game. The following information is provided for each:

- **Prerequisite Advances**—The Civilization Advance(s) that you must possess before you can research this Advance.
- **Units Allowed**—The units that can be produced as a result of discovering the Advance.
- **Improvements Allowed**—The City Improvements that can be built as a result of discovering the Advance.
- **Wonders Allowed**—The Wonders of the World that can be built as a result of discovering the Advance.
- **Special Functions**—New capabilities and functions made possible as a result of discovering the Advance. (This line is omitted if no special functions are made possible by the Advance.)
- **Advances Allowed**—The Civilization Advances that become available for research as a result of discovering the Advance. If a second Advance appears in parentheses next to the Advance allowed, it means that you must also research the Advance in parentheses before the first Advance becomes available.

Table 6-2 consolidates the statistical information for all Civilization Advances.

Provided along with the statistics for each Advance is a brief analysis of the pros and cons of pursuing each one. The purpose of this analysis is to help you choose which Advance to pursue next when you are offered a choice of research topics. Although there are a few Advances that are easily pegged as either "must have" or "should ignore," the truth is that, by design, very few Advances in *Civilization II* are useless or pointless. It is entirely possible that several items on your list of Advance choices are identified in this guide as being equally important. When this is the case, it is up to you to analyze the prevailing game situation and choose the Advance that most benefits you given your circumstances. Hopefully, the analysis provided will help you make an informed decision.

To get an overall picture of the research paths to and from each Advance, consult the Advances Chart included with the game. A portion of the Advances Chart, showing the immediate prerequisites of each Advance, can be found in the Civilopedia, the game's on-line encyclopedia, under the entry for each Advance.

❖ Table 6-2. Civilization Advance Statistics

ADVANCE	PREREQUISITES	UNITS ALLOWED	IMPROVEMENTS ALLOWED	WONDERS ALLOWED	ADVANCES ALLOWED
Advanced Flight	Radio Machine Tools	Bomber, Carrier	—	—	Combined Arms, Rocketry
Alphabet	—	—	—	—	Code of Laws, Map Making, Writing, Mathematics
Amphibious Warfare	Navigation Tactics	Marines	Port Facility	—	—
Astronomy	Mysticism, Mathematics	—	—	Copernicus' Observatory	Navigation, Theory of Gravity
Atomic Theory	Theory of Gravity, Physics	—	—	—	Nuclear Fission
Automobile	Combustion Steel	Battleship	Superhighways	—	Mass Production, Mobile Warfare
Banking	Trade Republic	—	Bank	—	Economics, Industrialization
Bridge Building	Iron Working, Construction	—	—	—	Railroad
Bronze Working	—	Phalanx	—	Colossus	Currency, Iron Working
Ceremonial Burial	—	—	Temple	—	Mysticism, Monarchy, Polytheism
Chemistry	University Medicine	—	—	—	Explosives, Refining
Chivalry	Feudalism, Horseback Riding	Knights	—	—	Leadership
Code of Laws	Alphabet	—	Courthouse	—	Literacy, Monarchy, Republic, Trade
Combined Arms	Mobile Warfare Advanced Flight	Helicopter Paratroopers	—	—	—
Combustion	Refining and Explosives	Submarine	—	—	Automobile, Flight
Communism	Philosophy Industrialization	—	Police Station	United Nations	Espionage, Guerrilla Warfare

Table 6-2. Civilization Advance Statistics *(continued)*

ADVANCE	PREREQUISITES	UNITS ALLOWED	IMPROVEMENTS ALLOWED	WONDERS ALLOWED	ADVANCES ALLOWED
Computers	Miniaturization Mass Production	—	Research Lab	SETI Program	Robotics, Space Flight
Conscription	Democracy, Metallurgy	Riflemen	—	—	Fundamentalism, Tactics
Construction	Currency, Masonry	—	Aqueduct, Colosseum	—	Bridge Building, Engineering
Corporation	Industrialization, Economics	Freight	Capitalization	—	Electronics, Genetic Engineering, Mass Production, Refining
Currency	Bronze Working	—	Marketplace	—	Construction, Trade
Democracy	Banking, Invention	—	—	Statue of Liberty	Conscription, Espionage, Recycling
Economics	University, Banking	—	Stock Exchange	Adam Smith's Trading Co.	Corporation
Electricity	Metallurgy, Magnetism	Destroyer	—	—	Electronics, Refrigeration, Steel, Radio
Electronics	Electricity, Corporation	—	Hydro Plant	Hoover Dam	Miniaturization, Nuclear Power, Rocketry
Engineering	The Wheel, Construction	—	—	King Richard's Crusade	Invention, Sanitation
Environmentalism	Recycling, Space Flight	—	Solar Plant	—	—
Espionage	Communism, Democracy	Spy	—	—	—
Explosives	Gunpowder, Chemistry	Engineers	—	—	Combustion
Feudalism	Monarchy, Warrior Code	Pikemen	—	Sun Tzu's War Academy	Chivalry, Theology

✦ Table 6-2. Civilization Advance Statistics *(continued)*

Advance	Prerequisites	Units Allowed	Improvements Allowed	Wonders Allowed	Advances Allowed
Flight	Combustion, Theory of Gravity	Fighter	—	—	Radio
Fundamentalism	Theology, Monotheism	Fanatics	—	—	—
Fusion Power	Nuclear Power, Superconductor	—	—	—	Future Technology 1
Future Technology	Fusion Power, Recycling	—	—	—	Future Technology
Genetic Engineering	Medicine, Corporation	—	—	Cure for Cancer	—
Guerrilla Warfare	Communism, Tactics	Partisans	—	—	Labor Union
Gunpowder	Invention, Iron Working	Musketeers	—	—	Explosives, Leadership, Metallurgy
Horseback Riding	—	Horsemen	—	—	The Wheel, Chivalry, Polytheism
Industrialization	Railroad, Banking	Transport	Factory	Women's Suffrage	Communism, Corporation, Steel
Invention	Engineering, Literacy	—	—	Leonardo's Workshop	Democracy, Gunpowder, Steam Engine
Iron Working	Bronze Working, Warrior Code	Legion	—	—	Bridge Building, Gunpowder, Magnetism
Labor Union	Mass Production, Guerrilla Warfare	Mech. Infantry	—	—	—
The Laser	Mass Production, Nuclear Power	—	SDI Defense	—	Superconductor
Leadership	Chivalry, Gunpowder	Dragoons	—	—	Tactics

Table 6-2. Civilization Advance Statistics *(continued)*

Advance	Prerequisites	Units Allowed	Improvements Allowed	Wonders Allowed	Advances Allowed
Literacy	Writing, Code of Laws	—	—	Great Library	Republic, Invention, Philosophy, Physics
Machine Tools	Steel, Tactics	Artillery	—	—	Advanced Flight, Miniaturization
Magnetism	Physics, Iron Working	Frigate, Galleon	—	—	Electricity
Map Making	Alphabet	Trireme	—	Lighthouse	Seafaring
Masonry	—	—	City Walls Palace	Great Wall Pyramids	Construction, Mathematics
Mass Production	Automobile Corporation	—	Mass Transit	—	Computers, Labor Union, The Laser, Nuclear Fission, Recycling
Mathematics	Alphabet, Masonry	Catapult	—	—	Astronomy, University
Medicine	Philosophy, Trade	—	—	Shakespeare's Theatre	Chemistry, Genetic Engineering, Sanitation
Metallurgy	Gunpowder, University	Cannon	—	—	Conscription, Electricity
Miniaturization	Machine Tools, Electronics	—	Offshore Platform	—	Computers
Mobile Warfare	Automobile, Tactics	Armor	—	—	Combined Arms, Robotics
Monarchy	Code of Laws, Ceremonial Burial	—	—	—	Feudalism
Monotheism	Philosophy, Polytheism	Crusaders	Cathedral	Michelangelo's Chapel	Theology, Fundamentalism
Mysticism	Ceremonial Burial	—	—	Oracle	Astronomy, Philosophy
Navigation	Seafaring, Astronomy	Caravel	—	Magellan's Expedition	Amphibious Warfare, Physics

♣ Table 6-2. Civilization Advance Statistics (*continued*)

Advance	Prerequisites	Units Allowed	Improvements Allowed	Wonders Allowed	Advances Allowed
Nuclear Fission	Atomic Theory, Mass Production	—	—	Manhattan Project	Nuclear Power
Nuclear Power	Nuclear Fission, Electronics	—	Nuclear Plant	—	Fusion Power, The Laser
Philosophy	Mysticism, Literacy	—	—	—	Communism, Medicine, Monotheism, University
Physics	Navigation, Literacy	—	—	—	Atomic Theory, Magnetism, Steam Engine
Plastics	Refining, Space Flight	—	Spaceship Component	—	Superconductor
Polytheism	Ceremonial Burial, Horseback Riding	Elephants	—	—	Monotheism
Pottery	—	—	Granary	Hanging Gardens	Seafaring
Radio	Flight, Electricity	—	Airport	—	Advanced Flight
Railroad	Steam Engine, Bridge Building	—	—	Darwin's Voyage	Industrialization
Recycling	Mass Production Democracy	—	Recycling Center	—	Environmentalism, Future Technology 1
Refining	Chemistry Corporation	—	Power Plant	—	Combustion, Plastics
Refrigeration	Electricity, Sanitation	—	Supermarket	—	—
Republic	Code of Laws, Literacy	—	—	—	Banking
Robotics	Computers, Mobile Warfare	Howitzer	Manufacturing Plant	—	Stealth
Rocketry	Advanced Flight, Electronics	AEGIS Cruiser Cruise Missile Nuclear Power	SAM Missile Battery	—	Space Flight

Table 6-2. Civilization Advance Statistics *(continued)*

ADVANCE	PREREQUISITES	UNITS ALLOWED	IMPROVEMENTS ALLOWED	WONDERS ALLOWED	ADVANCES ALLOWED
Sanitation	Engineering, Medicine	—	Sewer System	—	Refrigeration
Seafaring	Map Making, Pottery	Explorer	Harbor	—	Navigation
Space Flight	Computers, Rocketry	—	Spaceship Structural	Apollo Program	Environmentalism, Plastics
Stealth	Superconductor, Robotics	Stealth Bomber, Stealth Fighter	—	—	—
Steam Engine	Physics, Invention	Ironclad	—	Eiffel Tower	Railroad
Steel	Electricity, Industrialization	Cruiser	—	—	Automobile, Machine Tools
Superconductor	Plastics, The Laser	—	Spaceship Module	—	Fusion Power, Stealth
Tactics	Conscription, Leadership	Alpine Troops, Cavalry	—	—	Amphibious Warfare, Guerrilla Warfare, Machine Tools, Mobile Warfare
Theology	Monotheism, Feudalism	—	—	J.S. Bach's Cathedral	—
Theory of Gravity	Astronomy University	—	—	Isaac Newton's College	Atomic Theory, Flight
Trade	Currency, Code of Laws	Caravan	—	Marco Polo's Embassy	Banking, Medicine
University	Mathematics, Philosophy	—	University	—	Chemistry, Economics, Metallurgy
Warrior Code	—	Archers	—	—	Iron Working, Feudalism
The Wheel	Horseback Riding	Chariot	—	—	Engineering
Writing	Alphabet	Diplomat	—	—	Literacy

ADVANCED FLIGHT

Prerequisite Advances:	Radio and Machine Tools
Units Allowed:	Bomber, Carrier
Improvements Allowed:	None
Wonders Allowed:	None
Advances Allowed:	Combined Arms (with Mobile Warfare) Rocketry (with Electronics)

Advanced Flight not only provides the obvious and immediate results of allowing the construction of Bombers and Carriers, it is also one of the final steps in the direction of Nuclear Missiles (through Rocketry) and Paratroopers and Helicopters (through Combined Arms). Advanced Flight is also pivotal for nonviolent players because it is an important step in the direction of Space Flight and the beginning of the space race to Alpha Centauri.

ALPHABET

Prerequisite Advances:	None
Units Allowed:	None
Improvements Allowed:	None
Wonders Allowed:	None
Advances Allowed:	Code of Laws, Map Making, Writing Mathematics (with Masonry)

A glance at the statistics for the Alphabet provides a slightly skewed picture of the Advance when compared to the statistics of other early Advances. While it is true that no units, Improvements, or Wonders are available as a result of the Alphabet, this Advance is the most important to pursue. It should be your first choice, even if it means defending your cities with Warriors for a while. Many useful Advances are made available for study as a result of the discovery of the Alphabet, but the most important reason to pursue this Advance is that it is one of the first steps toward Monarchy and all intellectual and mystical pursuits including Mathematics, Philosophy, Polytheism, and Monotheism.

AMPHIBIOUS WARFARE

Prerequisite Advances:	Navigation and Tactics
Units Allowed:	Marines
Improvements Allowed:	Port Facility
Wonders Allowed:	None
Advances Allowed:	None

As it leads to no other Advances, Amphibious Warfare is obviously a late-game Advance. The importance of Amphibious Warfare varies depending on your goals, tactics, and strategies. Marines, though powerful, are not in and of themselves reason enough to drop other lines of research in order to pursue Amphibious Warfare (that is, unless your goal is primarily military). The Port Facility Improvement, on the other hand, is a more than adequate reason if you make heavy use of sea units and if you are involved in frequent naval conflicts. If your goals and methods are strictly peaceful, direct your research efforts elsewhere.

ASTRONOMY

Prerequisite Advances:	Mysticism and Mathematics
Units Allowed:	None
Improvements Allowed:	None
Wonders Allowed:	Copernicus' Observatory
Advances Allowed:	Navigation (with Seafaring)
	Theory of Gravity (with University)

Astronomy allows you to build Copernicus' Observatory, which helps to boost your research effort. However, the true importance of this Advance lies in the research paths it opens up. Astronomy is a crucial step in the direction of efficient sea travel (through Navigation). This line of research eventually leads to such important discoveries as Physics and Magnetism. Astronomy also allows you to research the Theory of Gravity, an important discovery that leads to Atomic Theory and starts you on the long road toward Flight.

ATOMIC THEORY

Prerequisite Advances:	Theory of Gravity and Physics
Units Allowed:	None
Improvements Allowed:	None
Wonders Allowed:	None
Advances Allowed:	Nuclear Fission (with Mass Production)

Atomic Theory is a quiet, transitory Advance that gives no immediate results. It's main purpose is to open the path to Nuclear Fission and Nuclear Power. This is an Advance that you can bypass for a while unless you are in desperate need of either a clean source of power or nuclear weapons. Eventually, there are a number of good reasons to pursue this line of research, both peaceful and military. Atomic Theory eventually leads to both Nuclear Power (which increases the speed of your ships and allows you to build Nuclear Power Plants) and the Manhattan Project (which, in turn, eventually allows Nuclear Missiles). This line of research also leads to Fusion Power, which increases the thrust of your spaceship and makes Nuclear Power Plants 100% safe.

AUTOMOBILE

Prerequisite Advances:	Combustion and Steel
Units Allowed:	Battleship
Improvements Allowed:	Superhighways
Wonders Allowed:	None
Advances Allowed:	Mass Production (with Corporation) Mobile Warfare (with Tactics)

The Automobile is an important Advance for warmongers and peaceniks alike. Warmongers love this Advance because of the immediate availability of the Battleship and the fact that the Automobile is one of the last steps toward Mobile Warfare (and, thus, Armor units). Peaceful players see the Automobile as a positive step toward increasing the productivity of their cities through Superhighways and the Improvements and research resulting from the eventual discovery of Mass Production. Any way you look at it, the Automobile is necessary for advancement, no matter what your style of play.

> **Note:** The Automobile also has two negative results that are, unfortunately, unavoidable. First, it increases the level of Population Pollution produced in all your cities. The second negative factor is that the discovery of the Automobile causes Leonardo's Workshop to become obsolete. If there is any reason to delay the discovery of the Automobile, it is to research Advances that take advantage of the abilities of Leonardo's Workshop before the Wonder is nullified.

BANKING

Prerequisite Advances:	Trade and Republic
Units Allowed:	None
Improvements Allowed:	Bank
Wonders Allowed:	None
Advances Allowed:	Economics (with University)
	Industrialization (with Railroad)

Banking is important both for its immediate benefits and the Advances it allows. Monetary and happiness problems alike are eased by the Bank Improvement, which increases a city's Taxes and Luxuries. Banking allows the research of both Economics and Industrialization, the two prerequisites to the Corporation which is a major prerequisite for just about every modern Advance. Banking is good for your economy and good for your technology.

BRIDGE BUILDING

Prerequisite Advances:	Iron Working and Construction
Units Allowed:	None
Improvements Allowed:	None
Wonders Allowed:	None
Special Functions:	Allows Settlers and Engineers to build roads in River squares

Advances Allowed:	Railroad (with Steam Engine)

Bridge Building is an important Advance that sometimes gets lost in the research shuffle. Although its only immediate effect is to allow the roads to be built over Rivers, the importance of Bridge Building lies in the fact that it is one of the Advances that leads to the Railroad. The Railroad, in turn, can dramatically improve your resource production and is one of the two prerequisites for Industrialization (along with Banking).

BRONZE WORKING

Prerequisite Advances:	None
Units Allowed:	Phalanx
Improvements Allowed:	None
Wonders Allowed:	Colossus
Advances Allowed:	Currency
	Iron Working (with Warrior Code)

Bronze Working has both economic and military importance. It is the technology that starts you on the road to such important economic and developmental Advances as Trade and Construction (through Currency), and it leads to important military and industrial Advances like Gunpowder and Bridge Building (through Iron Working). Perhaps most importantly, Bronze Working is one of the base Advances that leads toward Invention. Bronze Working also allows the construction of the Phalanx, one of the first effective defensive military units. It should, therefore, be considered a fairly high priority; especially if you have neighbors nearby!

CEREMONIAL BURIAL

Prerequisite Advances:	None
Units Allowed:	None
Improvements Allowed:	Temple
Wonders Allowed:	None
Advances Allowed:	Mysticism
	Monarchy (with Code of Laws)
	Polytheism (with Horseback Riding)

Ceremonial Burial should appear very close to the top of your "must research" list at the start of the game. Its immediate effect is to allow the construction of Temples, a very important Improvement especially when playing at a high difficulty level where early population unhappiness is a problem. Equally important are the Advances that become available after Ceremonial Burial is discovered. This Advance is one of the prerequisites of Monarchy, which should be your immediate goal at the start of the game. Ceremonial Burial also starts you on the path to Polytheism and Monotheism, two very significant Advances for keeping your people happy.

CHEMISTRY

Prerequisite Advances:	University and Medicine	
Units Allowed:	None	
Improvements Allowed:	None	
Wonders Allowed:	None	
Advances Allowed:	Explosives (with Gunpowder) Refining (with Corporation)	

Chemistry is an important research juncture in the pursuit of industrial and military Advances. It leads to Explosives (at which point Settlers are replaced by the more useful Engineers unit), and Refining, which in turn leads to such important Advances as Combustion (a step toward Mobile Warfare) and Plastics (vital for spaceship construction). If you have a need for the immediate benefits offered by other available Advances, the research of Chemistry can be postponed for a while. Only those pursuing a strictly military track, or those in desperate need of a Power Plant (which becomes available with Refining) need to pursue this Advance immediately. Don't let Chemistry slip for too long, however, since the Advances it leads to are important to any style of play.

CHIVALRY

Prerequisite Advances:	Feudalism and Horseback Riding	
Units Allowed:	Knights	
Improvements Allowed:	None	

Wonders Allowed:	None
Advances Allowed:	Leadership (with Gunpowder)

Chivalry was an Advance that usually fell by the wayside in *Civilization* because it was at the end of a short, dead-end branch of the Advances Chart (right behind Horseback Riding and Feudalism). In *Civilization II*, this is no longer the case. In fact, Chivalry is now the first in a long and fruitful line of military Advances, each of which dramatically improves your ability to wage war. Although Chivalry need not be your first choice in a peacetime situation, the research track it starts eventually becomes vital to your defensive and offensive survival. If you *are* at war when Chivalry becomes available, go for this Advance. The Knights unit is one of the best all-around military units of its era.

CODE OF LAWS

Prerequisite Advances:	Alphabet
Units Allowed:	None
Improvements Allowed:	Courthouse
Wonders Allowed:	None
Advances Allowed:	Literacy (with Writing)
	Monarchy (with Ceremonial Burial)
	Republic (with Literacy)
	Trade (with Currency)

Code of Laws is one of the vital Advances on the road to Monarchy. Barring any early-game military problems, this Advance should usually be among the first three that you research. In addition to allowing you to research Monarchy, Code of Laws allows you to move along the path of intellectual enlightenment and even higher forms of government (through Literacy), and gives you the opportunity to increase your Taxes, Science, and Luxuries through the construction of Courthouses and the discovery of Trade.

COMBINED ARMS

Prerequisite Advances:	Mobile Warfare and Advanced Flight
Units Allowed:	Helicopter, Paratroopers

Improvements Allowed:	None
Wonders Allowed:	None
Advances Allowed:	None

Combined Arms offers two of the best attack units available in the latter portion of the game, and is extremely valuable in a wartime situation. In fact, the prevailing military situation decides the value of this Advance. On the other hand, if you are at peace with your neighbors, Combined Arms is best left unexplored in favor of spaceship-building Advances, since it represents the end of a research path.

COMBUSTION

Prerequisite Advances:	Refining and Explosives
Units Allowed:	Submarine
Improvements Allowed:	None
Wonders Allowed:	None
Advances Allowed:	Automobile (with Steel)
	Flight (with Theory of Gravity)

Combustion is a very important Advance, especially in a military sense. Its only immediate effect is to make Submarines available, but the most important aspect of Combustion is the research it allows. It is the key to both Mobile Warfare and the Armor unit (through the Automobile), and it is the key to Flight and its related technologies. Also, combustion is vital to pacifists as well as warmongers, since the Flight research path leads to Space Flight eventually.

COMMUNISM

Prerequisite Advances:	Philosophy and Industrialization
Units Allowed:	None
Improvements Allowed:	Police Station
Wonders Allowed:	United Nations
Special Functions:	Communism becomes available as a form of government
Advances Allowed:	Espionage (with Democracy)
	Guerrilla Warfare (with Tactics)

Tip: Perhaps the best result of Communism is that it leads to Guerrilla Warfare and the accompanying Partisans unit. As explained in Chapter 8, Partisans are a tremendous asset when an enemy manages to capture one of your cities.

Besides giving you a new choice in your list of governments, Communism offers two immediate benefits: the United Nations Wonder, which is very useful (especially if you decide to govern through Democracy) and Police Stations. The Advances allowed by Communism, though they lead to such useful units as Partisans, Spies, and Mechanized Infantry, are very close to the end of their respective research lines. A negative aspect of Communism is that its discovery reduces the effectiveness of Cathedrals. The importance of researching this Advance is strictly a matter of personal preference. If you don't intend to govern through Communism, you don't need the United Nations. And since you don't need Communism to build Women's Suffrage (which substitutes for Police Stations), Communism can wait in favor of more pressing research.

COMPUTERS

Prerequisite Advances:	Miniaturization and Mass Production
Units Allowed:	None
Improvements Allowed:	Research Lab
Wonders Allowed:	SETI Program
Advances Allowed:	Robotics (with Mobile Warfare)
	Space Flight (with Rocketry)

Computers is an important Advance for a lot of reasons. In the long-term view, its discovery is pivotal to nearly every aspect of your space program, as well as many of the Improvements that allow you to diminish or eliminate pollution. The immediate benefits of Computers is to allow the construction of Research Labs, which significantly increase a city's Science output, and the SETI Program, which acts as a Research Lab in each city. If you are not in a position where war-like pursuits are a necessity, you should research Computers as soon as you can.

CONSCRIPTION

Prerequisite Advances:	Democracy and Metallurgy
Units Allowed:	Riflemen
Improvements Allowed:	None
Wonders Allowed:	None
Advances Allowed:	Fundamentalism (with Theology) Tactics (with Leadership)

Like Chivalry, Conscription was relegated to the end of a relatively short branch of the research tree in *Civilization*. In *Civilization II*, Conscription is a stepping stone to a new system of government (Fundamentalism) and, through Tactics, a number of powerful advanced military technologies and their accompanying units (Mobile Warfare, among others). It is actually good to be routed through Con-

Tip: If you have Leonardo's Workshop, make sure you research Conscription before the Wonder expires. That way, you'll receive free Riflemen for all your existing Musketeer units, significantly improving your defenses.

scription because it allows you to make use of Riflemen, who are better defenders than their predecessors the Musketeers. If a strong military is important to you, Conscription is an unavoidable stop along the military research path.

CONSTRUCTION

Prerequisite Advances:	Currency and Masonry
Units Allowed:	None
Improvements Allowed:	Aqueduct, Colosseum
Wonders Allowed:	None

Special Functions:	Allows Settlers and Engineers to build Fortresses
Advances Allowed:	Bridge Building (with Iron Working)
	Engineering (with The Wheel)

Construction is a very basic Advance that lays the groundwork for a myriad of important research paths. Most importantly, Construction is an early step in the direction of Invention (Leonardo's Workshop), which should, barring a major war situation, be your second short-term research goal after the Monarchy. Masonry's short-term benefits are also very important. Without Aqueducts, your cities can't grow past size eight, and Colosseums are an excellent (if expensive) way to appease an unhappy population. Construction should almost always be among your first ten Advances discovered.

CORPORATION

Prerequisite Advances:	Industrialization and Economics
Units Allowed:	Freight
Improvements Allowed:	Capitalization
Wonders Allowed:	None
Advances Allowed:	Electronics (with Electricity)
	Genetic Engineering (with Medicine)
	Mass Production (with Automobile)
	Refining (with Chemistry)

The Corporation serves many functions. First, it opens the modern era of trade by replacing Caravans with the Freight unit, which is twice as fast. The Corporation also allows Capitalization, an important new Improvement that can significantly boost your economy (see Chapter 7 for details). The main strength of this Advance, however, is that it is the doorway to nearly every technological and military line of research in the latter portion of the game. No matter what the prevailing circumstances, you can't go wrong by researching the Corporation.

CURRENCY

Prerequisite Advances:	Bronze Working
Units Allowed:	None
Improvements Allowed:	Marketplace
Wonders Allowed:	None
Advances Allowed:	Construction (with Masonry)
	Trade (with Code of Laws)

Because it is so important to achieve Monarchy as soon as possible, Currency can be allowed to slide until after the first revolution. At this point, Currency is one of the first steps along the path to what should be your next goal: Invention. In addition, Currency allows you to build the first of the "financial boost" Improvements, the Marketplace, which is a positive addition to all of your cities. This Advance is also necessary for the discovery of Trade, which allows for Caravans and trade routes.

Tip: If you choose to switch to a Republic early in the game, you should place a higher priority on the Currency Advance. Marketplaces in each city are a great help when trying to keep your citizens happy in a representative government.

DEMOCRACY

Prerequisite Advances:	Banking and Invention
Units Allowed:	None
Improvements Allowed:	None
Wonders Allowed:	Statue of Liberty
Special Functions:	Democracy becomes available as a form of government
Advances Allowed:	Conscription (with Metallurgy)
	Espionage (with Communism)
	Recycling (with Mass Production)

Democracy allows the use of the most advanced form of government available in the game, but its technological importance goes beyond that. It is also a conduit to most of the modern combat-oriented Advances (through Conscription), Spy units (through Espionage) and Recycling Centers (through Recycling). Even if you are a warfaring type who is unlikely to use Democracy as a form of government, Democracy is vital due to its connection to so many military Advances.

ECONOMICS

Prerequisite Advances:	University and Banking
Units Allowed:	None
Improvements Allowed:	Stock Exchange
Wonders Allowed:	Adam Smith's Trading Co.
Advances Allowed:	Corporation (with Industrialization)

Economics allows two immediate benefits that can vastly improve your civilization's economy: the Stock Exchange (which increases a city's Taxes and Luxuries by 150%) and Adam Smith's Trading Co. (which pays the Upkeep of some of your City Improvements). These two reasons alone are compelling enough to focus your research on Economics, but there's even more to the story. Economics is also one of the prerequisites of the Corporation, which opens up the paths to almost every modern Advance in the game. Economics is vital.

ELECTRICITY

Prerequisite Advances:	Metallurgy and Magnetism
Units Allowed:	Destroyer
Improvements Allowed:	None
Wonders Allowed:	None
Advances Allowed:	Electronics (with Corporation)
	Radio (with Flight)
	Refrigeration (with Sanitation)
	Steel (with Industrialization)

> **Tip:** Electricity also cancels the effects of the Great Library Wonder. If you want to stop an opponent who has built the Great Library from getting free Advances, you can do so by discovering Electricity.

The only immediate benefit of Electricity is the ability to build Destroyers, but don't let that delay your decision to move down this research path. Electricity is a vital link between the Renaissance-era Advances and the modern-era Advances. The Advances spawned by Electricity lead to all the spaceship-oriented Advances (through Electronics) and many of the modern military Advances (through Steel). Although Electricity can, theoretically, be put off for a while during a crisis situation, the longer you do so, the longer it takes you to achieve the modern Advances you need to compete with your opponents.

ELECTRONICS

Prerequisite Advances:	Electricity and Corporation
Units Allowed:	None
Improvements Allowed:	Hydro Plant
Wonders Allowed:	Hoover Dam
Advances Allowed:	Miniaturization (with Machine Tools)
	Nuclear Power (with Nuclear Fission)
	Rocketry (with Advanced Flight)

If your main goal is technological rather than military, you should follow the Electronics path as soon as you discover Electricity. You immediately benefit from the availability of Hydro Plants and the Hoover Dam, either of which provides both a boost in Shield production and a partial cure for Resource Pollution. From Electronics, you can quickly rise up the technological ladder through almost all of the spaceship-oriented Advances, though you will eventually be forced to follow the Steel path from Electricity in order to discover Rocketry. This way lies high-tech.

ENGINEERING

Prerequisite Advances:	The Wheel and Construction
Units Allowed:	None
Improvements Allowed:	None
Wonders Allowed:	King Richard's Crusade
Advances Allowed:	Invention (with Literacy) Sanitation (with Medicine)

Although the ability to build King Richard's Crusade is the only immediate effect of Engineering, don't put off the discovery of this Advance. Engineering is one of the final steps in achieving Invention, and the ever-so-important Leonardo's Workshop Wonder. Engineering is also one of the prerequisites of Sanitation, which allows the construction of Sewer Systems. If you follow the recommended research strategy of going for Invention right after you achieve Monarchy, Engineering falls in line as a matter of course.

ENVIRONMENTALISM

Prerequisite Advances:	Recycling and Space Flight
Units Allowed:	None
Improvements Allowed:	Solar Plant
Wonders Allowed:	None
Advances Allowed:	None

Environmentalism is one of the new, end-of-the-line Advances that is spawned off the high-tech branch of the research tree. The one and only reason for researching this Advance is to gain the ability to build Solar Plants. While Solar Plants are a wonderful way to curtail pollution (they eliminate a city's Resource Pollution altogether), adequate pollution control can usually be achieved through the combination of Mass Transit and a Recycling Center (or a Nuclear or Hydro Plant). Unless you have research time to spare, or you have an unstoppable pollution problem, Environmentalism can be put off indefinitely.

ESPIONAGE

Prerequisite Advances:	Communism and Democracy
Units Allowed:	Spy
Improvements Allowed:	None
Wonders Allowed:	None
Advances Allowed:	None

Espionage is another new Advance that falls at the end of a research path. It allows you to build Spies, which are undeniably useful units if subterfuge is your game (see Chapter 9). But, unfortunately, Spies are not enticing enough to abandon more important lines of research in most cases. If you are ahead of your opponents technologically, and you can spare the research time, Espionage can be fun. Of course, the opposite is also true. If you are way *behind* in technology, the Spy's ability to steal Advances from your neighbors can quickly close the scientific gap.

EXPLOSIVES

Prerequisite Advances:	Gunpowder and Chemistry
Units Allowed:	Engineers
Improvements Allowed:	None
Wonders Allowed:	None
Advances Allowed:	Combustion (with Refining)

Explosives sounds like it should be a major military Advance. It actually isn't, but it does lead to Combustion, which in turn leads to both the Automobile and Flight (two Advances which then lead to several very powerful military units). Explosives also makes it possible to build Engineers, a much more efficient and versatile version of Settlers. For all these reasons, Explosives is an important Advance to pursue.

FEUDALISM

Prerequisite Advances:	Monarchy and Warrior Code
Units Allowed:	Pikemen
Improvements Allowed:	None
Wonders Allowed:	Sun Tzu's War Academy
Advances Allowed:	Chivalry (with Horseback Riding) Theology (with Monotheism)

In *Civilization*, the research of Feudalism was a means to one, and only one, end: the ability to research Chivalry and obtain the Knights unit. Like the other "dead end" Advances in the original game, *Civilization II* places Feudalism in a much more important position in the research tree. It is now not only a prerequisite of Chivalry (which itself is no longer a dead end Advance), it is also a prerequisite of Theology, which allows the important J. S. Bach's Cathedral Wonder. In addition, Feudalism offers the immediate benefits of the Pikemen defensive unit and Sun Tzu's War Academy. Whereas in the original game it was an optional Advance, Feudalism can no longer be ignored.

FLIGHT

Prerequisite Advances:	Combustion and Theory of Gravity
Units Allowed:	Fighter
Improvements Allowed:	None
Wonders Allowed:	None
Advances Allowed:	Radio (with Electricity)

The obvious and immediate reason to research Flight is the ability to build Fighters and to start down the path toward Advanced Flight. The most *important* reason to discover Flight, however, is that it is the first step of many in the direction of Space Flight and the colonization of Alpha Centauri. If your goal is to quickly gain powerful military units, your best bet is to move on to Automobile after the discovery of Combustion. Otherwise, follow the Flight path.

FUNDAMENTALISM

Prerequisite Advances:	Monotheism and Conscription
Units Allowed:	Fanatics*
Improvements Allowed:	None
Wonders Allowed:	None
Special Features:	Fundamentalism becomes available as a system of government
Advances Allowed:	None

Fundamentalism allows the use of the new system of government by the same name, as well as the unique Fanatics unit. That's all. It is at the end of a research branch. While Fundamentalism offers some interesting possibilities as a system of government, especially for those who like to indulge their more violent tendencies, it is by no means crucial to the successful completion of the game. Fundamentalism should be researched only if you have the desire to experiment with this form of government. Otherwise, you needn't bother with it.

FUSION POWER

Prerequisite Advances:	Nuclear Power and Superconductor
Units Allowed:	None
Improvements Allowed:	None
Wonders Allowed:	None
Special Features:	Eliminates the possibility of Nuclear Plant meltdown
Advances Allowed:	Future Technology I (with Recycling)

Fusion Power is one of the last Advances you research in the game. In *Civilization*, the only advantage it really offered was to eliminate the already negligible chance of meltdown in any Nuclear Plants you might have. Fusion Power still has this effect, but now it offers something more. If you discover this Advance prior to the launch of your spaceship, the spaceship's thrust is increased by 25%.

---

* Fanatics units can only be built if your government type is Fundamentalism.

This new benefit makes Fusion Power well worth pursuing, since it can give you the edge you need to get to Alpha Centauri before your opponents.

FUTURE TECHNOLOGY

Prerequisite Advances:	Fusion Power and Recycling
Units Allowed:	None
Improvements Allowed:	None
Wonders Allowed:	None
Special Features:	Each Future Technology discovered adds five points to your Civilization Score
Advances Allowed:	Future Technology

Future Technology represents the ongoing march of science into the future. Theoretically, there is no limit to the number of Future Technologies you can discover. The only benefit derived from Future Technologies is a five-point addition to your Civilization Score for each one you discover. If your score is important to you, continue your research effort and discover as many Future Technologies as you can. If you are racing the other civilizations to complete and launch your spaceship, or you are mounting a major war effort, forget about Future Technologies and reallocate your Trade to Taxes in order to pay for spaceship parts.

GENETIC ENGINEERING

Prerequisite Advances:	Medicine and Corporation
Units Allowed:	None
Improvements Allowed:	None
Wonders Allowed:	Cure for Cancer
Advances Allowed:	None

There is only one reason to pursue the Genetic Engineering Advance: the ability to build the Cure for Cancer Wonder. This is important if you are having trouble with unhappiness throughout your civilization. If you are successful at keeping your people content through other means, Genetic Engineering is an end-of-the-line Advance that can be safely ignored.

GUERRILLA WARFARE

Prerequisite Advances:	Communism and Tactics
Units Allowed:	Partisans
Improvements Allowed:	None
Wonders Allowed:	None
Advances Allowed:	Labor Union (with Mass Production)

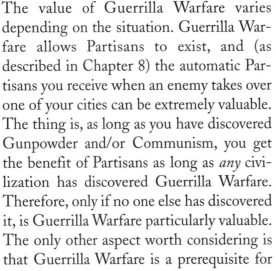

The value of Guerrilla Warfare varies depending on the situation. Guerrilla Warfare allows Partisans to exist, and (as described in Chapter 8) the automatic Partisans you receive when an enemy takes over one of your cities can be extremely valuable. The thing is, as long as you have discovered Gunpowder and/or Communism, you get the benefit of Partisans as long as *any* civilization has discovered Guerrilla Warfare. Therefore, only if no one else has discovered it, is Guerrilla Warfare particularly valuable. The only other aspect worth considering is that Guerrilla Warfare is a prerequisite for

Note: After you discover Guerrilla Warfare, the number of Partisans you receive when one of your cities is captured increases, while the number of Partisans your opponents receive when you capture one of their cities *decreases*.

Labor Union, which gives you the ability to build Mech. Infantry units (the best defensive units in the game). With the myriad of other powerful, modern units, the pursuit of Mech. Infantry alone is insufficient reason to pursue this path of research.

GUNPOWDER

Prerequisite Advances:	Invention and Iron Working
Units Allowed:	Musketeers
Improvements Allowed:	None
Wonders Allowed:	None
Special Features:	Makes existing Barracks obsolete

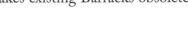

Advances Allowed:	Explosives (with Chemistry)
	Leadership (with Chivalry)
	Metallurgy (with University)

Gunpowder represents the first major military change in the game. It makes all your existing Barracks obsolete and marks the beginning of the end for units such as Knights, Crusaders, Pikemen, and Catapults. There is no need to mourn the loss of these units because Gunpowder opens up a whole new world of units that are much more powerful, both defensively and offensively. Gunpowder also paves the way for a number of important technological and military Advances.

HORSEBACK RIDING

Prerequisite Advances:	None
Units Allowed:	Horsemen
Improvements Allowed:	None
Wonders Allowed:	None
Advances Allowed:	The Wheel
	Chivalry (with Feudalism)
	Polytheism (with Ceremonial Burial)

Horseback Riding was an Advance that tended to fall by the wayside in the original *Civilization* because it led nowhere. In *Civilization II*, nothing could be farther from the truth. Horseback Riding is now critical to the discovery of almost every technological, military, and mystical Advance in the game. If you ignore this Advance for too long, you *will* fall behind in the technology race. Guaranteed. Horseback Riding is the Advance that starts you on the road toward Invention; so, if you follow the advice of making Invention your second short-term research goal, you won't be putting this Advance off for long.

INDUSTRIALIZATION

Prerequisite Advances:	Railroad and Banking
Units Allowed:	Transport
Improvements Allowed:	Factory
Wonders Allowed:	Women's Suffrage

Advances Allowed:	Communism (with Philosophy)
	Corporation (with Economics)
	Steel (with Electricity)

Industrialization represents a major turning point in the game: it is the beginning of every modern technological and military Advance. In addition to its long-term benefits, Industrialization also gives you the opportunity to boost your Shield production significantly by building Factories, and it allows you to build the important Women's Suffrage Wonder (see Chapter 7 for details). Industrialization is an important discovery both economically and technologically.

INVENTION

Prerequisite Advances:	Engineering and Literacy
Units Allowed:	None
Improvements Allowed:	None
Wonders Allowed:	Leonardo's Workshop
Advances Allowed:	Democracy (with Banking)
	Gunpowder (with Iron Working)
	Steam Engine (with Physics)

Tip: The road to Invention is a long one, and you acquire the ability to research many unrelated Advances along the way. It is safe to ignore some of these in favor of the push toward Invention, but some require more immediate attention. Important among these are Polytheism and Philosophy, both of which are required for the Monotheism and Cathedrals it allows. By the time you reach Invention, you are usually close to the time when you need the extra comfort of Cathedrals to make your people happy; so, if you have researched Polytheism and Philosophy along the way, you can proceed straight to Monotheism immediately after Invention.

It has been frequently stressed that Invention should be an important short-term research goal from the very start of the game. With a concerted effort, you can achieve this goal rather quickly, and you won't be disappointed by the opportunities it provides. Invention opens the door to the best governing system in the game (Democracy) and the first global military unit improvement (Gunpowder). But the real reason for rushing toward Invention is Leonardo's Workshop, arguably the finest Wonder available in the game (see Chapter 7 for details). Possessing this Wonder should be foremost in your mind from the moment you start the game.

IRON WORKING

Prerequisite Advances:	Bronze Working and Warrior Code
Units Allowed:	Legion
Improvements Allowed:	None
Wonders Allowed:	None
Advances Allowed:	Bridge Building (with Construction)
	Gunpowder (with Invention)
	Magnetism (with Physics)

If you are used to the research tree in *Civilization*, you may wonder why you can't research Iron Working when you have had Bronze Working for centuries. Unlike in the original game, Iron Working now has *two* prerequisites: you must research Warrior Code in addition to Bronze Working before you can move on to Iron Working. The new and improved Legion unit is an extra treat allowed after the discovery of this Advance. Whereas the Legion was a pretty good attacking unit in *Civilization*, *Civilization II's* Legions are good city defenders as well.

LABOR UNION

Prerequisite Advances:	Mass Production and Guerrilla Warfare
Units Allowed:	Mechanized Infantry
Improvements Allowed:	None

Wonders Allowed:	None
Advances Allowed:	None

Labor Union is an end-of-the-line Advance whose only function is to allow the production of Mech. Infantry units. While the Mech. Infantry unit is the best overall defensive unit in the game, it doesn't provide enough of an advantage over other contemporary military units to make research of the Labor Union an overwhelming priority. This Advance should be pursued only if you have research time to kill or you are experiencing serious defensive difficulties.

THE LASER

Prerequisite Advances:	Mass Production and Nuclear Power
Units Allowed:	None
Improvements Allowed:	SDI Defense
Wonders Allowed:	None
Advances Allowed:	Superconductor (with Plastics)

The importance of the SDI Defense was negligible in *Civilization* because the A.I. seldom, if ever, used Nuclear Missiles against your cities. The new, improved A.I. seems to greatly enjoy nuclear confrontations, however, making the SDI much more important—and the only way to build an SDI Defense is to discover The Laser. Another reason to pursue Laser technology is that it is one of the prerequisites for Superconductor, which is in turn a prerequisite for Stealth, and important to the space race. Still, unless you have a pressing need for nuclear protection or upgrades to your existing Bombers and Fighters, The Laser can wait in favor of other, more pressing research.

LEADERSHIP

Prerequisite Advances:	Chivalry and Gunpowder
Units Allowed:	Dragoons
Improvements Allowed:	None
Wonders Allowed:	None
Advances Allowed:	Tactics (with Conscription)

Leadership is one of the Advances in the most military-oriented research tracks in the game. This track, which actually starts with Horseback Riding, eventually goes on to such important modern military Advances as Mobile and Amphibious Warfare. The immediate benefit offered by Leadership is the Dragoons unit, which is the second most powerful mounted unit in the game. Because the impact of this Advance is strictly military in nature, it can be put off in favor of more pressing research needs if a peaceful climate prevails. On the other hand, if you can manage to discover Leadership before your opponents discover Gunpowder, you can make significant military progress by utilizing your Dragoons.

LITERACY

Prerequisite Advances:	Writing and Code of Laws
Units Allowed:	None
Improvements Allowed:	None
Wonders Allowed:	Great Library
Advances Allowed:	Republic
	Invention (with Engineering)
	Philosophy (with Mysticism)
	Physics (with Navigation)

Literacy makes a great many things possible. Its greatest impact is in the Advances it opens up to you, including the Republic, which allows you to utilize the second most powerful government type in the game. Literacy is also one of the prerequisites for the all-important Advance of Invention. The immediate benefit of Literacy, the Great Library, is also a strong inducement to research this Advance (see Chapter 7 for details on the Great Library Wonder). Because it leads to so many important and diverse lines of research, Literacy should not be put off for long.

MACHINE TOOLS

Prerequisite Advances:	Steel and Tactics
Units Allowed:	Artillery
Improvements Allowed:	None

Wonders Allowed:	None
Advances Allowed:	Advanced Flight (with Radio)
	Miniaturization (with Electronics)

Machine Tools gives you the ability to build Artillery units, which replace the Cannon as a siege weapon, and it is also a prerequisite for Advanced Flight. Because of these factors, Machine Tools has a significant military impact. The biggest long-term impact, however, is on your space program. If your plan is to start and/or win the space race as fast as possible, Machine Tools launches the line of research leading to all the elements of Space Flight.

MAGNETISM

Prerequisite Advances:	Physics and Iron Working
Units Allowed:	Frigate, Galleon
Improvements Allowed:	None
Wonders Allowed:	None
Advances Allowed:	Electricity (with Metallurgy)

The discovery of Magnetism has two major effects: it significantly updates your sea travel and battle capabilities by making it possible to build both the Galleon and the Frigate, and it makes it possible to research Electricity. While the former is extremely helpful, it is the latter that makes Magnetism important. Electricity is a sort of high-tech entry portal. It leads to the discovery of Electronics, which in turn leads to most of the technologies needed to pursue your space program. Although you can put Magnetism off for a while if more urgent needs arise, waiting too long to pursue this Advance can put you seriously behind in the technology race.

MAP MAKING

Prerequisite Advances:	Alphabet
Units Allowed:	Trireme
Improvements Allowed:	None
Wonders Allowed:	Lighthouse
Advances Allowed:	Seafaring (with Pottery)

The importance of Map Making early in the game depends largely on your starting position. If you start on a relatively small continent with few good city sites, Map Making is a necessity so that you can build Triremes to explore other nearby continents. Ultimately, Map Making starts you on the path towards all types of naval units, and towards Physics, a discovery that is vital to the research of many of the Advances that lead to modern warfare and technologies. However, if you have enough room to grow on your starting continent, Map Making can wait for a while.

MASONRY

Prerequisite Advances:	None	
Units Allowed:	None	
Improvements Allowed:	City Walls, Palace	
Wonders Allowed:	Great Wall, Pyramids	
Advances Allowed:	Construction (with Currency)	
	Mathematics (with Alphabet)	

Masonry provides many useful benefits. Especially useful are City Walls, which triple the strength of a city's defensive units without charging an Upkeep cost, and the Pyramids which can dramatically boost your population by acting as a Granary in every city. As for long-term benefits, Masonry allows Feudalism and the line of powerful military units to which that line of research ultimately leads. It also leads to Mathematics, which allows you to build Catapults, and Construction, which is a step toward Invention.

MASS PRODUCTION

Prerequisite Advances:	Automobile and Corporation	
Units Allowed:	None	
Improvements Allowed:	Mass Transit	
Wonders Allowed:	None	

Advances Allowed:	Computers (with Miniaturization)
	Labor Union (with Guerrilla Warfare)
	The Laser (with Nuclear Power)
	Nuclear Fission (with Atomic Theory)
	Recycling (with Democracy)

Mass Production leads to everything. It is the only Advance in the game that is a prerequisite for five other Advances. One of these Advances, Computers, is particularly important to the pursuit of Space Flight. The immediate benefit offered by Mass Production is the Mass Transit Improvement, which eliminates all Population Pollution in any city where it is built. This is only fair, since the mere discovery of Mass Production increases the level of Population Pollution in your cities by 25%. For technological reasons, it is impossible to put off this Advance for long.

MATHEMATICS

Prerequisite Advances:	Alphabet and Masonry	
Units Allowed:	Catapult	
Improvements Allowed:	None	
Wonders Allowed:	None	
Advances Allowed:	Astronomy (with Mysticism)	
	University (with Philosophy)	

The immediate effect of Mathematics is the ability to build Catapults, the first major siege weapon in the game. The Advances allowed as a result of the discovery of Mathematics are more important, however. Through Astronomy, Mathematics paves the way for Advances in the area of sea exploration and warfare and, ultimately, the cornerstones of the pursuit of Flight. Through the University, Mathematics ultimately leads to many important military Advances, such as Gunpowder. Despite these benefits, Mathematics can usually wait while you pursue either the Monarchy or the Invention research track—unless there is some pressing military need for Catapults or exploratory need for sea units more advanced than Triremes.

MEDICINE

Prerequisite Advances:	Philosophy and Trade
Units Allowed:	None
Improvements Allowed:	None
Wonders Allowed:	Shakespeare's Theatre
Advances Allowed:	Chemistry (with University)
	Genetic Engineering (with Corporation)
	Sanitation (with Engineering)

If Shakespeare's Theatre and the ability to research Genetic Engineering were the only benefits of Medicine, this Advance could be safely left behind until very late in the game—or even ignored entirely, without causing any problems. However, Medicine is a vital link in the chain leading toward some of the most advanced military units in the game and to the pursuit of Space Flight. Medicine allows Chemistry, which allows Explosives and Refining, two of the key Advances in the research of such important discoveries as the Automobile, Flight, and Rocketry. When Medicine becomes available, it is best to get it out of the way; it is very easy for the importance of this Advance to slip your mind.

Tip: Since Medicine is not vital in the short-run, you might want to obtain this Advance by trading for it or by stealing it from one of your opponents.

METALLURGY

Prerequisite Advances:	Gunpowder and University
Units Allowed:	Cannon
Improvements Allowed:	None
Wonders Allowed:	None
Advances Allowed:	Conscription (with Democracy)
	Electricity (with Magnetism)

Tip: f you have Leonardo's Workshop, Metallurgy is an excellent choice if you want to take advantage of unit upgrades. After Catapults are converted to Cannons, you can easily follow the Conscription path and get your Musketeers upgraded to Riflemen before the Wonder expires.

Metallurgy is the Advance that provides access to a newer, more powerful siege unit to replace your Catapults: the Cannon. It also opens the door to a long string of military research and improved units, starting with Conscription and the accompanying Riflemen unit. As if the benefits of this Advance weren't already bountiful enough, Metallurgy is also a prerequisite for Electricity, which is the beginning of a fruitful technological path that includes such important Advances as Steel and Electronics. There are no drawbacks to researching this Advance as soon as it becomes available.

MINIATURIZATION

Prerequisite Advances:	Machine Tools and Electronics
Units Allowed:	None
Improvements Allowed:	Offshore Platform
Wonders Allowed:	None
Advances Allowed:	Computers (with Mass Production)

Miniaturization's major role in the game is as one of the prerequisites of Computers, a vital high-tech Advance that leads to Space Flight (and, ultimately, the ability to colonize Alpha Centauri). Miniaturization is one of those Advances whose value is based entirely on your current goals. If you are determined to win the game by winning the space race, you must pursue Miniaturization as soon as possible. Otherwise, this Advance can wait (unless you have a pressing need for Howitzers and Stealth, which are also indirectly dependent on the discovery of Computers).

MOBILE WARFARE

Prerequisite Advances:	Automobile and Tactics
Units Allowed:	Armor
Improvements Allowed:	None
Wonders Allowed:	None
Special Functions:	Makes existing Barracks obsolete
Advances Allowed:	Combined Arms (with Advanced Flight) Robotics (with Computers)

In *Civilization*, Armor units were available after the discovery of the Automobile. Now, Armor is the result of Mobile Warfare, one Advance further down the line. Mobile Warfare is close to the pinnacle of advanced ground warfare, and the Armor unit is one of the most well-rounded ground units when it comes to attack and defense. The research paths beyond Mobile Warfare lead to a number of other useful and powerful military units and one nonviolent Improvement (the Manufacturing Plant, through Robotics). If the prevailing climate is peaceful, there is no reason why Mobile Warfare can't wait in favor of making progress toward Space Flight.

MONARCHY

Prerequisite Advances:	Code of Laws and Ceremonial Burial
Units Allowed:	None
Improvements Allowed:	None
Wonders Allowed:	None
Special Features:	Monarchy becomes available as a system of government
Advances Allowed:	Feudalism (with Warrior Code)

Because of the strict corruption, waste, and resource production penalties placed on Despotism, it is important to change to a better form of government as quickly as you can. Monarchy is usually the earliest government you can achieve, and the benefits gained by changing from Despotism to Monarchy are dramatic (see Chapter 9 for complete details). Monarchy should be your first

> **Tip:** Despite the fact that Despotism had similar drawbacks in terms of resource production in the original *Civilization*, many players shied away from Monarchy because of the high support cost for units. *Civilization II's* version of Monarchy is much improved over its original counterpart, because the first three units in each city are support-free. So, don't be afraid to make the switch—you'll be glad you did.

short-term research goal. The resource production benefits you receive when you switch from Despotism to Monarchy have a profound effect on your civilization's early growth.

MONOTHEISM

Prerequisite Advances:	Philosophy and Polytheism
Units Allowed:	Crusaders
Improvements Allowed:	Cathedral
Wonders Allowed:	Michelangelo's Chapel
Advances Allowed:	Theology (with Feudalism)
	Fundamentalism (with Conscription)

Monotheism, along with Theology, more or less replace "Religion" from the original *Civilization*. Monotheism is extremely important, especially if you are playing on higher difficulty levels and/or you are using one of the two representative governments (Republic or Democracy), where population unhappiness is a common

> **Tip:** The Crusaders unit is a wonderful gift of an otherwise peaceful line of research. This powerful (if vulnerable) unit allows you to hold your own in a military campaign even if most of your research has been geared primarily toward intellectual pursuits.

problem. This is the Advance that allows you to build Cathedrals, which are very helpful in easing civil unrest. Better still, Mono-theism allows you to build Michelangelo's Chapel, an extremely desirable Wonder that acts as a Cathedral in all your cities. Since building Cathedrals (or Michelangelo's Chapel) is one of the best ways to keep your people happy, you should strive to achieve this Advance before unhappiness gets out of hand.

MYSTICISM

Prerequisite Advances:	Ceremonial Burial
Units Allowed:	None
Improvements Allowed:	None
Wonders Allowed:	Oracle
Special Functions:	Doubles the effectiveness of Temples
Advances Allowed:	Astronomy (with Mathematics)
	Philosophy (with Literacy)

Mysticism is an offshoot of Ceremonial Burial that eventually leads down both scientific and intellectual paths to such important discoveries as Navigation (through Astronomy) and Democracy (through Philosophy). Mysticism can be allowed to fall by the wayside for a short time in favor of military or other important research, but it should not be ignored for long. In situations where the happiness of your population is a problem, such as high difficulty levels and ruling through representative governments, the Temple-enhancing benefit of Mysticism, and the ability to build the Oracle, can do much to ease your problems. If you have the time to spare, the early discovery of Mysticism can really pay off.

NAVIGATION

Prerequisite Advances:	Seafaring and Astronomy
Units Allowed:	Caravel
Improvements Allowed:	None
Wonders Allowed:	Magellan's Expedition

Tip: Because Navigation is required in order to discover Physics which, in turn, eventually leads to important Advances such as the Railroad and Flight, it isn't a good idea to put off Navigation for too long. Any time you have a bit of spare research time, slip Navigation into the cycle just to stay on top of things.

Advances Allowed:	Amphibious Warfare (with Tactics)
	Physics (with Literacy)

Navigation drastically improves your ability to explore and travel the sea by making Triremes obsolete and making it possible to build Caravels. Another short-term bonus is the ability to build Magellan's Expedition, which increases the movement ability of all your sea units through the end of the game. If you have the time, early research of this Advance can be quite beneficial in terms of exploration and overseas trade routes. Otherwise, if naval power is not a priority, you can put Navigation on the back burner in favor of other, more pressing needs.

NUCLEAR FISSION

Prerequisite Advances:	Atomic Theory and Mass Production
Units Allowed:	None
Improvements Allowed:	None
Wonders Allowed:	Manhattan Project
Advances Allowed:	Nuclear Power (with Electronics)

Nuclear Fission is potentially the deadliest Advance in the game. It allows the construction of the Manhattan Project, which in turn, uncorks the bottle and lets out the atomic genie by allowing all civilizations to build Nuclear Missiles. The peaceful effects of this line of research are the eventual ability to build Nuclear Plants and the SDI Defense. On the more violent side, Stealth Fighters and Bombers, and the possibility of Nuclear Missiles await you. Although many of the results are war-oriented, Nuclear Fission is part of the final path leading to the ability to construct Spaceship Modules. This means that you must pursue this line of research even if you are at peace.

NUCLEAR POWER

Prerequisite Advances:	Nuclear Fission and Electronics
Units Allowed:	None
Improvements Allowed:	Nuclear Plant
Wonders Allowed:	None
Special Features:	Increases the Movement Factor of your sea units by one
Advances Allowed:	Fusion Power (with Superconductor) The Laser (with Mass Production)

The immediate benefit of Nuclear Power, the Nuclear Plant Improvement, can be very helpful if you are suffering from the effects of pollution. Nuclear Plants have the same positive impact on pollution as Hydro Plants, but are less expensive. The movement bonus for your sea units is also incredibly helpful. There's not much left to research along this particular branch of the tree, but this is a path that must be followed to the end if you intend to build a spaceship. The Superconductor, which makes it possible to build Spaceship Modules, lies at the very end of the line, right after The Laser.

PHILOSOPHY

Prerequisite Advances:	Mysticism and Literacy
Units Allowed:	None
Improvements Allowed:	None
Wonders Allowed:	None
Special Features:	Grants a free Civilization Advance to the first civilization to discover it
Advances Allowed:	Communism (with Industrialization) Monotheism (with Polytheism) University (with Mathematics) Medicine (with Trade)

Philosophy is a critical Advance for most non-combat purposes. In fact, it is so important that you should pause in your rush toward Invention to pick up Philosophy on the way. Because of the bonus Advance you get if you are the first to discover it, your overall research plan won't even feel the impact. With Philosophy under your belt, you are ready to move quickly into Monotheism and the happiness it can bring.

PHYSICS

Prerequisite Advances:	Navigation and Literacy
Units Allowed:	None
Improvements Allowed:	None
Wonders Allowed:	None
Advances Allowed:	Atomic Theory (with Theory of Gravity)
	Magnetism (with Iron Working)
	Steam Engine (with Invention)

The discovery of Physics gives you no immediate benefits but more than makes up for this with the Advances it allows. It is the gateway to the research of all nuclear Advances (through Atomic Theory); it begins a new era in sea travel (through Magnetism), and it is a critical link in discovering the Railroad (through Steam Engine). After you make your way to Invention, Physics should be one of your top priorities.

PLASTICS

Prerequisite Advances:	Refining and Space Flight
Units Allowed:	None
Improvements Allowed:	Spaceship Component
Wonders Allowed:	None
Advances Allowed:	Superconductor (with The Laser)

Plastics serves two vital roles when you are building a spaceship. It immediately allows you to build Spaceship Components (engines and fuel). Then, through research of the Superconductor, it allows the construction of Spaceship Modules.

The other benefit of Plastics that it eventually leads to both Fusion Power and Stealth. Plastics is only somewhat useful for war, but vital for the space program.

POLYTHEISM

Prerequisite Advances:	Ceremonial Burial and Horseback Riding
Units Allowed:	Elephants
Improvements Allowed:	None
Wonders Allowed:	None
Advances Allowed:	Monotheism (with Philosophy)

Polytheism is most significant in its role as a prerequisite of Monotheism. Although it is not part of the path to either Monarchy or Invention, you should try to fit this Advance in somewhere along the way, along with Philosophy, so that you are ready to pursue Monotheism as soon as citizen unhappiness demands it. The immediate benefit of Polytheism, the Elephants unit, provides a fairly powerful attack unit for players whose research is primarily peaceful in nature.

POTTERY

Prerequisite Advances:	None
Units Allowed:	None
Improvements Allowed:	Granary
Wonders Allowed:	Hanging Gardens
Advances Allowed:	Seafaring (with Map Making)

In *Civilization*, Pottery was an Advance that led absolutely nowhere. As such, you could make a decision on its worth just by weighing the importance of Granaries and the Hanging Gardens to your society. In *Civilization II*, things aren't quite so simple. Pottery now leads to Seafaring, which improves your sea travel abilities and eventually leads to replacements for your Triremes. If naval power is important to you, you should try to fit Pottery into your research scheme fairly early in the game, or obtain the technology from another civilization through knowledge exchange or by stealing it.

RADIO

Prerequisite Advances:	Flight and Electricity
Units Allowed:	None
Improvements Allowed:	Airport
Wonders Allowed:	None
Special Features:	Settlers and Engineers can build Air Bases
Advances Allowed:	Advanced Flight (with Machine Tools)

Radio is a vital technology in the pursuit of air superiority and mobility. One immediate benefit is the ability to build Airports in your cities, which allow you to airlift or instantly move units from one city to another, if both cities are equipped with this Improvement. It also lets you repair damaged air units completely in a single turn. Radio effectively increases your flight range and capabilities by allowing Settlers and Engineers to build Air Bases. Fighters and all other types of aircraft can utilize a remote Air Base instead of returning to a city or Carrier to refuel, thus increasing the flexibility of these units. Finally, Radio opens up the entire Advanced Flight branch of the research tree, which eventually leads to Space Flight and its related technologies.

RAILROAD

Prerequisite Advances:	Steam Engine and Bridge Building
Units Allowed:	None
Improvements Allowed:	None
Wonders Allowed:	Darwin's Voyage
Special Features:	Settlers and Engineers can build railroads
Advances Allowed:	Industrialization (with Banking)

Railroad is important for many reasons. First, it allows Settlers and Engineers to convert existing roads to railroads, which dramatically increase your cities' resource production while, at the same time, acting as a means of free travel for all your ground units. Railroad also allows you to build Darwin's Voyage, a Wonder that automatically grants you two free Civilization Advances. Finally, Railroad is the gateway to the modern age through Industrialization. Because of its many advantages, you should research this Advance as soon as you possibly can.

RECYCLING

Prerequisite Advances:	Mass Production and Democracy
Units Allowed:	None
Improvements Allowed:	Recycling Center
Wonders Allowed:	None
Advances Allowed:	Environmentalism (with Space Flight)
	Future Technology I (with Fusion Power)

Recycling and Environmentalism sit together at the end of one branch of the research tree. The sole purpose of either of these Advances is to reduce the amount of Resource Pollution produced by your civilization. Recycling allows the Recycling Center, which eliminates two-thirds of a city's Resource Pollution. While this is an excellent reduction in pollution, you can usually achieve adequate pollution control with a combination of a "clean" power source (a Nuclear or Hydro Plant) and Mass Transit. Unless you have a pollution problem that just won't quit, you can safely ignore this line of research indefinitely.

REFINING

Prerequisite Advances:	Chemistry and Corporation
Units Allowed:	None
Improvements Allowed:	Power Plant
Wonders Allowed:	None
Advances Allowed:	Combustion (with Explosives)
	Plastics (with Space Flight)

Refining is the key to two very important branches of the research tree. First, it leads to the discovery of Combustion, which in turn leads the way to both Flight and Mobile Warfare. Later in the game, after the discovery of Space Flight, it leads to Plastics, which is needed to build Spaceship Components. The Power Plant, Refining's short-term benefit, can significantly increase the Shield output of any city that has a Factory (although it does lack the environmental bonuses of all other forms of power generation). You might be better off passing on the Power Plant as a source of energy, but the long-term benefits of Refining are important enough to make it a high priority.

REFRIGERATION

Prerequisite Advances:	Electricity and Sanitation
Units Allowed:	None
Improvements Allowed:	Supermarket
Wonders Allowed:	None
Special Features:	Settlers and Engineers can create farmland
Advances Allowed:	None

Refrigeration is one of the new, end-of-the-line Advances. This particular technology is very important if you have cities that are experiencing a Food crisis. Once you build a Supermarket in any city, any farmland within the City Radius produces 50% more Food. This is an Advance that can go unexplored for a long time if your cities are having no problem generating Food, but cities equipped with Supermarkets and extensive tracts of farmland tend to grow to enormous sizes.

Note: The extra Food produced farmland/Supermarket combination replaces the effect of railroads on Food in *Civilization*. In *Civilization II*, only Shield and Trade production are enhanced by the presence of a railroad in a Terrain square.

REPUBLIC

Prerequisite Advances:	Code of Laws and Literacy
Units Allowed:	None
Improvements Allowed:	None
Wonders Allowed:	None
Special Features:	Republic becomes available as a system of government
Advances Allowed:	Banking (with Trade)

Republic allows the second most advanced form of government in the game. The Republic is a logical step up from Monarchy as a system of government, but it isn't practical until you have a stable population attitude and financial base. However, that is no reason to put off researching the Republic Advance: it leads to Banking, which usually comes in handy at earlier stages of the game.

ROBOTICS

Prerequisite Advances:	Computers and Mobile Warfare
Units Allowed:	Howitzer
Improvements Allowed:	Manufacturing Plant
Wonders Allowed:	None
Advances Allowed:	Stealth (with Superconductor)

Robotics is a combination military- and production-oriented Advance. Its immediate benefits are the Manufacturing Plant (which increases Shield output in conjunction with a Factory) and the Howitzer, the most powerful offensive ground weapon in the game. The only Advance that Robotics leads to is Stealth, which allows Stealth Bombers and Stealth Fighters. Unless you need the production boost or the weapons it allows, you can leave this research path unexplored until you have some research time to spare.

Note: Veterans of *Civilization* should note that Robotics is no longer required in order to build Spaceship Modules. The Superconductor, which lies along a similar but separate research path, is now the Advance that allows you to produce Spaceship Modules.

ROCKETRY

Prerequisite Advances:	Advanced Flight and Electronics
Units Allowed:	AEGIS Cruiser, Cruise Missile, Nuclear Missile*

---

* After someone has built the Manhattan Project.

Improvements Allowed:	SAM Missile Battery
Wonders Allowed:	None
Advances Allowed:	Space Flight (with Computers)

No other Advance allows the construction of more units than Rocketry. Three powerful military units, including the devastating Nuclear Missile, are made possible by this Advance. In addition, Rocketry provides a useful defensive Improvement, the SAM Missile Battery. Despite all its war-oriented aspects, Rocketry is also a prerequisite of Space Flight, the Advance that ultimately leads to the ability to build your spaceship and colonize Alpha Centauri. If your intent is to head for space, you should avidly follow this research path, stopping for nothing short of immediate need for military research of some sort.

SANITATION

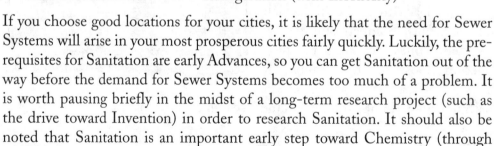

Prerequisite Advances:	Engineering and Medicine
Units Allowed:	None
Improvements Allowed:	Sewer System
Wonders Allowed:	None
Advances Allowed:	Refrigeration (with Electricity)

If you choose good locations for your cities, it is likely that the need for Sewer Systems will arise in your most prosperous cities fairly quickly. Luckily, the prerequisites for Sanitation are early Advances, so you can get Sanitation out of the way before the demand for Sewer Systems becomes too much of a problem. It is worth pausing briefly in the midst of a long-term research project (such as the drive toward Invention) in order to research Sanitation. It should also be noted that Sanitation is an important early step toward Chemistry (through Medicine).

SEAFARING

Prerequisite Advances:	Map Making and Pottery
Units Allowed:	Explorer
Improvements Allowed:	Harbor

Wonders Allowed:	None
Special Features:	Decreases the likelihood of Triremes being lost at sea
Advances Allowed:	Navigation (with Astronomy)

Seafaring is an intermediate step that ultimately leads to many of the Advances that allow early sea unit upgrades. It allows the construction of Harbors, which can be especially useful in a city with lots of Ocean Terrain inside its City Radius. Seafaring also allows the Explorer unit (which can be useful for quick exploration of unknown Terrain and for checking out villages) and upgraded survivability for Triremes. There is no mistaking this Advance for what it is—a half-step toward more important discoveries. If you have the need or desire to use sea units, you shouldn't hesitate too long before pursuing this line of research. Keep in mind also that Navigation is one of the prerequisites of Physics, so Seafaring must be discovered before you can explore the high-tech paths that lead from Navigation.

SPACE FLIGHT

Prerequisite Advances:	Computers and Rocketry
Units Allowed:	None
Improvements Allowed:	Spaceship Structural
Wonders Allowed:	Apollo Program
Advances Allowed:	Environmentalism (with Recycling)
	Plastics (with Refining)

Space Flight represents the true beginning of your space program. Before you can begin construction of your spaceship, one of the civilizations in the world must build the Apollo Program. Afterwards, Space Flight allows you to build Spaceship Structural Pieces, which form the framework of your spaceship. Once Space Flight is discovered and you have committed yourself to the notion of being the first civilization to reach Alpha Centauri, you need to aggressively pursue the Plastics research path so you can gain the ability to build Spaceship Components and Modules to complete your craft.

STEALTH

Prerequisite Advances:	Superconductor and Robotics
Units Allowed:	Stealth Bomber, Stealth Fighter
Improvements Allowed:	None
Wonders Allowed:	None
Advances Allowed:	None

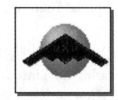

Stealth is an end-of-the-line military Advance that allows the construction of the two most advanced air units in the game. Like all dead-end Advances, the only compelling reason to research Stealth is to take advantage of its immediate benefits. If air war and bomb runs are your game, Stealth-based units offer the ultimate in air attack power. Often, however, an air war can be successfully fought and won using Fighters, Bombers, and/or Helicopters—thus relegating the research of Stealth to a fairly low priority.

STEAM ENGINE

Prerequisite Advances:	Physics and Invention
Units Allowed:	Ironclad
Improvements Allowed:	None
Wonders Allowed:	Eiffel Tower
Advances Allowed:	Railroad (with Bridge Building)

The Steam Engine is one of the final steps required on the way to Industrialization. But besides being a key to the future, this Advance offers other important developments of its own. It immediately allows you to build the Eiffel Tower, a Wonder that has dramatic effects on the attitude that other civilizations have toward you. The Steam Engine is also one of the prerequisites for the Railroad, an Advance that can be used to dramatically improve your mobility and productivity. If no immediate military crisis exists after you discover Invention, the Steam Engine is a good track to take.

STEEL

Prerequisite Advances:	Electricity and Industrialization
Units Allowed:	Cruiser
Improvements Allowed:	None
Wonders Allowed:	None
Advances Allowed:	Automobile (with Combustion)
	Machine Tools (with Tactics)

Civilization veterans might be disappointed that Steel no longer allows the construction of Battleships; the Cruiser is now the unit allowed by Steel. The long-term benefits of Steel are still important, however; in fact, Steel now spawns two lines of research rather than one. First, it leads to Mobile Warfare (through the Automobile) and the Armor units that Advance allows. Second, Steel allows the study of Machine Tools, an Advance that eventually leads to military Advances such as Advanced Flight, and high-tech Advances such as Computers. Even though some of its immediate appeal is lost due to the replacement of the Battleship by the Cruiser, Steel is still an important Advance.

SUPERCONDUCTOR

Prerequisite Advances:	Plastics and The Laser
Units Allowed:	None
Improvements Allowed:	Spaceship Module
Wonders Allowed:	None
Advances Allowed:	Fusion Power
	Stealth (with Robotics)

The Superconductor in *Civilization* was a leftover Advance that had only limited usefulness. In *Civilization II* it has become a vital Advance, required for the construction of the most important parts of your spaceship. Superconductor also leads to Stealth and Fusion Power, both of which are optional technologies. If you are engaged in building a spaceship, you would be wise to move as quickly as possible to research this Advance.

TACTICS

Prerequisite Advances:	Conscription and Leadership
Units Allowed:	Alpine Troops and Cavalry
Improvements Allowed:	None
Wonders Allowed:	None
Advances Allowed:	Amphibious Warfare (with Navigation)
	Guerrilla Warfare (with Communism)
	Machine Tools (with Steel)
	Mobile Warfare (with Automobile)

Tactics spews forth a veritable fountain of military-oriented Advances that eventually lead to such diverse units as Marines, Partisans, Artillery, and Armor. Tactics itself also provides two powerful units: Alpine Troops, one of the best defensive units available, and Cavalry, the best of the mounted units. Other lines of research can be pursued in lieu of Tactics if there is no pressing need for the powerful military units it provides. Don't put Tactics on the back burner for too long, though, because Machine Tools is an Advance required in the pursuit of both the Advanced Flight and the Computer paths that eventually lead to Space Flight.

THEOLOGY

Prerequisite Advances:	Monotheism and Feudalism
Units Allowed:	None
Improvements Allowed:	None
Wonders Allowed:	J. S. Bach's Cathedral
Special Functions:	Adds one content citizen to every city that has a Cathedral
Advances Allowed:	None

Theology is a new Advance that encompasses part of the Religion Advance from the original *Civilization* (the rest of Religion being covered by Monotheism). There are two compelling reasons to research this Advance. First, the discovery of Theology offsets the negative effect of Communism on your Cathedrals by adding one content citizen to every city that has a Cathedral. The other reason to pursue Theology is J. S. Bach's Cathedral. This high-priority Wonder is an excellent way to mollify unhappy citizens.

THEORY OF GRAVITY

Prerequisite Advances:	Astronomy and University
Units Allowed:	None
Improvements Allowed:	None
Wonders Allowed:	Isaac Newton's College
Advances Allowed:	Atomic Theory (with Physics)
	Flight (with Combustion)

In *Civilization*, there was little need to rush into studying the Theory of Gravity other than to reap the benefits of Isaac Newton's College. Theory of Gravity is now a prerequisite of Flight (which it logically should be), so the value of studying this Advance earlier in the game is clear. While the benefits of the Advances spawned from Atomic Theory don't appear until the later stages of the game, Flight and its benefits become available much earlier. Theory of Gravity is also one of the first Advances in the long climb toward Space Flight.

TRADE

Prerequisite Advances:	Currency and Code of Laws
Units Allowed:	Caravan
Improvements Allowed:	None
Wonders Allowed:	Marco Polo's Embassy
Advances Allowed:	Banking (with Republic)
	Medicine (with Philosophy)

Trade is one of those early discoveries that is worth exploring even if it means a diversion from a long-term research project. The main reason for this is that Trade allows you to build Caravans, which are helpful not only in their capacity to establish trade routes, but to help build Wonders as well. Trade is also the cornerstone for scientific advancement through Medicine and financial advancement through Banking. Trade is definitely a discovery that should be made early in the game, especially if a peaceful victory is your goal.

UNIVERSITY

Prerequisite Advances:	Mathematics and Philosophy
Units Allowed:	None
Improvements Allowed:	University
Wonders Allowed:	None
Advances Allowed:	Chemistry (with Medicine)
	Economics (with Banking)
	Metallurgy (with Gunpowder)

In *Civilization*, the University had one major disadvantage in that it caused the Great Library to expire. Now that this is no longer the case, all of the results of this Advance are positive. Besides allowing you to build Universities to increase your cities' Science output, the University leads to a number of lines of research that, in turn, lead to important military and social Advances such as Steel and the Corporation. Although you can put off researching it for a while, the University is eventually vital to your continued advance toward the Modern era.

WARRIOR CODE

Prerequisite Advances:	None
Units Allowed:	Archers
Improvements Allowed:	None
Wonders Allowed:	None
Advances Allowed:	Iron Working (with Bronze Working)
	Feudalism (with Monarchy)

Warrior Code is a brand new Advance that allows a brand new unit: Archers. Archers are one of the best early attack units that also provide a good defense; but they aren't the reason that Warrior Code is important. The reason this Advance is vital is that it leads to Iron Working, which is required for many other important Advances; and to Feudalism and the powerful Knights unit. Those used to the research tree in *Civilization* might be caught off guard by this and put off researching Warrior Code. Luckily, if you intend to take the fast track toward Invention, Warrior Code is inevitable, and it won't fall by the wayside accidentally.

The Wheel

Prerequisite Advances:	Horseback Riding
Units Allowed:	Chariot
Improvements Allowed:	None
Wonders Allowed:	None
Advances Allowed:	Engineering (with Construction)

Though occasionally handy for exploring or marauding, Chariots are not a compelling reason to pursue this Advance. The importance of The Wheel in the real world is that it is a basic element that plays a role in almost every aspect of everyday life. This is reflected in the game: The Wheel is one of the earliest elements in the research path leading the way toward the important Invention Advance. If you take the early route to Invention, The Wheel is a natural part of your research progression. If not, The Wheel is still an Advance you can't avoid for long.

Writing

Prerequisite Advances:	Alphabet
Units Allowed:	Diplomat
Improvements Allowed:	None
Wonders Allowed:	None
Advances Allowed:	Literacy (with Code of Laws)

In *Civilization*, Writing led to both Literacy and Religion. Since Religion has been subdivided into Monotheism and Theology, both of which appear further down the research path, Writing now only allows Literacy. This, by no means, diminishes the importance of this Advance. Literacy leads the way to all things scientific by allowing Invention, and it also leads the way to Monotheism through Philosophy. Writing also allows you to build Diplomats, whose special abilities can be a valuable asset in dealing with other civilizations (see Chapter 9 for details).

Research Strategies

The research paths you choose should be based upon both your personal preference and your style of play. The prevailing game conditions and difficulty level also play key roles in how things progress, so your methods and strategies must vary slightly from game to game accordingly. Because of all the variables involved, there is no way to plot a definitive course through the technology tree. There are, however certain guidelines that you can use to achieve your desired goals as efficiently as possible. The remainder of this chapter is dedicated to presenting effective research strategies to achieve various goals.

THE FIRST STEP

The first step in *any* strategy should be the acquisition of a new government type to replace Despotism. The penalties on resource production are too great to stay in Despotism for more time than you have to.

The best government to replace Despotism is usually Monarchy. Several key modifications have been made to this form of government both to make it more

Note: Please note that despite the fact that their prerequisites have been discovered, all Advances might not be available on the menu when you are prompted to choose a new Advance due to a random element of the game. If no Advances that lead to your goal are currently available, choose an Advance that provides you with immediate benefits that you can exploit, or one that leads in the direction of your next planned research path.

> **Tip:** If you are prepared to deal with the possible consequences, you can bypass ruling by Monarchy in favor of ruling through a Republic. Getting to Republic is just as easy as getting to Monarchy if you follow this simple research path: Alphabet, Writing, Literacy, Code of Laws, Republic. Remember, the reason Monarchy is the advisable first step up from Despotism is that Monarchy is less restrictive of troop movement, allowing you to spread out, colonize, and explore without fear of unhappy citizens.

desirable and to ease the transition from Despotic rule (see Chapter 9 for details). The path to Monarchy is an easy one: start by researching Ceremonial Burial (so you can build Temples as early as possible). From there, research Alphabet, Code of Laws, and finally Monarchy. Once you achieve Monarchy, immediately change over to the new government and watch your production rates soar.

The only thing that should cause you to waver from your pursuit of a new government is early hostilities from your neighbors. If you experience such problems, take the time to research Bronze Working or Warrior Code so you can build better units to defend your cities.

Choosing the "early Republic" strategy (see the "Tip" above) also does wonders for your research and production. If you choose this course of action, just make sure that you build Temples and strive to build the Oracle so that your people stay happy.

THE INVENTION STRATEGY

Throughout the analysis of Advances earlier in this chapter, the need to achieve Invention is something that was repeatedly stressed. The reason for this can be summed up in two words: Leonardo's Workshop. Those who doubt the importance of this Wonder have never built it and reaped its benefits. The unwavering pursuit of Invention is vital if you intend to build Leonardo's Workshop: your A.I. opponents are strong believers in its ability, and they will certainly build it if you don't. Your only chance is to get to Invention first.

> **Note:** There are several important Advances that become available along the way as you move toward Invention. These include Iron Working, Sanitation, and Philosophy. If you are ahead of your opponents technologically, or you are in dire need of one of these subsidiary Advances and its benefits, you shouldn't hesitate to stray briefly from the Invention path in order to pursue them.

The path to Invention is long, but you discover many important Advances along the way. The order in which you research these Advances is up to you (aside from restrictions due to prerequisites, of course . . .), but you should base the order on which Advances provide the best short-term benefits in the prevailing situation. The complete path to Invention is illustrated in Figure 6-1.

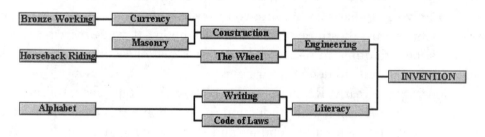

Figure 6-1 The research path leading to Invention.

ON THE WAR PATH

In a "Bloodlust" game, or any game in which you are attempting to win through global conquest, you need to follow the path that leads to the most expedient discovery of Advances that provide you with the units and abilities to suit your violent needs.

The best government under which to conduct a war is Fundamentalism. Luckily, both the Monarchy and the Invention paths described earlier lead in

> Tip: When there is a lull in the battlefield action, move your units back to their home cities and switch to Democracy or Republic for a while to accumulate a few Civilization Advances.

that general direction, so you can pursue these tracks first. Leonardo's Workshop is extremely useful for staying "one up" on your neighbors when conducting a military campaign.

Under Fundamentalism, your Science output is cut in half, so once you switch to this government you need to generate as much Science as you can in order to maintain your research effort. The best way to do this is to build as many Science-enhancing Improvements and Wonders as you can. Even though you capture technology from your enemies every time you take a city, that is not enough to keep you even in the technology race. You should also use Diplomats and Spies to steal Advances whenever possible.

The most lucrative path for producing powerful military units is the one shown in Figure 6-2. This is a line of research you shouldn't pass up when attempting to conquer the world.

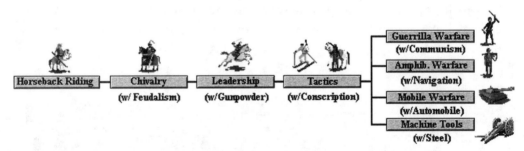

Figure 6-2 A lucrative research path for producing combat units

GIVE PEACE A CHANCE

A peaceful game is usually more challenging than an all-out military conflict because it involves finding a way to grow your civilization while maintaining peace with your neighbors. Because the A.I. is more aggressive and the diplomacy system is more involved in *Civilization II* than it was in the original game, peaceful coexistence is now more difficult than ever.

As for technology, you should start your game by following the Monarchy and Invention research paths. From Invention, backtrack through Polytheism, then go for Philosophy, Monotheism, and Theology. Once you are well on your way down this path, switch over to Republic or Democracy, and concentrate on building Wonders and Improvements that increase your Science and keep your people happy.

Continue to pour as much Trade as possible into Science. Your goal is to reach Space Flight as fast as possible, so unless you are forced to do so by an impending attack, ignore the Advance paths that are primarily military in favor of those that produce industrial and scientific Advances. Even as a result of peace-oriented research, you gain sufficiently powerful military units to mount an effective defense against a moderate attack. Just keep your international relations as friendly as possible to prevent wars from happening. (The United Nations can be a big help in this respect.)

Once you start building your spaceship, it is very possible that your opponents might gang up on you in order to prevent its launch. This is especially true at higher levels of difficulty. This is the time to go back and get some of the powerful military Advances that you might have skipped on your way to Space Flight. Build a super-strong defensive force and, if need be, launch several small counter-offensives to protect your cities until your spaceship reaches its destination.

Tip: If you lose track of what you need to research next in order to achieve the desired Advance, use the "Goal" button at the bottom of the menu listing possible research topics. Choose your goal from the resulting menu of Advances. A message is displayed telling you which of the available Advances should be researched next in order to reach your goal.

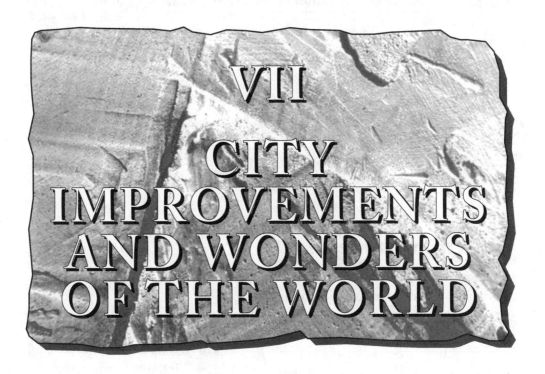

VII
CITY IMPROVEMENTS AND WONDERS OF THE WORLD

*T*he development of cities involves an ongoing series of decisions. You need to determine the needs of each individual city and its citizens, and you need to decide which City Improvement is needed most. At the same time, you need to balance the needs of individual cities against the needs of your civilization as a whole: can the current Tax Rate cover the maintenance cost of new Improvements? Even if it can, would your society benefit more from the construction of a unit or Wonder, rather than an Improvement, at this time?

These questions cannot be analyzed properly until you know all of the Improvements and Wonders. The purpose of this chapter is to provide you with that information. The following statistics are listed for each Improvement and Wonder:

* **Cost**—The number of Shields it costs to build the Improvement or Wonder.

* **Upkeep**—The amount of money that must be paid each turn to maintain the Improvement. (Since they have no Upkeep cost, this statistic is not listed for Wonders.)

* Prerequisite—The Civilization Advance that must be discovered in order to build the Improvement or Wonder.

* Expiration—The Civilization Advance that cancels the effects of a Wonder. (Since their effects never expire, this statistic is not listed for most City Improvements.)

* Effects—The function or functions served by the Improvement or Wonder.

City Improvements

Just about every City Improvement is an important addition to the infrastructure of your cities. In practice, larger cities eventually build almost every City Improvement by the end of the game. The most important thing you need to learn is to build Improvements in a logical order, so that your cities can reap their benefits without your civilization going broke trying to maintain them.

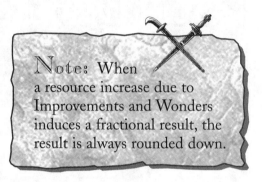

Note: When a resource increase due to Improvements and Wonders induces a fractional result, the result is always rounded down.

This section lists the statistics of all the City Improvements in the game, along with an analysis of the pros and cons of each Improvement. The statistics for all Improvements are consolidated for easy reference in Table 7-1.

AIRPORT

Cost:	160
Upkeep:	3
Prerequisite:	Radio
Effects:	Completely repairs any damaged air unit that spends an entire turn in the city. City produces Veteran air units. Allows airlifts.

✤ **Table 7-1.** Statistics and Effects of City Improvements

IMPROVEMENT	COST	UPKEEP	PREREQUISITE	EFFECTS
Airport	160	3	Radio	Repairs any damaged air unit that spends an entire turn in the city. Allows airlifts.
Aqueduct	80	2	Construction	Required for a city to grow beyond the size of 8.
Bank	120	3	Banking	Increases the city's Taxes and Luxuries by 50% (cumulative with Marketplace)
Barracks	40	1	—	All units produced in the city are automatically Veterans.
Capitalization	—	—	Corporation	Converts all the city's Shield output into Taxes.
Cathedral	120	3	Monotheism	Makes 3 content citizens happy. (2 after the discovery of Communism) +1 after the discovery of Theology
City Walls	80	0	Masonry	Triples the Defense Factor of units inside city.
Coastal Fortress	80	1	Metallurgy	Doubles the Defense Factor of units inside city against sea bombardments.
Colosseum	100	4	Construction	Makes 3 unhappy citizens content (4 with Electronics).
Courthouse	80	1	Code of Laws	Decreases corruption and waste by 50%. (Makes one unhappy citizen content under Democracy).
Factory	200	4	Industrialization	Increases the city's Shield output by 50%.
Granary	60	1	Pottery	Only half the city's Food is depleted when the city increases in size.
Harbor	60	1	Seafaring	Allows every Ocean square within the City Radius to produce one extra Food.
Hydro Plant	240	4	Electronics	Increases Factory output by 50%. Decreases Resource Pollution by 50%.
Library	80	1	Writing	Increases the city's Science output by 50%.
Manufacturing Plant	320	6	Robotics	Increases the city's Shield output by 50% (cumulative with Factory).
Marketplace	80	1	Currency	Increases the city's Tax and Science output by 50%.
Mass Transit	160	4	Mass Production	Eliminates all Population Pollution.
Nuclear Plant	160	2	Nuclear Power	Increases Factory output by 50%. Decreases Resource Pollution by 50%.

✤ Table 7-1. Statistics and Effects of City Improvements *(continued)*

IMPROVEMENT	COST	UPKEEP	PREREQUISITE	EFFECTS
Offshore Platform	160	3	Miniaturization	All Ocean squares in the City Radius can produce one Shield.
Palace	100	0	Masonry	Eliminates all corruption and waste in the city, and reduces them in nearby cities.
Police Station	60	2	Communism	Decreases the number of unhappy citizens due to units in the field by one.
Port Facility	80	3	Amphibious Warfare	Repairs any damaged sea unit that spends an entire turn in the city.
Power Plant	160	4	Refining	Increases Factory output by 50%.
Recycling Center	200	2	Recycling	Reduces Resource Pollution by 2/3.
Research Lab	160	3	Computers	Increases the city's Science output by 50% (cumulative with Library and University)
SAM Missile Battery	100	2	Rocketry	Doubles the Defense Factor of units inside city against air and Cruise Missile attacks.
SDI Defense	200	4	The Laser	Protects everything within three squares of the city from Nuclear Missile attacks.
Sewer System	120	2	Sanitation	Required for a city to grow beyond size 12.
Solar Plant	320	4	Environmentalism	Increases Factory output by 50%. Eliminates Resource Pollution in the city.
Spaceship Component	160	0	Plastics	See description in the City Improvements section of this chapter.
Spaceship Module	320	0	Superconductor	See description in the City Improvements section of this chapter.
Spaceship Structural	80	0	Space Flight	Forms the structural framework for your spaceship.
Stock Exchange	160	4	Economics	Increases the city's Tax and Luxury output by 50% (cumulative with Marketplace and Bank).
Superhighways	160	3	Automobile	All squares with roads or railroads produce 50% more Trade.
Supermarket	120	3	Refrigeration	Farmland squares produce 50% more Food.
Temple	40	1	Ceremonial Burial	Two unhappy citizens are made content.
University	160	3	University	Increases the city's Science output by 50% (cumulative with Library).

Tip: If you conquer a city on a distant continent, consider rush-building an Airport. That way, you can airlift units to that city for protection.

If your military strategy depends heavily on the use of air units, Airports are indispensable. Building Airports in every city is an unnecessary expense; you should only build them in selected, strategic locations. The presence of Airports in front-line cities can greatly extend the life span of your expensive air units, and decrease their down-time for repairs. The ability to "airlift" units between cities is also very powerful. When a unit is in a city with an Airport, you can select the Airlift command from the Orders menu and instantly transport the unit into any other friendly city with an Airport. This is a great way to keep fresh troops on the front lines. Finally, Airports can enhance the value of trade routes (if both the source and destination cities have Airports).

AQUEDUCT

Cost:	80
Upkeep:	2
Prerequisite:	Construction
Effects:	Required for a city to grow beyond the size of eight

Aqueducts are "must have" Improvements: unless a city has an Aqueduct, its growth comes to a grinding halt at a population of eight. Because Aqueducts increase your operating expenses, you shouldn't build them right away. You can safely wait until a city reaches size six or seven before you start construction on this Improvement.

BANK

Cost:	120
Upkeep:	3
Prerequisite:	Banking
Effects:	Increases the city's Tax and Luxury output by 50% (cumulative with Marketplace)

Eventually, the cost of maintaining the Improvements in all of your cities becomes a heavy Tax burden that even the combination of Marketplaces and raising the Tax rate can't keep up with. Banks are very helpful in this respect, working in combination with the city's Marketplace to cumulatively double the city's Tax revenues. The Luxury effects of the Bank/Marketplace combination are also significant, and can do much to help prevent Civil Disorder.

Tip: If your city's economy is good and at least 20% of your Trade is being used for Luxuries, you might want to try building a Bank before resorting to expensive "happiness" Improvements like Cathedrals and Colosseums.

BARRACKS

Cost:	40
Upkeep:	1
Prerequisite:	None
Expiration:	Gunpowder and Mobile Warfare (Barracks must be rebuilt)
Effects:	All units produced by the city are automatically given Veteran status. Damaged units are repaired in a single turn.

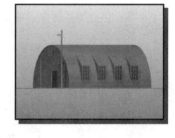

Barracks is the first Improvement you can build, and it gives you the ability to produce Veteran units and instantly repair damaged units, both of which lend you a military edge. However, building Barracks early in the game creates an unnecessary financial burden. In addition, all existing Barracks are lost upon the discovery of both Gunpowder and

Tip: During a sustained military campaign, consider building one or more Barracks in high-production cities near the front line. These can act as repair centers to support your war effort.

Mobile Warfare, forcing you to build new ones. If you want to produce Veteran units early in the game, consider researching your way to Feudalism and build Sun Tzu's War Academy.

Note: Unlike the original game, *Civilization II* compensates you for the loss of your old Barracks. When they become obsolete, every existing Barracks is sold, and the money is added to your treasury.

CAPITALIZATION

Cost:	N/A
Upkeep:	N/A
Prerequisite:	Corporation
Effects:	Converts all the city's Shield production into Taxes

Capitalization is unique. It isn't quite an Improvement, and it isn't quite a Wonder. When a city is "building" Capitalization, all of its surplus Shields are converted to money which is then added to your treasury each turn. This is one of the most useful additions to the game from a financial standpoint—when there is nothing left to build in the city, either while waiting for a new Advance or after everything has been discovered and built, you can temporarily switch over to Capitalization and fill your coffers with money that can be used later to finance your military or space efforts. Capitalization also provides a quick fix to short-term financial deficits.

CATHEDRAL

Cost:	120
Upkeep:	3
Prerequisite:	Monotheism

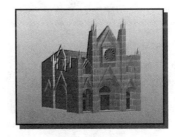

Effects: Makes three content citizens happy (two after the discovery of Communism). After the discovery of Theology, the number of content citizens produced by the Cathedral is increased by one.

Cathedrals are important additions to your cities, especially at higher difficulty levels and when governing with Republic or Democracy, where population unhappiness is more frequent. Although their effect diminishes somewhat after you discover Communism, this decrease is offset if you research Theology. A Cathedral in each city is one of the best ways to keep your population content.

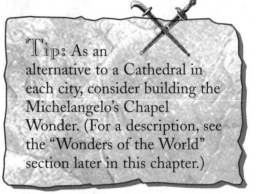

Tip: As an alternative to a Cathedral in each city, consider building the Michelangelo's Chapel Wonder. (For a description, see the "Wonders of the World" section later in this chapter.)

CITY WALLS

Cost:	80
Upkeep:	0
Prerequisite:	Masonry
Effects:	Triples the Defense Factor of any unit inside the city

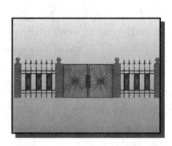

Those familiar with the original *Civilization* have probably noticed a subtle but significant change in the City Walls Improvement: no Upkeep cost. Because of this change, there is no excuse for *any* city to be without this extra layer of protection. With City Walls in place, your cities are much more secure from invaders. Remember, the benefits of this Improvement are based on the Defense Factor of the units defending the city. The better the defender, the safer the city.

Note: City Walls do not provide a bonus when the attacking unit is a Howitzer, a sea unit, or an air unit.

COASTAL FORTRESS

Cost:	80
Upkeep:	1
Prerequisite:	Metallurgy
Effects:	Doubles the Defense Factor of any units inside the city against bombardments by enemy ships

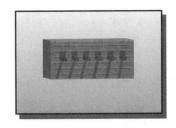

Coastal Fortresses are essentially City Walls that protect against ships. The A.I. has a tendency to make heavy use of naval units when fighting a war, so coastal cities in high-traffic areas tend to be the frequent victims of sea attacks. This low-maintenance, high-powered Improvement is a must in war time.

Tip: Cities located next to inland "lakes" can build Coastal Fortresses because the "lake" is actually an isolated Ocean square. It is a waste of time, Shields, and money to build a Coastal Fortress in such a city, since it could never be attacked from the sea.

COLOSSEUM

Cost:	100
Upkeep:	4
Prerequisite:	Construction
Effects:	Makes three unhappy citizens content. (Four after the discovery of Electronics.)

At first, Colosseums are not as effective at maintaining population attitude as Cathedrals. But after the discovery of Electronics, they are actually *more* effective. Colosseums have the advantage of being available earlier than Cathedrals at a lower initial cost; however, the Upkeep for Colosseums is higher. If you have a stable economic base, and you need something to keep your people happy before the discovery of Monotheism, Colosseums are the way to go.

COURTHOUSE

Cost:	80
Upkeep:	1
Prerequisite:	Code of Laws
Effects:	Decreases corruption and waste by 50%, and makes the city more resistant to bribery by enemy Diplomats and Spies. Under a Democracy, a Courthouse makes one citizen in the city happy.

If your early-game strategy involves spreading out as quickly as possible, Courthouses are very important. Under less-sophisticated forms of government, cities that are far-removed from your capital tend to lose a great deal of their Trade and Shield production to corruption and waste. Courthouses help your research, finances, happiness, and production to operate more effectively under these conditions. The happy citizen produced by a Courthouse when you switch to Democracy is an added bonus. Under Democracy, you can use every happy person you can get.

FACTORY

Cost:	200
Upkeep:	4
Prerequisite:	Industrialization
Effects:	Increases the city's Shield production by 50%

Factories are both a godsend and a curse. They are an excellent way to significantly increase the Shield output of a city, thus increasing its rate of unit, Improvement, and Wonder production. Factories are especially useful in cities built in areas with sparse Shield production to increase Shield output to an acceptable level. The curse of Factories is that, in cities with high Shield output, they significantly increase the amount of pollution the city produces. The spread of pollution and the construction of Factories often go hand in hand.

GRANARY

Cost:	60
Upkeep:	1
Prerequisite:	Pottery
Effects:	Only half of the city's Food stores are depleted when the city increases in size.

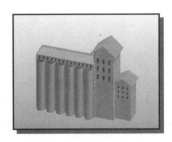

No other Improvement inspires such a diversity of opinions amongst players than the Granary. There are those who say you should build Granaries in every city as soon as possible to induce rapid city growth. On the other side of the argument, there are those who say you should hold off on building Granaries because the rapid population growth they bring about often outpaces your ability to keep the citizens happy. The truth lies somewhere in between. There are a number of factors you need to consider before building a Granary.

On higher levels of difficulty, automatically unhappy citizens appear earlier. When playing at King level or above, it is probably best to hold off building Granaries until after the discovery of Ceremonial Burial (so that you can counteract unhappiness by building Temples). On any difficulty level, if you have chosen Food-rich city sites and your cities are experiencing steady growth, Granaries need not be a priority. Only when a city is growing at an extremely slow rate is a Granary necessary early in the game.

> **Tip:** Instead of building Granaries in all your cities, consider building the Pyramids Wonder instead. (For a complete description, see the "Wonders of the World" section later in this chapter.)

HARBOR

Cost:	60
Upkeep:	1
Prerequisite:	Seafaring

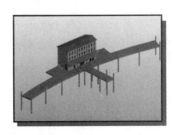

Effects: Allows every Ocean square within the City Radius
                    to produce one extra unit
                    of Food

Harbors are relatively inexpensive
both to build and to maintain. They
can be a good investment for any
city that has a large number of
Ocean squares under its control,
especially if one or more of these
squares contain Fish or Whales.
However, the benefits of this
Improvement are dependent on how
many of the Ocean squares are being utilized. Cities with few Ocean squares
and/or not enough citizens to utilize them should spend their Shields elsewhere.

> **Note:** Like the Coastal Fortress, Harbors can be built by cities bordering "lakes." Such cities gain little advantage from the presence of a Harbor.

HYDRO PLANT

Cost: 240
Upkeep: 4
Prerequisite: Electronics
Effects: Increases the Factory output of
                 a city by 50%, and decreases
                 pollution caused by Shield
                 production by 50% (not
                 cumulative with Power Plants, Nuclear Plants, or Solar
                 Plants)

The Hydro Plant serves a dual purpose: it helps to ease a city's pollution, and it
improves Shield production if the city has a Factory. (The antipollution benefit is gained even if there is no Factory in the city.) Hydro and Nuclear Plants
are equally "clean" forms of energy, but the Hydro Plant is preferable because of
the possibility of meltdown with a Nuclear Plant. Unfortunately, Hydro Plants
can only be built in cities adjacent to Oceans, Rivers, or Mountains.

The antipollution benefit alone is enough reason to build this Improvement. The Shield-output increase in cities with Factories is just an added
bonus.

> Tip: Instead of building power plants of any type in your cities, consider building the Hoover Dam Wonder. (For a complete description, see the "Wonders of the World" section later in this chapter.)

LIBRARY

Cost:	80
Upkeep:	1
Prerequisite:	Writing
Effects:	Increases the city's Science output by 50%

As you are probably aware by now, the research of Civilization Advances is vital to your success in the game. Anything that increases the speed at which Advances are discovered is beneficial. The Library is the first of three Improvements that cumulatively increase the Science output of a city. With their low Upkeep and important effect, Libraries have no downside. The construction of Libraries in every city should be a priority as soon as you discover Writing.

MANUFACTURING PLANT

Cost:	320
Upkeep:	6
Prerequisite:	Robotics
Effects:	Increases the city's Shield output by 50% (cumulative with Factory)

In order to build a Manufacturing Plant, a city must first have a Factory. These two Improvements work together to double the Shield output of the city, increasing the rate at which the city can build units, Improvements, and Wonders. Manufacturing Plants come with the same warning as Factories, only more so: the Shield-output increase greatly increases a city's likelihood to pollute. If you intend to build Manufacturing Plants, it is a good idea to reduce the pollution by building a Recycling Center or by building a Hydro, Nuclear, or Solar Plant in the city as soon as one of these Improvements becomes available. You should also consider the high Upkeep of this Improvement versus its potential benefits for the city before you rush to build it.

MARKETPLACE

Cost:	80
Upkeep:	1
Prerequisite:	Currency
Effects:	Increases the city's Tax and Luxury output by 50%

The Marketplace (along with Banks and Stock Exchanges) are often ignored until a financial crisis is looming on the horizon. Early construction of Marketplaces in your cities can help to keep your financial outlook bright. The Tax benefits of a Marketplace are more than sufficient to make this Improvement self-sustaining. The potential happiness benefits should also be taken into consideration: Marketplaces magnify the Luxuries produced by Entertainers as well as the Luxuries produced by Trade. If at least 20% of your Trade is allocated to Luxuries, you should attempt to mollify your citizens with Marketplaces before you resort to more expensive "happiness" Improvements like Cathedrals and Colosseums.

MASS TRANSIT

Cost:	160
Upkeep:	4
Prerequisite:	Mass Production
Effects:	Eliminates all Population Pollution

Considering its beneficial effects, the cost of building and maintaining the Mass Transit Improvement are negligible. By building Mass Transit in a city, you completely eliminate population from the pollution formula. The larger the city, the more dramatic the pollution reduction. As a preventive measure against the devastating effects of global warming, Mass Transit should be high on your "Improvements to build" list as soon as you discover Mass Production.

NUCLEAR PLANT

Cost:	160
Upkeep:	2
Prerequisite:	Nuclear Power
Effects:	Increases the Factory output of a city by 50%, and decreases pollution caused by Shield production by 50% (not cumulative with Power Plants, Hydro Plants, or Solar Plants). Poses a danger of a meltdown if the city remains in Civil Disorder for two consecutive turns (until the discovery of Fusion Power).

Nuclear Plants produce the same benefits as Hydro Plants at a significantly lower price and maintenance cost. They also have the advantage of being available for construction in every city, not just the ones near water or Mountains. The only drawback to this Improvement is the possibility of nuclear meltdown, which reduces the city's population and generates lots of pollution. This possibility is negligible—and considering the cost and Upkeep difference between Nuclear and Hydro Plants, it's worth the risk.

OFFSHORE PLATFORM

Cost:	160
Upkeep:	3
Prerequisite:	Miniaturization
Effects:	Allows all Ocean squares inside the City Radius to produce one Shield

Offshore Platforms add value to the already resource-rich Ocean Terrain by allowing Ocean squares to produce Shields. The overall value of this Improvement is based on two factors: the number of Ocean Squares within the City

Radius and the number of these squares currently in use. In cities with few Ocean squares, the Upkeep cost of the Offshore Platform often outweighs the Shield benefit it provides. Likewise, in smaller cities where only a few Ocean squares are being used for production purposes, the limited return in Shields makes this Improvement an unnecessary expense. Only in large cities with a large number of Ocean squares is the Offshore Platform a worthwhile investment.

> **Note:** Like Coastal Fortresses, Offshore Platforms are available in cities built near "lakes." The benefit of building Offshore Platforms in cities such as these is minimal at best.

PALACE

Cost:	100
Upkeep:	0
Prerequisite:	Masonry
Effects:	Eliminates all corruption and waste in the city and reduces it in nearby cities

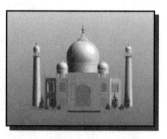

The city containing your Palace is the capital city of your civilization. You receive a Palace automatically when you build your first city. You can only have one Palace at any given time; when you choose to build a Palace in a city, you

> **Tip:** The best reason to move your Palace is to prevent your enemies from capturing your capital city after you launch your spaceship. If the capital is captured while your spaceship is en route to Alpha Centauri, the spaceship is destroyed. If your capital city is in danger of being captured, quickly move the Palace to a safer location. If your Palace is captured at any time, build a new one as soon as possible to prevent corruption and waste from becoming a problem.

are actually relocating the Palace from its original location to a new one. When the Palace is moved to a new city, the old Palace disappears and the new city becomes your capital. Unlike Palaces in the original *Civilization*, Palaces in *Civilization II* cannot be sold.

POLICE STATION

Cost:	60
Upkeep:	2
Prerequisite:	Communism
Effects:	Decreases the number of citizens unhappy because of units away from the city by one

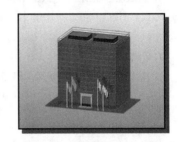

Police Stations are invaluable when your government is a Republic or a Democracy, especially if you happen to be at war. The more units you have away from the city under these forms of government, the more trouble you have with unhappy citizens. Police Stations allow you to more easily conduct military and exploratory operations away from the city. If you are not governing through Republic or Democracy, Police Stations are an unnecessary expense.

Tip: Instead of building Police Stations in every city, consider building the Women's Suffrage Wonder. (For complete details, see "Wonders of the World" later in this chapter.)

PORT FACILITY

Cost:	80
Upkeep:	3
Prerequisite:	Amphibious Warfare
Effects:	Repairs any damaged sea unit that spends an entire turn in the city. City produces Veteran sea units.

Port Facilities are important if you intend to utilize a large number of sea units. Just as Airports keep air units operating at peak efficiency, Port Facilities quickly repair ships, improving their performance by getting damaged units back in business faster. Because of their high Upkeep cost, Port Facilities are too expensive to be built in every coastal city. Limit their construction to the cities closest to your major shipping routes and battle lines.

Note: Once again, beware of the ability to build Port Facilities in cities adjacent to "lakes." A Port Facility on an inland sea is a waste of resources.

POWER PLANT

Cost:	160
Upkeep:	4
Prerequisite:	Refining
Effects:	Increases the Factory output of a city by 50 %, and decreases pollution caused by Shield production by 50% (not cumulative with Hydro Plants, Nuclear Plants, or Solar Plants)

Power Plants are the first "energy source" Improvements you can build. They are also the least beneficial: Power Plants don't provide any antipollution benefits, even though you get the same Shield-boost you get from Hydro, Nuclear, and Solar Plants,. This unfortunate drawback, at a cost equal to that of a Nuclear Plant and a maintenance cost *twice* that of a Nuclear Plant, makes Power Plants less than desirable. Unless a city desperately needs Shields, it is best to avoid Power Plants and wait until cleaner forms of energy are available. If you must build Power Plants, however, build them in one or two of your most productive cities. That way, you can get some of the Shield benefits without causing a runaway pollution problem.

RECYCLING CENTER

Cost:	200
Upkeep:	2
Prerequisite:	Recycling
Effects:	Reduces Resource Pollution by two-thirds

Until you able to build Solar Plants, Recycling Centers are the most effective way to cut the amount of Resource Pollution produced by a city. Cities equipped with both Recycling Centers and Mass Transit are virtually pollution-free. It should be noted, however, that adequate pollution control can usually be achieved through a combination of either a Nuclear or Hydro Plant and Mass Transit.

Note: The anti-pollution effects of Recycling Centers supersede those of a Nuclear or Hydro Plant that exists in the same city; the bonuses are not cumulative.

RESEARCH LAB

Cost:	160
Upkeep:	3
Prerequisite:	Computers
Effects:	Increases the city's Science output by 50% (cumulative with Library and University)

Tip: As an alternative to Research Labs in every city, consider building the SETI Program Wonder. (For details, see "Wonders of the World" later in this chapter.)

Research Labs are the Stock Exchange of Science. Their effect combines with those of the Library and University to give the city a total Science increase of 150%. A Research Lab in each city is highly recommended if you want to stay ahead in the research race in the later stages of the game.

SAM MISSILE BATTERY

Cost:	100
Upkeep:	2
Prerequisite:	Rocketry
Effects:	Doubles the Defense Factor of all units inside the city against air attacks and Cruise Missile attacks

SAM Missile Batteries defend a city against air units and Cruise Missiles in the same way that City Walls defend against ground units and Coastal Fortresses defend against sea units. If your enemies are fond of using air units and missiles against your cities, a SAM Missile Battery in each city is a good investment. The value of this defensive

Note: SAM Missile Batteries provide no defense against Nuclear Missile attacks.

Improvement is based on how frequently a city experiences airborne attacks; build them as necessary to suit the prevailing situation.

SDI DEFENSE

Cost:	200
Upkeep:	4
Prerequisite:	Laser
Effects:	Protects everything within three squares of the city from Nuclear Missile attacks. Increases the city's defense against Cruise Missiles by 50%

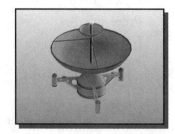

In the original *Civilization*, the A.I. seldom, if ever, used nuclear weapons against you; but your enemies in *Civilization II* do not hesitate to use Nuclear Missiles—in fact, they seem to revel in the practice. As a result, the SDI Defense plays a much more important role than it once did. As soon as any

> Tip: Every city might not need its own SDI Defense, depending on their proximity to one another. If two cities are within three squares of one another, building an SDI Defense in one of the cities protects both of them from Nuclear Missile attacks.

civilization with whom you have questionable relations gains the ability to build nuclear weapons (you can tell who these people are because their ". . . words are backed by nuclear weapons . . ." during negotiations), you should start protecting your most important cities by building SDI Defense systems. You should also do so before you start a war with a civilization that possesses nuclear capability.

The SDI Defense also protects against Cruise Missiles, doubling the city's defense against these weapons. The defensive bonus against Cruise Missiles is cumulative with that of the SAM Missile Battery.

SDI Defense systems do not protect against nuclear devices planted by spies.

SEWER SYSTEM

Cost:	120
Upkeep:	2
Prerequisite:	Sanitation
Effects:	Required for a city to grow beyond size 12

Like Aqueducts, the Sewer System is a "must have" Improvement if you want your cities to continue growing. Although you might gain the ability to build Sewer Systems relatively early in the game, you should wait until a city reaches a size of 10 or 11 before you bother to add this Improvement; building them earlier incurs many turns of unnecessary Upkeep costs.

SOLAR PLANT

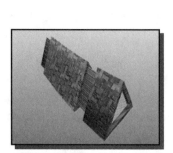

Cost:	320
Upkeep:	4
Prerequisite:	Environmentalism
Effects:	Increases Factory output by 50%, and eliminates all Resource Pollution in the city (not cumulative with Power Plant, Hydro Plant, or Nuclear Plant). Helps to prevent global warming by partially neutralizing existing pollution.

Solar Plants are the ultimate in clean power generation. They greatly improve the pollution situation by eliminating Resource Pollution in the city. Solar Plants also help to slow the effects of global warming. Each Solar Plant you build neutralizes one-half of one polluted square. In other words, if there are currently six polluted Terrain squares in your territory and four of your cities have Solar Plants, only four polluted squares are counted toward the global warming total. (For details on global warming, see Chapter 5.)

Whether or not you should build a Solar Plant depends on the situation. If a city already has Mass Transit, a Recycling Center, and/or a "clean" power plant of some variety, and the amount of pollution generated by the city is causing no problems, a Solar Plant is of little benefit. It is usually possible to get through the entire game without building a Solar Plant.

SPACESHIP COMPONENT

Cost:	160
Upkeep:	0
Prerequisite:	Plastics
Effects:	*Thrust Component:* Increases your spaceship's thrust by 25 percent
	Fuel Component: Provides enough fuel for one Thrust Component

Spaceship Components are obviously vital to the success of a spaceship's mission—without fuel and engines, the ship can't be launched. In order to function, every Thrust Component must have an accompanying Fuel Component. Spaceship Components are unavailable if you select the "Bloodlust" option during game setup.

SPACESHIP MODULE

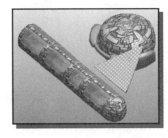

Cost:	320
Upkeep:	0
Prerequisite:	Superconductor
Effects:	*Population Module:* Provides enough living space for 10,000 colonists
	Life Support Module: Provides support facilities for one Population Module
	Solar Panel: Provides power for two other Modules

Like Spaceship Components, Spaceship Modules are vital to the completion of your spaceship. In order to function, a spaceship must have, at a minimum, one of each type of Module. Each Habitation Module must have a Life Support Module to keep its inhabitants alive. Each Life Support/Habitation Module pair must have an accompanying Solar Panel Module in order to function.

SPACESHIP STRUCTURAL

Cost:	80
Upkeep:	0
Prerequisite:	Space Flight
Effects:	Forms the structural framework for your spaceship

In order for any Spaceship Components or Modules to function, they must be completely connected to the framework of the spaceship. The framework is made up of many Spaceship Structural pieces, which are automatically linked together as they are constructed. Components and Modules not properly connected to the Structural framework are highlighted on the Spaceship View (see Figure 7-1).

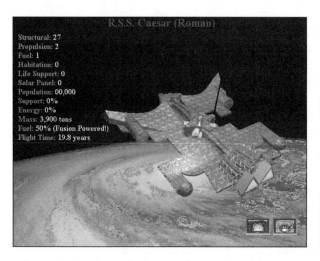

R.S.S. Caesar (Roman)

Structural: 27
Propulsion: 2
Fuel: 1
Habitation: 0
Life Support: 0
Solar Panel: 0
Population: 00,000
Support: 0%
Energy: 0%
Mass: 3,900 tons
Fuel: 50% (Fusion Powered!)
Flight Time: 19.8 years

Figure 7-1 *A partially completed spaceship.*

Tip:
Spaceship Structural pieces are the first spaceship parts you are able to build. Since you need a lot of them in order to complete even the smallest spaceship, you should have several of your cities start producing Spaceship Structural pieces while you complete the research required to produce Spaceship Components and Modules.

STOCK EXCHANGE

Cost:	160
Upkeep:	4
Prerequisite:	Economics
Effects:	Increases the city's Tax and Luxury output by 50% (cumulative with Marketplace and Bank)

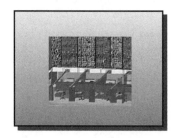

Civilization II provides a third Improvement to boost a city's Tax and Luxury output in conjunction with the Marketplace and Bank. The incredible 150% Tax and Luxury boost collectively generated by these Improvements makes this three-Improvement combination impossible to resist, especially since they more than pay for their own Upkeep. As soon as it becomes feasible, every city should have a Stock Exchange.

SUPERHIGHWAYS

Cost:	160
Upkeep:	3
Prerequisite:	Automobile
Effects:	All squares inside the City Radius with roads or railroads produce 50% more Trade. Adds a 50% bonus to trade route income

Superhighways provide an excellent Trade boost in any city that is surrounded by roads. Cities surrounded by railroads receive a particularly good Trade increase because the effect of Superhighways is cumulative with that of the railroad itself. For a mid-to-late game augmentation to your research efforts and Taxes, as well as a big boost in trade route income, Superhighways in all your cities are a tremendous asset.

SUPERMARKET

Cost:	80
Upkeep:	3
Prerequisite:	Refrigeration
Effects:	All farmland squares within the City Radius produce 50% more Food

Until a city builds a Supermarket, double-irrigated (farmland) squares within the City Radius produce the same amount of Food as normally irrigated Terrain. A Supermarket Improvement combined with a number of farmland squares is an excellent way to improve the Food production of cities with lower than average Food output or those experiencing a Food deficit, inducing them to grow larger. When used in cities with average or better Food production, the Supermarket/farmland combination creates mega-cities, with huge populations. Except in cities with a Food deficit Supermarkets needn't be high on your production priority list unless runaway growth is your goal.

TEMPLE

Cost:	40
Upkeep:	1
Prerequisite:	Ceremonial Burial
Effects:	One unhappy citizen is made content (two after the discovery of Mysticism).

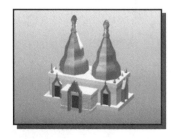

Depending on the research path you choose, Temples are one of the earliest Improvements available. Temples should, arguably, be the first Improvement built in each city, especially on the higher difficulty levels where your citizens become unhappy more quickly. Once each city has a Temple in place, steady city growth can proceed with less chance of the population becoming unhappy.

UNIVERSITY

Cost:	160
Upkeep:	3
Prerequisite:	University
Effects:	Increases the city's Science output by 50% (cumulative with Library)

Once again, the importance of research cannot be over emphasized. The cumulative effect of the Library and University is to double a city's Science output. As soon as you can afford it, a University in every city is highly recommended in order to remain competitive in the quest for knowledge.

Wonders of the World

Wonders of the World are built in the same way as City Improvements. Although they are much more expensive than most City Improvements, their effects are more far-reaching and dramatic. In fact, several Wonders allow all of your cities to reap the benefits of certain City Improvements without having to construct the Improvements themselves. Most of the Wonders in the game are well worth the investment in time and Shields required to construct them. Because of their powerful nature, only one of each Wonder of the World can exist in the game.

This section provides statistics and analysis of the 28 Wonders of the World. The statistics of the Wonders are also consolidated in Table 7-2 for easy reference.

Note: The effects produced by Wonders of the World expire when *any* civilization in the game discovers the Expiration Advance listed.

Tip: Keep the expiration Advances of your opponents' Wonders in mind. If you want to rob an opponent of the effects of a Wonder, make a concerted effort to research the technology that makes the Wonder expire.

ADAM SMITH'S TRADING CO.

Cost:	400
Prerequisite:	Economics
Expiration:	Does not expire
Effects:	Pays the maintenance costs of all City Improvements with an Upkeep cost of one. Improvements with an Upkeep greater than one are not affected.

As you know, most City Improvements require that you pay an Upkeep cost each turn in order to maintain them. Adam Smith's Trading Company offers a partial solution to the high cost of maintenance by absorbing the Upkeep costs for all Improvements with an Upkeep of one. Seven Improvements fall into this category. This Wonder can save you a significant amount of money; for example, in

* Table 7-2. Statistics and Effects of the Wonders of the World

WONDER	COST	PREREQUISITE	EXPIRATION	EFFECTS
Adam Smith's Trading Co.	400	Economics	—	Pays the Upkeep of all Improvements with an Upkeep cost of one.
Apollo Program	600	Space Flight	—	Allows all civilizations to build spaceships. Reveals entire map.
Colossus	200	Bronze Working	Flight	Generates one extra unit of Trade in any square already producing Trade in the city where built.
Copernicus' Observatory	300	Astronomy	—	Increases Science output by 50% in the city where it is built.
Cure for Cancer	600	Genetic Engineering	—	Makes one content citizen happy in every city.
Darwin's Voyage	400	Railroad	—	Automatically grants two Civilization Advances.
Eiffel Tower	300	Steam Engine	—	Shifts attitudes of rival civilizations 25 points in your favor. Rivals forget your transgressions more quickly.
Great Library	300	Literacy	Electricity	Automatically gives you an Advance when it is discovered by two other civilizations.
Great Wall	300	Masonry	Metallurgy	Acts as City Walls in all friendly cities. Unit Attack Factors doubled versus Barbarians. Rival civilizations are forced to offer peace.
Hanging Gardens	200	Pottery	Railroad	Makes three content citizens happy in the city where built, and one content citizen happy in every other city.
Hoover Dam	600	Electronics	—	Acts as a Hydro Plant in every friendly city.
Isaac Newton's College	400	Theory of Gravity	—	Doubles Science output in the city where it is built.
J. S. Bach's Cathedral	400	Theology	—	Decreases the number of unhappy citizens by 2 in every friendly city.
King Richard's Crusade	300	Engineering	Industrialization	Every square in the City Radius of the city where it is built produces one extra Shield.

♣ Table 7-2. Statistics and Effects of the Wonders of the World (*continued*)

Wonder	Cost	Prerequisite	Expiration	Effects
Leonardo's Workshop	400	Invention	Automobile	Automatically upgrades obsolete units free of charge.
Lighthouse	200	Map Making	Magnetism	Triremes cannot be lost at sea. Movement Rate of sea units increased by one. All new sea units are Veterans.
Magellan's Expedition	400	Navigation	—	Increases the Movement Rate of all sea units by 2.
Manhattan Project	600	Nuclear Fission	—	Allows all civilizations to build Nuclear Missiles (once they discover Rocketry).
Marco Polo's Embassy	200	Trade	Communism	Automatically gives you an embassy with all other civilizations.
Michelangelo's Chapel	400	Monotheism	—	Acts as a Cathedral in all your cities.
Oracle	300	Mysticism	Theology	Doubles the effectiveness of all Temples.
Pyramids	200	Masonry	—	Acts as a Granary in all your cities.
SETI Program	600	Computers	—	Acts as a Research Lab in all your cities.
Shakespeare's Theatre	300	Medicine	—	Eliminates unhappy citizens in the city where it is built.
Statue of Liberty	400	Democracy	—	Eliminates Anarchy when changing governments. Allows the choice of any government type.
Sun Tzu's War Academy	300	Feudalism	Mobile Warfare	All new units are Veterans. All non-Veteran units automatically become Veterans when they win a battle.
United Nations	600	Communism	—	Automatically gives you an embassy with all other civilizations. Rivals forced to offer peace. You can declare war on a civilization with whom you have a treaty 50% of the time under a Democracy.
Women's Suffrage	600	Industrialization	—	Acts as a Police Station in all your cities.

a civilization with 20 cities, each of which has all seven of the one-Upkeep Improvements, Adam Smith's Trading Company saves you 140 gold every turn. If you have the chance to build it, this Wonder is highly recommended.

APOLLO PROGRAM

Cost:	600
Prerequisite:	Space Flight
Expiration:	Does not expire.
Effects:	Allows all civilizations to build spaceships. Reveals the entire world map.

The Apollo Program is a pivotal Wonder if you intend to win the game by sending a spaceship to Alpha Centauri. It is not necessarily important that your civilization be the one to build it, however. No matter who builds the Apollo Program, *all* civilizations in the game gain the ability to build spaceships, and the map is revealed to *all* civilizations. If you are about to build the Apollo Program and you receive notice that another civilization is building it, abandon the project and let your opponent build it for you. There is no reason to build this Wonder yourself unless you are in a tremendous hurry or you want the points for your Civilization Score.

COLOSSUS

Cost:	200
Prerequisite:	Bronze Working
Expiration:	Flight
Effects:	Generates one extra unit of Trade in any square already producing Trade around the city where it is built.

The Colossus provides a good Trade boost for the city that builds it. As Wonders go, it is relatively inexpensive; it is available very early in the game; and its benefits can be great if it is built in the right city. The Colossus naturally functions best in a city that produces a lot of Trade.

Tip: Building Wonders early in the game can be very time consuming. You should wait until you have several cities before you attempt your first Wonder, since the city producing the Wonder often has its production tied up hundreds of game years. If you have several cities, the others can build any units you need while the Wonder-city is busy.

COPERNICUS' OBSERVATORY

Cost:	300
Prerequisite:	Astronomy
Expiration:	Does not expire
Effects:	Increases Science output in the city where it is built by 50%

Anything you do to increase the amount of Science generated by your civilization can only improve your game performance. Copernicus' Observatory is cumulative with the effects of Libraries, Universities, and Research Labs. In fact, the effects of the Wonder are calculated *after* the effects of City Improvements and Scientists, yielding a significant amount of additional Science. Although its overall importance is not as great as some of the other Wonders, Copernicus' Observatory is very useful, especially if built in a city with an already generous Science output.

Tip: For really super Science output, build Copernicus' Observatory in the same city as other Science-enhancing Wonders, like Isaac Newton's College.

CURE FOR CANCER

Cost:	600
Prerequisite:	Genetic Engineering
Expiration:	Does not expire
Effects:	Makes one content citizen happy in every friendly city

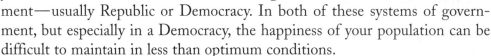

Chances are that by the latter portion of the game you have switched to an advanced form of government—usually Republic or Democracy. In both of these systems of government, but especially in a Democracy, the happiness of your population can be difficult to maintain in less than optimum conditions.

Cure for Cancer offers late-game assistance in this area. It produces essentially the same effect as having a permanent Entertainer in each of your cities. If you anticipate a war-torn climate or other conditions that could cause your citizens to be unhappy (like a decrease in the Luxuries rate), it is a good idea to build this Wonder when it becomes available. You'll be surprised how helpful an additional happy person in each city can be.

Tip: The unhappiness effects of military units abroad under the Republic and the Democracy are resolved *after* the effects of such unhappiness-quelling Improvements such as Temples and Cathedrals. The only way to balance unit-induced unhappiness is with extra "happy" citizens that are added through Luxuries and Wonders. This makes both the Cure for Cancer and Hanging Gardens Wonders extremely valuable under these systems of government.

DARWIN'S VOYAGE

Cost:	400
Prerequisite:	Railroad
Expiration:	Functions only once (on the turn it is built).
Effects:	Automatically grants two Civilization Advances.

Darwin's Voyage is unique in that it neither expires nor continues to function after its initial construction. It is also of no real value (other than score) when it is captured by another civilization. Nevertheless, this Wonder provides a nice bonus when you build it: it instantly completes research on the Advance currently being studied and then grants another free Advance of your choice. You should give this Wonder serious attention when it becomes available. Darwin's Voyage gives your research effort a big boost right at the start of the Industrial age (when research is starting to get expensive). And remember: if *you* build it, you deprive one of your opponents of two instant Advances.

EIFFEL TOWER

Cost:	300
Prerequisite:	Steam Engine
Expiration:	Does not expire.
Effects:	When first built (or captured), the attitudes of all rival civilizations shift dramatically in your favor and continue to improve over time, barring conflicts. Also, computer-controlled civilizations forget your transgressions more quickly.

There are two good reasons to build the Eiffel Tower: to atone for your past sins and to ease the consequences later in the game as you revel in your ruthless nature. Because of the complex diplomacy system in *Civilization II* (see Chapter 9), it is much more difficult to get away with the frequent breaking of peace treaties than it was in the original game. Your opponents have a long memory and are unlikely to deal peacefully with you if you are have a bad reputation. Possessing the Eiffel Tower tends to ease this situation somewhat. This is a low-priority Wonder if you have little difficulty dealing peacefully with your neighbors. If you like to break treaties, or if your opponents tend to anger easily, you should consider the Eiffel Tower as one possible way to ease your political woes.

GREAT LIBRARY

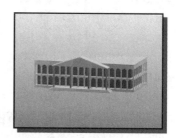

Cost:	300
Prerequisite:	Literacy
Expiration:	Electricity
Effects:	Automatically gives you every Civilization Advance discovered by at least two other civilizations.

In the original *Civilization*, the Great Library was of limited use because it expired quickly, usually yielding only three or four Advances. Now that the life of this Wonder has been significantly extended, the Great Library is a much more worthwhile investment. It is most valuable when you have fallen behind your opponents in research. The free Advances given by the Great Library ensure that you remain at least somewhat current in the research race.

Tip: One of the nice things about the Great Library is that it allows you to discover Advances from a number of different research paths simultaneously. For example, if you are pursuing a pacifistic line of research and two of your opponents are going for militaristic Advances, with the Great Library you can accumulate free military Advances, and the units they allow, while continuing your preferred line of research.

GREAT WALL

Cost:	300
Prerequisite:	Masonry
Expiration:	Metallurgy
Effects:	Acts as City Walls in all friendly cities. Unit Attack Factor is double versus Barbarians. Rival civilizations are forced to offer peace during negotiations.

The Great Wall is among the earliest Wonders available. Whereas this Wonder was a fairly low priority in the original *Civilization*, the Great Wall's new abilities (acting as City Walls and doubling your Attack Factor against Barbarians) make the Great Wall worth your consideration. Still, you should weigh the pros and cons. If you tend to switch to Republic early in the game, the constant offers of peace can get in your way when you want to attack your enemies: your Senate has a tendency to force peace upon you when it is offered. Also, you must consider the vulnerability your cities will experience when the Great Wall expires. You'll have to drop everything and build City Walls in all your cities to regain the level of security you enjoyed while the Wonder was in effect.

Note: Unlike the original *Civilization*, *Civilization II* enforces the peace treaty restrictions imposed by the Great Wall against you as well as the computer-controlled players.

HANGING GARDENS

Cost:	200
Prerequisite:	Pottery
Expiration:	Railroad
Effects:	Makes three content citizens happy in the city where it is built, and one content citizen happy in every other friendly city

This Wonder is, essentially, the ancient version of Cure for Cancer with an added bonus. The importance of the Hanging Gardens depends on the level of game difficulty: on higher levels of difficulty, where citizen unhappiness can be a problem early in the game, the Hanging Gardens can be extremely helpful in keeping the peace. This Wonder is particularly beneficial in its home city because of the extra two happy citizens it creates, making "We Love the King Day" a common occurrence there. If you want a city to grow quickly early in the game, build the Hanging Gardens.

HOOVER DAM

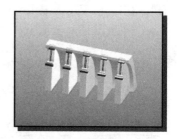

Cost:	600
Prerequisite:	Electronics
Expiration:	Does not expire
Effects:	Acts as a Hydro Plant in all friendly cities. Effects are *not* cumulative with existing Power Plants, Hydro Plants, Nuclear Plants, or Solar Plants.

Building the Hoover Dam is an excellent way to ease pollution and increase Shield production throughout your entire civilization. This Wonder should be relegated to high-priority whether or not you have a pollution and/or Shield-deficit problem: sooner or later, you are bound to need some sort of power plant, so it might as well be a clean one. Hoover Dam also saves you all the money you would normally spend maintaining individual power plants in all your cities.

Note:
Unlike its predecessor in the original *Civilization*, the Hoover Dam now affects all of your cities (not just those on the same continent).

> **Tip:** If you build Hoover Dam, sell off all your existing Power Plants and Nuclear Plants for extra cash—you won't need them anymore. Do not, however, sell Solar Plants: their environmental effects supersede those of the Hoover Dam.

ISAAC NEWTON'S COLLEGE

Cost:	400
Prerequisite:	Theory of Gravity
Expiration:	Does not expire
Effects:	Doubles the Science output in the city where it is built.

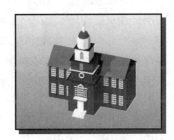

This Wonder is a more modern, more powerful version of Copernicus' Observatory. Like Copernicus' Observatory, Isaac Newton's College bases its Science bonus on the amount of Science produced by its home city *after* the bonuses for Improvements and Scientists are taken into account. This Wonder can be extremely beneficial to your research efforts, especially if it is built in a city that is already producing a generous amount of Science. Despite the fact that its effects don't extend beyond one city, Isaac Newton's College is not a Wonder to be ignored.

> **Tip:** If you intend to build both Copernicus' Observatory and Isaac Newton's College, consider building them in the same city. Since the effects are cumulative, you can get a TREMENDOUS Science bonus by doing so.

J. S. BACH'S CATHEDRAL

Cost: 400
Prerequisite: Theology
Expiration: Does not expire
Effects: Decreases the number of unhappy citizens by two in all friendly cities.

J. S. Bach's Cathedral is one of the three highest priority Wonders in the game. When playing at higher difficulty levels and/or governing by Republic or Democracy, this Wonder goes a long way toward keeping the peace in your empire. Two less unhappy people per city means two extra units that can be away from their home city in a Republic (one extra unit under a Democracy.) When you discover Theology, make the construction of J. S. Bach's Cathedral one of your top priorities.

Note: Those familiar with the original *Civilization* should note that the effects of J. S. Bach's Cathedral are no longer limited to the continent where it is built, thus increasing the power of this already desirable Wonder.

KING RICHARD'S CRUSADE

Cost: 300
Prerequisite: Engineering
Expiration: Industrialization
Effects: Every square inside the City Radius of the city where the Wonder is built produces one extra Shield.

On the surface, King Richard's Crusade seems to be a good way to increase Shield production. This is true to an extent, but there are better ways to increase Shield output in most cases. This Wonder is most useful in a city that has low overall Shield output. The city also needs to be fairly large to reap the full benefits of King Richard's Crusade, since only Terrain squares that are being worked by one of your citizens produce the bonus Shield. Due to these factors, plus its limited life span, King Richard's Crusade is definitely a low priority Wonder.

Note: As always, there are dissenting opinions. It should be noted that Brian Reynolds (designer and programmer of the game) builds this Wonder every game.

LEONARDO'S WORKSHOP

Cost:	400
Prerequisite:	Invention
Expiration:	Automobile
Effects:	Whenever an existing unit becomes obsolete due to the discovery of a new Civilization Advance, it is automatically upgraded to its modern equivalent free of charge.

It is impossible to convey the true value and importance of this Wonder. Leonardo's Workshop is, hands down, the most desirable Wonder in the game. If you plan your city production and research carefully while you control this

Tip: There are a number of good strategies concerning Leonardo's Workshop. First, keep the expiration Advance of this Wonder in mind when deciding what to research. Plan your research path so that you get as many unit upgrades as possible before you are forced to research the Automobile. Consult Chapter 6 of this book and the Advances Chart included with the game to strategically plan your research.

Wonder, you can receive dozens of free unit upgrades as you make new discoveries. Meanwhile, the Shields you save by not having to pay for upgrading your units can be used to build new Improvements and other Wonders. When you discover Invention, drop whatever you are doing and turn all your efforts to producing Leonardo's Workshop. You won't be sorry.

Another related strategy actually increases the value of the weak Warrior unit. Before you discover Feudalism, build a Warrior in all of your cities. When you discover Gunpowder, Leonardo's Workshop transforms all of these worthless Warriors into Musketeers. Essentially, you have built a whole army of Musketeers for a measly ten Shields apiece.

Finally, be sure that you discover Explosives before this Wonder expires. That way, all of your existing Settlers are converted to Engineers for free.

LIGHTHOUSE

Cost:	200
Prerequisite:	Map Making
Expiration:	Magnetism
Effects:	Eliminates the risk of Triremes being lost at sea, and increases the Movement Rate of all other sea units by one. All sea units produced are automatically granted Veteran status.

The Lighthouse's importance is based entirely upon how much you depend on the use of sea units early in the game. If you are forced, either by continent size or by nearby neighbors, to expand your civilization to another continent while you are still using Triremes, the Lighthouse allows you to do so without fear of losing your Triremes, and the units they are carrying, at sea. The movement rate bonus is a great aid to early exploration, and the automatic Veteran status for new sea units makes early naval battles easier to win. But because of the Lighthouse's expiration date, the movement and Veteran bonuses are short-lived (the Trireme bonus is even shorter-lived, as Triremes become obsolete when Caravels become available). As early Wonders go, there are several better choices than the Lighthouse.

MAGELLAN'S EXPEDITION

Cost:	400
Prerequisite:	Navigation
Expiration:	Does not expire
Effects:	Increases the Movement Rate of all sea units by two

Magellan's Expedition is a much more useful Wonder than its early predecessor, the Lighthouse. Although it doesn't give sea units automatic Veteran status, it provides twice the movement bonus of the Lighthouse, and it never expires. The benefits of Magellan's Expedition are more subtle than those of many of the other Wonders; but they are useful if you find yourself making extensive use of naval units late in the game. Magellan's Expedition is not a "drop everything" Wonder, but it can be useful if you have the time and resources.

MANHATTAN PROJECT

Cost:	600
Prerequisite:	Nuclear Fission
Expiration:	Does not expire
Effects:	Allows all civilizations to build nuclear weapons

The Manhattan Project opens the door to the horrors of nuclear warfare. Because of the power it imparts, players often assign more importance to this Wonder than it really deserves. Unless you have an overwhelming need or desire to start a nuclear war, the Manhattan Project can safely be ignored. Since *any* civilization that has discovered Rocketry can build Nuclear Missiles once this Wonder is built, why not let some other civilization spend the time and resources to build it? You stand to reap the same benefits, and the only thing you have to lose are a few points off your Civilization Score.

Tip: Marco Polo's Embassy also allows you to contact and negotiate with all the other races in the world. By making friends with everyone, you can become a "dealer in information" by trading technologies with others. You can quickly build your level of technology by acting as the middleman. For example, trade Advances "A" and "B" to the Chinese for Advances "C" and "D". Then, trade "B" and "C" to the French in exchange for "E" and "F", and so on. Not only do you tend to make friends quickly in this manner, you also experience technological growth in leaps and bounds.

MARCO POLO'S EMBASSY

Cost:	200
Prerequisite:	Trade
Expiration:	Communism
Effects:	You automatically establish an embassy with all other civilizations.

Marco Polo's Embassy gives you a free peek at all the other civilizations in the game. Because this Wonder can usually be built so early in the game, this sneak-peek at your opponents often comes before you have met some or all of them. Marco Polo's Embassy is especially useful if you plan to win by conquering the world. The earlier you begin your conquest the easier it is, and your task is made even easier if you know exactly what you are up against.

MICHELANGELO'S CHAPEL

Cost:	400
Prerequisite:	Monotheism
Expiration:	Does not expire
Effects:	Acts as a Cathedral in all your cities

Tip: The ability to build Michelangelo's Chapel coincides with the ability to build Cathedrals. Once you discover Monotheism, throw all of your efforts and resources into building the Wonder rather than wasting resources building Cathedrals. You can always build Cathedrals later if someone beats you to the Wonder.

Michelangelo's Chapel is the third of the "must have" Wonders (the others being J. S. Bach's Cathedral and Leonardo's Workshop). The effects of Michelangelo's Chapel are different now than they were in the original *Civilization*, but equally (if not more) powerful. By acting as a Cathedral in every city, Michelangelo's Chapel not only gives you a population happiness bonus in every city you control, it also saves you the time and resources required to build Cathedrals everywhere and eliminates a healthy chunk of your Upkeep costs. This Wonder is too good to pass up.

ORACLE

Cost:	300
Prerequisite:	Mysticism
Expiration:	Theology
Effects:	Doubles the effectiveness of all Temples

The Oracle is one of the more useful early Wonders, especially on the high difficulty levels. If all your cities have Temples, the Oracle's effect is to make two additional unhappy citizens in every city content. This goes a long way toward easing any unhappiness problems that occur early in the game. The effects of the Temple-Oracle combination now overlap the ability to build Cathedrals, so there should be no transitional unhappiness. Even on lower levels of difficulty, where unhappiness is not as much of a problem in the early stages of play, building the Oracle can't hurt if you have some excess resources and time.

PYRAMIDS

Cost:	200
Prerequisite:	Masonry
Expiration:	Does not expire
Effects:	Acts as a Granary in all friendly cities

Those familiar with *Civilization* might be surprised at the effects of the Pyramids in *Civilization II*. The former effects of this Wonder have been transferred to the Statue of Liberty.

The usefulness of the Pyramids depends on your viewpoint regarding Granaries. If you are a player who likes to build Granaries early, spare no time and expense to get the Pyramids built as soon as possible. Even if you don't normally build Granaries early, you might want to reconsider your strategy in light of the long-term benefits of the Pyramids: if you control this Wonder throughout the game, you never have to build or pay maintenance for any Granaries. That can save you lots of Shields and money.

The only caution about this Wonder is the same one that applies to Granaries themselves: on higher levels of difficulty, rapid, early growth of cities can outpace your ability to keep the population happy. Be prepared.

Tip: It is possible (even likely) that you will gain the ability to build Granaries before you can build the Pyramids. If you plan on taking advantage of this Wonder, don't waste time and Shields building Granaries before you make an attempt at building the Pyramids. If another civilization beats you to the Pyramids, you can always build Granaries later.

SETI PROGRAM

Cost:	600
Prerequisite:	Computers
Expiration:	Does not expire
Effects:	Acts as a Research Lab in all friendly cities

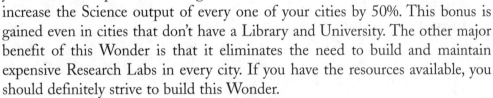

The SETI Program is the single best way to boost your Science output late in the game. Its effect is to increase the Science output of every one of your cities by 50%. This bonus is gained even in cities that don't have a Library and University. The other major benefit of this Wonder is that it eliminates the need to build and maintain expensive Research Labs in every city. If you have the resources available, you should definitely strive to build this Wonder.

SHAKESPEARE'S THEATRE

Cost:	300
Prerequisite:	Medicine
Expiration:	Does not expire
Effects:	All unhappy citizens in the city are made content

Tip: One possible use for Shakespeare's Theatre is to use the city where the Wonder is built as a staging point for exploration and military expeditions in a Republic or a Democracy. The effects of this Wonder nullify the unhappiness usually experienced under these governments when units are away from the city. As long as the city has sufficient Shields to support them, the city can send as many units as it wants into the field with no unhappiness penalty.

Shakespeare's Theatre has a dramatic effect, but an extremely limited scope. It essentially allows you to create a small pocket of contentment; a city where no one is ever unhappy. The limited scope of its effect makes Shakespeare's Theatre a low-priority Wonder. Under Fundamentalism, this Wonder has no value whatsoever.

STATUE OF LIBERTY

Cost:	400
Prerequisite:	Democracy
Expiration:	Does not expire
Effects:	Eliminates the period of Anarchy usually experienced when switching government types. Allows the choice of any government type regardless of whether the prerequisite technologies have been discovered

The Statue of Liberty performs the function that was performed by the Pyramids in *Civilization*. Because this Wonder doesn't become available until the discovery of Democracy, the ability to switch to any government type is almost moot; once you reach Democracy, you have already discovered most forms of government. The real power of The Statue of Liberty is the ability to switch government types without experiencing a period of Anarchy. This is a valuable ability if you anticipate the need to break treaties frequently by switching governments, which is an important ability because of the strict enforcement of Senate rulings in *Civilization II*.

SUN TZU'S WAR ACADEMY

Cost:	300
Prerequisite:	Feudalism
Expiration:	Mobile Warfare
Effects:	All new ground units produced are automatically given Veteran status. All existing non-Veteran units automatically become Veterans when they win a battle.

Building Barracks creates Veterans, and the power of Veteran units should not be underestimated. But there are two major drawbacks of building a Barracks in every city early in the game—and they are the Upkeep costs and the fact that they must be rebuilt twice due to obsolescence (once when Gunpowder is discovered and again when Mobile Warfare is discovered). Sun Tzu's War Academy gives you the opportunity to produce Veteran units in all your cities without experiencing either of the Barracks' early drawbacks. Both of the Barracks expirations are bypassed when utilizing this Wonder: you only have to build a Barracks once in each city instead of three times, and the one you build after Sun Tzu's Academy expires lasts through the end of the game. If Veteran units are a priority to you, build this Wonder.

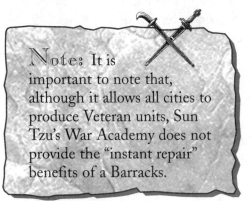

Note: It is important to note that, although it allows all cities to produce Veteran units, Sun Tzu's War Academy does not provide the "instant repair" benefits of a Barracks.

UNITED NATIONS

Cost:	600
Prerequisite:	Communism
Expiration:	Does not expire
Effects:	You automatically establish an embassy with all rival civilizations. Rivals are forced to offer peace during negotiations. Under a Democracy, you can successfully override Senate decisions 50% of the time.

The United Nations is a combination of the Great Wall and Marco Polo's Embassy in the modern era, with a twist. The automatic peace offer helps to quell your violent neighbors and keeps them from declaring war on you, which can be helpful when it seems that everyone is ganging up on you. Wars can be ended simply by requesting an audience with your enemy. The best power of the United Nations is the ability to override the decisions imposed by your Senate.

> **Note:** Like the Great Wall, the peace treaty restrictions imposed by the United Nations are now enforced against human players as well as computer-controlled players.

A 50% chance is better than none at all, and when successful you can avoid the nastiness of staging a revolution to start a war. Much more useful than its ancient counterpart, the United Nations is a good Wonder to have if you have the time and resources to build it.

WOMEN'S SUFFRAGE

Cost:	600
Prerequisite:	Industrialization
Expiration:	Does not expire
Effects:	Acts as a Police Station in all friendly cities

If your warlike attitude is constantly causing unhappiness in your Republic or Democracy, Women's Suffrage is an important Wonder for you to acquire. By acting as a Police Station in all your cities, this Wonder gives you more leeway to send units into the field. It also eliminates the need to pay the construction and maintenance costs incurred by building a separate Police Station in every city. If war under Democracy or Republic is your game, Women's Suffrage is for you.

Tips and Strategies for Building Improvements and Wonders

In addition to the specific information regarding each City Improvement and Wonder of the World, there are a number of general production strategies that can help you when deciding how to best develop your cities. The remainder of this chapter presents these strategies.

USING CARAVANS AND FREIGHT TO ACCELERATE WONDER PRODUCTION

One of the built in features of Caravans and Freight units is their ability to accelerate the production of Wonders of the World. When you move either of these units into a friendly city that is producing a Wonder, you are given the option to add the unit's Shield value (50 Shields in either case) to the production effort. This is a good way to speed the completion of Wonders.

This idea can be taken one step further. If you know in advance that you want to build a Wonder as soon as it becomes available, planning ahead can allow you to build the Wonder almost instantly. When you start researching the Advance that makes the desired Wonder possible, dedicate your cities to producing as many Caravans or Freight units as possible, and then move them into positions surrounding the city where the Wonder is to be built. As soon as you discover the Advance, switch the city's production to the desired Wonder, move all the surrounding Caravans or Freight units into the city on the same turn and order them to help build the Wonder. Poof! Instant Wonder.

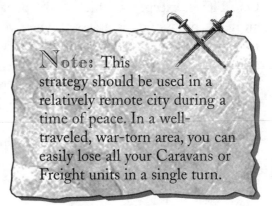

Note: This strategy should be used in a relatively remote city during a time of peace. In a well-traveled, war-torn area, you can easily lose all your Caravans or Freight units in a single turn.

SPEEDING THE PRODUCTION OF IMPROVEMENTS

Although there is no provision that allows Caravans and Freight units to help with the production of City Improvements as they do with Wonders of the World, a similar strategy is a available. When you disband a unit inside one of your cities, half of that unit's original Shield cost is added to the production of whatever item is currently being built in that city. Making use of this feature allows you to use any type of unit as a sort of mini-Caravan for the purposes of speeding up Improvements production in other cities. Although you lose half of the unit's value in Shields every time you do this, this strategy is a good way to accelerate the production of a critical Improvement in a city with slow production.

ote: The strategy of disbanding units to
speed production works equally well to speed the production
of new units, and to speed the production of Wonders before
the development of Trade. This strategy should not be used
for Wonders after Caravans become available.

Avoid Production Type Changes

On all levels except for Chief, a 50% penalty of the Shields already allocated to an item's production is assessed when you change to a different item type in mid-production. In other words, if you are building a unit, you are penalized for switching production to an Improvement or Wonder; if you are building a Wonder, you are penalized for switching to an Improvement or unit; and so on. This penalty is assessed if any Shields whatsoever have been allocated to the current production item.

The production penalty can make things a little tricky when you want to disband a unit in a city to add Shields to production. If you intend to switch to a new type of production on the same turn that you are adding Shields by dis-

Note: The production penalty is applied only
the first time you change production types in a city on a given turn.
For instance, if you switch from producing a unit to producing an
Improvement, and then switch from the Improvement to a
Wonder, you are charged only for the first production change and
not the second. This penalty is assessed for each city individually.

banding a unit, make the production switch *first*, and then disband the unit. Otherwise, half of the Shields gained by disbanding the unit are lost to the production change penalty.

MAKE USE OF THE "GLOBAL IMPROVEMENT" WONDERS

As you have seen from the descriptions in this chapter, there are several Wonders of the World that act as a specific Improvement in every city in your civilization. The value of these Wonders cannot be stressed enough. If the Improvement mimicked by the Wonder is one that you normally construct in every city, build the Wonder instead. The overall savings in time, Shields, and maintenance costs is very significant. Do the math!

Along the same lines, if you have built one or more Improvements and, afterwards, you build or acquire control of a Wonder that produces the same effects, sell the existing Improvements for some extra cash. You won't need them anymore.

There is, of course, one drawback to using Wonders instead of individual Improvements. If the city containing the Wonder is captured by an enemy, the benefits produced by that Wonder are lost in all your cities. Depending on the Wonder, this can be devastating to your empire. To avoid this problem build "global Improvement" Wonders in well-protected cities that are isolated from the front lines of any ongoing wars.

DON'T CENTRALIZE YOUR WONDERS

Because they are so expensive to build, the temptation is to build every Wonder in the city that generates the most Shields. While this might seem like a sound idea from a resource standpoint, it is a potentially dangerous practice.

The primary reason to build Wonders of the World is to reap the benefits they offer. In fact, once certain Wonders are built, you quickly come to count on their effects to balance one or more aspects of your civilization. Imagine, then, a city that contains five important Wonders being captured by an enemy civilization. Not only have you lost a city, you might well have lost all your Cathedrals (Michelangelo's Chapel), all your Granaries (the Pyramids), all your Police Stations (Women's Suffrage), and so on. The results of losing that one city could very well bring about the downfall of your civilization.

To avoid this scenario, scatter your Wonders amongst several cities, and keep the cities containing Wonders well protected. If the Wonders are decentralized in this manner, you don't have to worry about losing the game through the loss of a single city.

Note: The exception to the "Wonder scattering" rule is in the case of Wonders that compound the effects of one another, such as Copernicus' Observatory and Isaac Newton's College. Wonders such as these produce greater benefits if built in the same city.

VIII
UNITS AND COMBAT

*M*uch of your success in *Civilization II* is based on the steady but orderly expansion of your empire. A single city or small group of cities cannot survive the economic pressures of the game and the social pressure imposed by neighboring civilizations. If your empire's growth stagnates, your research is bound to fall behind. Once you are sufficiently behind in research, your more advanced neighbors are likely to remove you permanently from the game.

At the heart of your expansion effort are the units you produce. Even if you choose a non-militaristic style of play, the growth of your civilization still relies on combat units used in a defensive role to protect your cities, as well as the work of non-combat units such as Settlers and Engineers to build new cities and improve the surrounding Terrain.

The first section of this chapter identifies and describes all the combat and special units available in the game, followed by a brief discussion concerning the production of units. The final section of the chapter describes the game's combat system and discusses the strategies involved in armed conflicts.

Units Described

There are many different units to choose from in *Civilization II*. Some of these units perform unique functions, while others are capable of performing similar tasks with differing degrees of success. The following two sections describe the characteristics of the special and combat units available, giving you the information you need to get the most out of your unit budget.

The following information is presented for each unit type:

- ❖ **Cost**—The cost to produce the unit (in Shields)
- ❖ **Movement Factor**—The number of movement points the unit has each turn
- ❖ **Attack Factor**—The unit's attack strength in combat
- ❖ **Defense Factor**—The unit's defensive strength in combat
- ❖ **Hit Points**—The amount of damage the unit can sustain before being destroyed
- ❖ **Firepower**—The amount of damage the unit causes as the result of a successful attack
- ❖ **Special Features**—Special abilities possessed by the unit
- ❖ **Prerequisite**—The Civilization Advance that must be discovered in order to build the unit
- ❖ **Obsolete**—The Civilization Advance that makes the unit obsolete (When a unit becomes obsolete, it can no longer be built.)

The statistics for all units in the game can also be found in Table 8-1.

In addition to raw statistics, a brief analysis of each unit's uses and usefulness is included.

Chapter VIII: Units and Combat

❖ Table 8-1. Unit Statistics

Unit	Cost	Move	Att.	Def.	H.P.	Fire.	Special Features	Prerequisite	Obsolete
AEGIS Cruiser	120	5	8	8	3	2	Def. x 2 vs. air and missile units. Can see Submarines.	Rocketry	—
Alpine Troops	50	1	5	5	2	1	Move cost = 1/3 (any Terrain)	Tactics	—
Archers	30	1	3	2	1	1	—	Warrior Code	Gunpowder
Armor	80	3	10	5	3	1	—	Mobile Warfare	—
Artillery	50	1	10	1	2	2	—	Machine Tools	Robotics
Battleship	160	4	12	12	4	2	—	Automobile	—
Bomber	120	8	12	1	2	2	Ignores City Walls	Advanced Flight	Stealth
Cannon	40	1	8	1	2	1	—	Metallurgy	Machine Tools
Caravan	50	1	0	1	1	1	Ignores enemy zones of control	Trade	Corporation
Caravel	40	3	2	1	1	1	Can transport 3 ground units	Navigation	Magnetism
Carrier	160	5	9	1	4	2	Can transport 8 air or missile units	Advanced Flight	—
Catapult	40	1	6	1	1	1	—	Mathematics	Metallurgy
Cavalry	60	2	8	3	2	1	—	Tactics	Mobile Warfare
Chariot	30	2	3	1	1	1	—	The Wheel	Polytheism
Cruise Missile	40	12	20	0	1	3	Ignores enemy zones of control	Rocketry	—
Cruiser	80	5	6	6	3	2	Can see Submarines	Steel	Superconductor
Crusaders	40	2	5	1	1	1	—	Monotheism	Leadership
Destroyer	60	6	4	4	3	1	Can see Submarines	Electricity	—
Diplomat	30	2	0	0	1	1	Ignores enemy zones of control. Diplomatic functions	Writing	Espionage

♣ Table 8-1. Unit Statistics *(continued)*

Unit	Cost	Move	Att.	Def.	H.P.	Fire.	Special Features	Prerequisite	Obsolete
Dragoons	50	2	5	2	2	1	—	Leadership	Tactics
Elephants	40	2	4	1	1	1	—	Polytheism	Monotheism
Engineers	40	2	0	2	2	1	Terrain improvement. Ignores enemy zones of control	Explosives	—
Explorers	30	1	0	1	1	1	Move cost = 1/3 (any Terrain)	Seafaring	Guerrilla Warfare
Fanatics	20	1	4	4	2	1	No support required under Fundamentalism	Fundamentalism	—
Fighter	60	10	4	2	2	2	Can attack air units. Ignores City Walls.	Flight	Stealth
Freight	50	2	0	1	1	1	Ignores enemy zones of control	Corporation	—
Frigate	50	4	4	2	2	1	Can transport 2 ground units	Magnetism	Electricity
Galleon	40	4	0	2	2	1	Can transport 4 ground units	Magnetism	Industrialization
Helicopter	100	6	10	3	2	2	Can see Submarines. Ignores City Walls. Can fly indefinitely.	Combined Arms	—
Horsemen	20	2	2	1	1	1	—	Horseback Riding	Chivalry
Howitzer	70	2	12	2	3	2	Ignores effects of City Walls	Robotics	—
Ironclad	60	4	4	4	3	1	—	Steam Engine	Electricity
Knights	40	2	4	2	1	1	—	Chivalry	Leadership
Legion	40	1	4	2	1	1	—	Iron Working	Gunpowder
Marines	60	1	8	5	2	1	Can make amphibious assaults	Amphibious Warfare	—
Mech. Infantry	50	3	6	6	3	1	—	Labor Union	—

✤ **Table 8-1.** Unit Statistics *(continued)*

UNIT	COST	MOVE	ATT.	DEF.	H.P.	FIRE.	SPECIAL FEATURES	PREREQUISITE	OBSOLETE
Musketeers	30	1	3	3	2	1	—	Gunpowder	Conscription
Nuclear Missile	160	16	99	0	1	1	Must hit its target at the end of its turn, or end up in a city or Carrier	Rocketry	—
Paratroopers	60	1	6	4	2	1	Can make paradrops	Combined Arms	—
Partisans	50	1	4	4	2	1	Ignores enemy zones of control. Move cost = 1/3 (any Terrain)	Guerrilla Warfare	—
Phalanx	20	1	1	2	1	1	—	Bronze Working	Feudalism
Pikemen	20	1	1	2	1	1	Def. x 2 vs. mounted units	Feudalism	Gunpowder
Riflemen	40	1	5	4	2	1	—	Conscription	—
Settlers	40	1	0	1	2	1	Terrain improvements	—	Explosives
Spy	30	3	0	0	1	1	Ignores enemy zones of control. Spy functions.	Espionage	—
Stealth Bomber	160	12	14	3	2	2	Ignores City Walls	Stealth	—
Stealth Fighter	80	14	8	3	2	2	Can attack air units. Ignores City Walls.	Stealth	—
Submarine	60	3	10	2	3	2	Invisible to most enemy ships	Combustion	—
Transport	50	5	0	3	3	1	Can transport 8 ground units	Industrialization	—
Trireme	40	3	1	1	1	1	Can transport 2 ground units. Must end turn adjacent to land.	Map Making	Navigation
Warriors	10	1	1	1	1	1	—	—	Feudalism

SPECIAL UNITS

While most units are designed specifically for combat, there are some that are built to serve in non-combat roles. These units are known as "special units."

CARAVAN

Cost:	50
Movement Factor:	1
Attack Factor:	0
Defense Factor:	1
Hit Points:	1
Firepower:	1
Special Features:	Ignores enemy zones of control. Trade functions
Prerequisite:	Trade
Obsolete:	Corporation

Although it is theoretically possible to play an entire game without utilizing a Caravan (or a Freight unit, the modern version of a Caravan), this unit nevertheless offers a number of important capabilities. Caravans can increase a city's Trade income by establishing trade routes (see Chapter 9 for details). Caravans can also help with the construction of Wonders of the World by contributing their entire Shield value to the Wonder's production. This ability should definitely be exploited when you are racing with another civilization to complete an important Wonder.

DIPLOMAT

Cost:	30
Movement Factor:	2
Attack Factor:	0
Defense Factor:	0
Hit Points:	1
Firepower:	1
Special Features:	Ignores enemy zones of control. Diplomatic functions (see Chapter 9)

| Prerequisite: | Writing |
| Obsolete: | Espionage |

The basic functions of a Diplomat—establishing embassies and examining your opponents' cities—are very useful from the standpoint of knowing what your enemies are up to. The more sinister abilities of the Diplomat, such as sabotaging production and subverting units and cities, should be used with discretion, as these functions are often the last thing you do before the onset of a bloody war (see Chapter 9 for details.)

Tip: You can use your Diplomats (and, later, your Spies) to "guide" military units behind enemy lines. Since Diplomats ignore enemy zones of control, move the Diplomat into the enemy square you want your military unit to enter. You can now move your military unit into the square occupied by the Diplomat (since you can always move into a space occupied by a friendly unit regardless of enemy zones of control). (Zones of control are explained in the game manual.)

ENGINEERS

Cost:	40
Movement Factor:	2
Attack Factor:	0
Defense Factor:	2
Hit Points:	2
Firepower:	1
Special Features:	Can establish cities, build roads and railroads, improve Terrain, and transform Terrain. Ignores enemy zones of control
Prerequisite:	Explosives
Obsolete:	Never

Like the Settlers they replace, Engineers perform vital duties such as building cities, road and railroad construction, irrigation, and mining that can be performed by no other unit type. Engineers perform all these tasks twice as fast as Settlers, and they have the added ability to perform major transformations of Terrain. Any Settlers still in use after the discovery of Explosives should be replaced with Engineers as soon as possible.

Tip: If you have any Settlers active after Engineers have made them obsolete, use the Settlers to establish new cities. The fact that they are twice as slow as Engineers makes leftover Settlers a burden when used for any other task.

EXPLORERS

Cost:	30
Movement Factor:	1
Attack Factor:	0
Defense Factor:	1
Hit Points:	1
Firepower:	1
Special Features:	Treats all Terrain as roads (movement cost = $\frac{1}{3}$ point per square)
Prerequisite:	Seafaring
Obsolete:	Guerrilla Warfare

As their name implies, the main use for Explorers is scouting and exploration. They have no combat potential, and are therefore usually lost if they encounter hostile opposing units. The most practical use for an Explorer is examining large, empty continents and seeking out and exploring villages ("goodie huts").

FREIGHT

Cost:	50
Movement Factor:	2
Attack Factor:	0
Defense Factor:	1
Hit Points:	1
Firepower:	1
Special Features:	Ignores enemy zones of control
Prerequisite:	Corporation
Obsolete:	Never

The Freight unit is the modern equivalent of the Caravan, the main difference being that it moves at twice the Caravan's speed. Under the new trade route formula, trade routes established by Freight units are more profitable than those established by Caravans. (See the description for Caravan for more information.)

GALLEON

Cost:	40
Movement Factor:	4
Attack Factor:	0
Defense Factor:	2
Hit Points:	2
Firepower:	1
Special Features:	Can transport up to four friendly ground units
Prerequisite:	Magnetism
Obsolete:	Industrialization

The Galleon is the old-world equivalent of the Transport unit. With twice the cargo capacity of the Frigate, the Galleon is the ship of choice when you need to transport ground units across the sea—as long as you know that no sea battles are imminent. Although it can defend itself, the Galleon cannot initiate combat. If your purpose is to engage in sea battles or to bombard and take over an enemy coastal city, the Frigate is a better choice.

SETTLERS

Cost:	40
Movement Factor:	1
Attack Factor:	0
Defense Factor:	1
Hit Points:	2
Firepower:	1
Special Features:	Can establish cities, build roads and railroads, and improve Terrain
Prerequisite:	None
Obsolete:	Explosives

The Settler is the most basic yet irreplaceable unit in the game. Prior to the discovery of Explosives, the Settler is the only unit capable of improving terrain and building cities. Settlers (and, later, Engineers) play a vital role throughout the entire game.

Tip: In *Civilization II*, the time it takes for Settlers and Engineers to accomplish their various tasks can be reduced by assigning the task to two or more units. For example, it normally takes a Settler 10 turns to convert a Grassland square to Forest through mining. If two Settlers are assigned to this task, it takes only 5 turns. The more Settlers/Engineers you assign, the faster the job gets done.

SPY

Cost:	30
Movement Factor:	3
Attack Factor:	0
Defense Factor:	0
Hit Points:	1
Firepower:	1

Special Features:	Ignores enemy zones of control. Diplomatic and terrorist functions (see Chapter 9)
Prerequisite:	Espionage
Obsolete:	Never

The Spy comes with the same caveat as its predecessor, the Diplomat: its basic abilities are extremely useful, but its advanced abilities are a fine way to start a war if the mission is bungled. However, the added destructive abilities of the Spy over the Diplomat might be enough to induce you to attempt a life of subterfuge (see Chapter 9 for details).

Note: Under a Communist government, all Spies produced are automatically Veterans. Veteran Spies have a 50% higher rate of success in all Spy missions.

COMBAT UNITS

AEGIS CRUISER

Cost:	100
Movement Factor:	5
Attack Factor:	8
Defense Factor:	8
Hit Points:	3
Firepower:	2
Special Features:	Defense Factor doubled against air and missile attacks. Can spot Submarines in adjacent squares
Prerequisite:	Rocketry
Obsolete:	Never

In addition to its enhanced abilities versus airborne attacks, the AEGIS cruiser has a 50% greater attack and defense capability than its predecessor, the Cruiser. The AEGIS Cruiser is most successful when used as an escort for your Transports and weaker ships. Once enemy Cruise Missiles become a factor, there is no better way to protect your shipping lanes.

ALPINE TROOPS

Cost:	50
Movement Factor:	1
Attack Factor:	5
Defense Factor:	5
Hit Points:	2
Firepower:	1
Special Features:	Treats all Terrain as roads (movement cost = $\frac{1}{3}$ point per square)
Prerequisite:	Tactics
Obsolete:	Never

The enhanced movement capabilities of Alpine Troops provide a tactical advantage over most other units. However, the major strength of this unit is its ability to defend a city. Only the Mech. Infantry unit provides better city defense at such a reasonable cost.

ARCHERS

Cost:	30
Movement Factor:	1
Attack Factor:	3
Defense Factor:	2
Hit Points:	1
Firepower:	1
Special Features:	None
Prerequisite:	Warrior Code
Obsolete:	Gunpowder

As early defensive and attack units, Archers are a good choice. While not as powerful on the attack as a Legion, the less expensive Archers are nevertheless powerful enough to handle most of their contemporary opponents. They also provide the same amount of defense as a Phalanx, though the Phalanx is more cost effective if you need a unit for a strictly defensive role. Archers are a nice compromise between Phalanxes and Legions.

ARMOR

Cost:	80
Movement Factor:	3
Attack Factor:	10
Defense Factor:	5
Hit Points:	3
Firepower:	1
Special Features:	None
Prerequisite:	Mobile Warfare
Obsolete:	Never

No other ground unit offers the combination of attack, defense, and mobility provided by the Armor unit. This unit can mount a devastating attack against an enemy city and, once the city is captured, it can provide the city with an effective temporary defense until the city can build its own defensive units. Despite the Armor unit's defensive capabilities, less expensive units such as Alpine Troops and Mech. Infantry can defend your cities just as effectively.

ARTILLERY

Cost:	50
Movement Factor:	1
Attack Factor:	10
Defense Factor:	1
Hit Points:	2
Firepower:	2
Special Features:	None
Prerequisite:	Machine Tools
Obsolete:	Robotics

Artillery is, essentially, the mobile attack unit that fills the gap between the obsolescence of the Cannon and the ability to build Armor units. Although the attack factor of Artillery is equal to that of Armor, Artillery suffers from the same drawback as its forerunners, the Catapult and the Cannon: it has little in the way of defensive capabilities. Although excellent on the attack, Artillery cannot be used effectively to secure captured cities against enemies attempting to retake them.

Note: The unit known as "Artillery" in *Civilization* is now the Howitzer unit. In *Civilization II*, the Artillery unit represents 19th century technology.

BATTLESHIP

Cost:	160
Movement Factor:	4
Attack Factor:	12
Defense Factor:	12
Hit Points:	4
Firepower:	2
Special Features:	None
Prerequisite:	Automobile
Obsolete:	Never

Undeniably the queen of the seas, the Battleship is unmatched by any sea unit for attack or defense. No other ship is more effective for shore bombardment of enemy cities; several hits from a Battleship can easily eliminate the city's defending units, leaving the city open for occupation. Battleships also make good defenders for coastal cities, although they are subject to the same Firepower restrictions as other ships when they are in port (as explained later in this chapter).

BOMBER

Cost:	120
Movement Factor:	8
Attack Factor:	12
Defense Factor:	1
Hit Points:	2
Firepower:	2

Special Features:	Ignores enemy zones of control. Ignores the effects of City Walls. Must end every other turn at a friendly city, Air Base, or Carrier
Prerequisite:	Advanced Flight
Obsolete:	Stealth

The range, movement abilities, Attack Factor, and Firepower of the Bomber make it one of the most effective means of attack in the game. Like Battleships, Bombers can be used effectively to pave the way for a surface attack by destroying all the units inside an enemy city. The low Defense Factor is less important for air units than it is for other units, since the Bomber can only be attacked by Fighters and Stealth Fighters. The two drawbacks to this unit are its high cost and the movement restrictions that force it to return to a base, city, or Carrier every other turn. Once available, Helicopters provide a less expensive, more durable alternative to the Bomber.

CANNON

Cost:	40	
Movement Factor:	1	
Attack Factor:	8	
Defense Factor:	1	
Hit Points:	2	
Firepower:	1	
Special Features:	None	
Prerequisite:	Metallurgy	
Obsolete:	Machine Tools	

The Cannon is the first replacement available for the Catapult. Although it is more powerful on the attack and has twice the Hit Points of its predecessor, the Cannon still suffers the same weakness of the Catapult: a low Defense Factor. Cannons are effective at capturing enemy cities, but they are unable to hold them against anything but minimal attack forces. The best way to use this unit is to land it via ship next to the city you are about to capture. If forced to traverse a battle zone by land, the Cannon is unlikely to reach its target.

CARAVEL

Cost:	40
Movement Factor:	3
Attack Factor:	2
Defense Factor:	1
Hit Points:	1
Firepower:	1
Special Features:	Can transport up to three friendly ground units
Prerequisite:	Navigation
Obsolete:	Magnetism

The Caravel is the first "real" seagoing vessel you can build. Its attack and cargo-hauling abilities surpass those of the Trireme, and the Caravel can be used to explore large sections of the map since it isn't forced to remain close to land like its predecessor. This unit's active life span is often short-lived: it is replaced by the Frigate and the Galleon once Magnetism is discovered. Although the Caravel can be used to bombard cities, it is seldom very successful in this area.

CARRIER

Cost:	160
Movement Factor:	5
Attack Factor:	9
Defense Factor:	1
Hit Points:	4
Firepower:	2
Special Features:	Can carry up to eight friendly air units or missiles
Prerequisite:	Advanced Flight
Obsolete:	Never

In military history, the Carrier superseded the Battleship as the most powerful vessel at sea. In the game, this is true only if you can afford the cost involved to make it so. A Carrier with a full complement of Bombers or Stealth Bombers surpasses the Battleship's shore bombardment capabilities and can launch attacks on separate cities simultaneously. The Carrier extends the range of air units by providing a mobile refueling base to which they can return when necessary. The cost of supporting the Carrier plus its air wing is often prohibitive, especially if you experience heavy losses.

CATAPULT

Cost:	40
Movement Factor:	1
Attack Factor:	6
Defense Factor:	1
Hit Points:	1
Firepower:	1
Special Features:	None
Prerequisite:	Mathematics
Obsolete:	Metallurgy

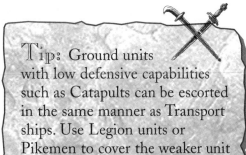

The Catapult is the first "heavy" attack unit that appears in the game. Its high Attack Factor makes it a tempting choice for the bombardment of an annoying neighbor's cities and units. However, the Catapult suffers a major drawback: it has very little in the way of defense. When you get the chance to attack first, the Catapult is often successful; but when the Catapult is attacked, it is usually

Tip: Ground units with low defensive capabilities such as Catapults can be escorted in the same manner as Transport ships. Use Legion units or Pikemen to cover the weaker unit as it approaches its target.

defeated. If forced to travel by land through enemy territory, Catapults seldom reach the cities they are sent to attack. You are better served by units like Knights who have a lower Attack Factor but who are able to defend themselves.

CAVALRY

Cost:	60
Movement Factor:	2
Attack Factor:	8
Defense Factor:	3

Hit Points:	2
Firepower:	1
Special Features:	None
Prerequisite:	Tactics
Obsolete:	Mobile Warfare

The most advanced of the mounted units, Cavalry units are fast and effective on the attack, with enough defensive strength to hold a city when they capture one. Because it has a higher Defense Factor, Cavalry makes a good alternative to Cannons or Artillery.

> **Note:** The "Cavalry" unit from *Civilization* is now the Horsemen unit. *Civilization II* Cavalry represents 19th century mounted forces like those common in the American Civil War rather than the mounted troops of the ancient world.

CHARIOT

Cost:	30
Movement Factor:	2
Attack Factor:	3
Defense Factor:	1
Hit Points:	1
Firepower:	1
Special Features:	None
Prerequisite:	The Wheel
Obsolete:	Polytheism

The Chariot is one of the first fast-attack units. While slightly more powerful on the attack than Horsemen, Chariots are also slightly more expensive. They have little in the way of defense, so they tend to lose when attacked. Although Chariots can be used effectively to intercept slower enemy units, there are other units available early in the game (Knights, for example) that make better attack units when laying siege to enemy cities.

CRUISE MISSILE

Cost:	40
Movement Factor:	12
Attack Factor:	20
Defense Factor:	0
Hit Points:	1
Firepower:	3
Special Features:	Ignores enemy zones of control
Prerequisite:	Rocketry
Obsolete:	Never

For those of you who enjoy launching missile attacks but don't want all that nasty nuclear pollution, the Cruise Missile is the unit for you. Unfortunately, the effects of a Cruise Missile attack aren't nearly as devastating. However, using a couple of Cruise Missiles to destroy a city's defending units followed by a paradrop can be an effective city-capture strategy. Cruise Missiles can also provide an effective means of dealing with enemy shipping. The only drawback of this unit is that it is destroyed when it is used. This makes the continued use of Cruise Missiles less cost-effective than using Bombers in the long run.

CRUISER

Cost:	80
Movement Factor:	5
Attack Factor:	6
Defense Factor:	6
Hit Points:	3
Firepower:	2
Special Features:	Can spot Submarines in adjacent squares
Prerequisite:	Steel
Obsolete:	Superconductor

The Cruiser has the advantage of being one of the first modern naval units you can build. As such, it is more than a match for your opponents' navies if they are behind you technologically. The best use for a Cruiser is as an escort for Transports and as a raider to destroy enemy Transports. In a shore bombardment or an all-out sea battle role, Cruisers are invariably inferior to Battleships.

CRUSADERS

Cost:	40
Movement Factor:	2
Attack Factor:	5
Defense Factor:	1
Hit Points:	1
Firepower:	1
Special Features:	None
Prerequisite:	Monotheism
Obsolete:	Leadership

Crusaders are a more zealous version of Knights, with a higher Attack Factor but a lower Defense Factor. On an Attack Factor-to-Cost ratio, Crusaders are about the best deal in the game; however, their low defensive capabilities make them a second choice to Knights. Crusaders can often be ignored in favor of other, more defense-oriented units.

Note: The nicest thing about Crusaders is that they become available as a result of a peace-oriented Advance. As such, they provide a viable means of attack for players engaged in primarily peaceful lines of research.

DESTROYER

Cost:	60
Movement Factor:	6
Attack Factor:	4
Defense Factor:	4
Hit Points:	3
Firepower:	1
Special Features:	Can spot Submarines in adjacent squares
Prerequisite:	Electricity
Obsolete:	Never

If you have an enemy that likes to use Submarine warfare, one or two Destroyers are a valuable addition to your fleet. When used to escort Transports and other ships, the chances of a Submarine sneak-attack are greatly reduced. With Attack and Defense Factors lower than those of a Cruiser, Destroyers are inadequate when it comes to shore bombardments and full-scale naval conflicts.

DRAGOONS

Cost:	50
Movement Factor:	2
Attack Factor:	5
Defense Factor:	2
Hit Points:	2
Firepower:	1
Special Features:	None
Prerequisite:	Leadership
Obsolete:	Tactics

As soon as Dragoons come along, you should replace any existing Knights with these units. Dragoons have the attack capabilities of Crusaders combined with the same Defense Factor and twice the Hit Points of Knights. This makes the Dragoon a better all-around unit than any of its mounted predecessors. Dragoons are a good alternative to Cannons as attack units because of their defensive capabilities.

ELEPHANTS

Cost:	40
Movement Factor:	2
Attack Factor:	4
Defense Factor:	1
Hit Points:	1
Firepower:	1
Special Features:	None
Prerequisite:	Polytheism
Obsolete:	Monotheism

Elephants are mounted units that serve as a half-step between Horsemen and Crusaders: they have the same movement and defensive capabilities of the former with almost as much attack strength as the latter. Because they are transitory units, Elephants are only available for a relatively short time. If you have no early contact with other civilizations, Elephants often come and go without a single one ever being built.

Note: Like Crusaders, Elephants become available as the result of discovering a peaceful Advance. Therefore, they provide a means of attack for players preferring to pursue a non-violent technology track.

FANATICS

Cost:	20
Movement Factor:	1
Attack Factor:	4
Defense Factor:	4
Hit Points:	2
Firepower:	1
Special Features:	Can only be built under Fundamentalism. No Shield support required under a Fundamentalist government
Prerequisite:	Fundamentalism
Obsolete:	Never

The ability to produce Fanatics is unique in the game: if you never use Fundamentalism as your system of government, you never have the opportunity to build them. Their two major advantages are low price and the fact that they require no Shield support under Fundamentalism. However, the true benefits of Fanatics cannot be enjoyed unless you are willing to stick with a Fundamentalist government. Despite the lure of this strong but inexpensive unit, it isn't worth the loss in Science to switch governments temporarily just to build Fanatics.

FIGHTER

Cost:	60
Movement Factor:	10
Attack Factor:	4
Defense Factor:	2
Hit Points:	2
Firepower:	2
Special Features:	Ignores enemy zones of control. Ignores the effects of City Walls. Can attack air units in flight. Must end their turn in a friendly city, on a Carrier, or at an Air Base
Prerequisite:	Flight
Obsolete:	Stealth

Fighters are the first air units you can produce under normal circumstances. While not as useful overall as a Bomber, the Fighter has the ability to move anywhere and attack anything at will, with little fear of retaliation. Only other Fighters (or Stealth Fighters), AEGIS Cruisers, and cities with a SAM Missile Battery pose a major threat to these units. Because of their limited range, Fighters are most useful when used to defend cities and Carriers against enemy air units.

FRIGATE

Cost:	50
Movement Factor:	4
Attack Factor:	4
Defense Factor:	2
Hit Points:	2
Firepower:	1
Special Features:	Can transport up to 2 friendly ground units
Prerequisite:	Magnetism
Obsolete:	Electricity

The Frigate is the first effective attack ship. It can hold its own against other ships of its era, and it can perform shore bombardments with reasonable effectiveness against enemies of the same technology level. The Frigate's ability to fight combined with its ability to transport ground units makes it the perfect choice in its era for the transportation of troops into hostile territory.

HELICOPTER

Cost:	100
Movement Factor:	6
Attack Factor:	10
Defense Factor:	3
Hit Points:	2
Firepower:	2
Special Features:	Ignores enemy zones of control. Ignores the effects of City Walls. Can fly indefinitely without refueling. Can spot Submarines in adjacent squares
Prerequisite:	Combined Arms
Obsolete:	Never

Helicopters are unique among the air units in the game because they are never forced to return to a city, base, or Carrier to refuel. Because of their ability to spot Submarines, Helicopters make excellent escorts for sea units. Although they possess neither the attack strength or the per-turn range of Bombers and Stealth Bombers, Helicopters are, neverthe-less, viable alternatives to either of these units: they possess the same defensive capabilities, and their unlimited fuel more than compensates for their shorter per-turn range.

Note: Although they don't require refueling, Helicopters gradually lose Hit Points each turn they remain away from a friendly city, Airbase, or Carrier.

HORSEMEN

Cost:	20
Movement Factor:	2
Attack Factor:	2
Defense Factor:	1
Hit Points:	1
Firepower:	1
Special Features:	None
Prerequisite:	Horseback Riding
Obsolete:	Chivalry

Horsemen are the first mounted units you can build. Because of their Movement Factor, Horsemen make good explorers, but their combat capabilities are strictly average. Often, the time of the Horsemen passes before you are able to build many of them, since they become obsolete when you gain the ability to build Knights.

Note: "Horsemen" in *Civilization II* are the equivalent of "Cavalry" in the original *Civilization*.

HOWITZER

Cost:	70
Movement Factor:	2
Attack Factor:	12
Defense Factor:	2
Hit Points:	3
Firepower:	2
Special Features:	Ignores the effects of City Walls
Prerequisite:	Robotics
Obsolete:	Never

The Howitzer represents the apex in the development of heavy field weapons. Though somewhat stronger defensively than their predecessors, Howitzers still make poor defensive units. They are, however, the best ground units available in the game for attacking cities. When attacking a city with a Howitzer, the units defending the city do not receive the normal defensive bonus provided by City Walls. If you can get them to their targets intact, Howitzers make devastating weapons.

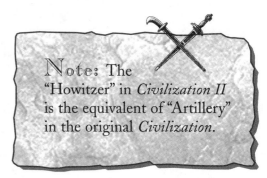

Note: The "Howitzer" in *Civilization II* is the equivalent of "Artillery" in the original *Civilization*.

IRONCLAD

Cost:	60
Movement Factor:	4
Attack Factor:	4
Defense Factor:	4
Hit Points:	3
Firepower:	1
Special Features:	None
Prerequisite:	Steam Engine
Obsolete:	Electricity

Technologically, Ironclads usually appear shortly after Frigates and Galleons. Because they have a greater Hit Point capacity, Ironclads have a slight defensive edge over Frigates, making the Ironclad more likely to survive prolonged bombardments and battles. Ironclads are less useful and versatile than Frigates, however, due to their inability to transport ground units.

KNIGHTS

Cost:	40
Movement Factor:	2
Attack Factor:	4
Defense Factor:	2
Hit Points:	1
Firepower:	1
Special Features:	None
Prerequisite:	Chivalry
Obsolete:	Leadership

Knights were available in the original Civilization, but they often went unbuilt because Chivalry was the last stop on an early dead-end research path. Now that Chivalry is a mainstream Advance, the ability to build Knights is a matter of course in every game. This is fortunate, because Knights are very powerful and versatile units. Their combination of speed, attack, and defense make Knights the dominant ground units of their era.

LEGION

Cost:	40
Movement Factor:	1
Attack Factor:	4
Defense Factor:	2
Hit Points:	1
Firepower:	1
Special Features:	None
Prerequisite:	Iron Working
Obsolete:	Gunpowder

Legions are usually the first dedicated attack units available in the game. Players of the original Civilization will note that the Legions' Attack and Defense Factors have been upgraded, making them more formidable. Although Legions still suffer from a lack of movement speed, their upgraded offensive and defensive capabilities improve their ability to successfully attack and hold a city early in the game.

MARINES

Cost:	60
Movement Factor:	1
Attack Factor:	8
Defense Factor:	5
Hit Points:	2
Firepower:	1
Special Features:	Can make amphibious assaults (attack directly from a ship)

Prerequisite:	Amphibious Warfare
Obsolete:	Never

Marines are powerful modern units with a number of noteworthy abilities. Marines have 80% of the Attack Factor and 100% of the Defense Factor of Armor units at a significantly lower price. Even though they have less Hit Points, Marines are a viable alternative to Armor in an all-out war situation, since they can be produced more quickly. In addition, Marines can attack directly from a ship, an ability that comes in handy when attempting to capture a coastal city. Marines are capable of holding a captured city as well, due to their high Defense Factor. For purely defensive purposes, however, the less expensive Alpine Troops units are just as effective.

MECHANIZED INFANTRY

Cost:	50
Movement Factor:	3
Attack Factor:	6
Defense Factor:	6
Hit Points:	3
Firepower:	1
Special Features:	None
Prerequisite:	Labor Union
Obsolete:	Never

The Mechanized Infantry unit is the best unit available for defending cities. Its high Defense Factor and Hit Point rating make it difficult to destroy, while its reasonably high Attack Factor allows it to be rather successful on the offense as well. Mech. Infantry provides all these features at the same price of the less powerful Alpine Troops unit. Unfortunately, Mech. Infantry seldom makes an appearance in the game because Labor Union is an optional, dead-end Advance.

MUSKETEERS

Cost:	30
Movement Factor:	1
Attack Factor:	3
Defense Factor:	3
Hit Points:	2
Firepower:	1
Special Features:	None
Prerequisite:	Gunpowder
Obsolete:	Conscription

Musketeers represent a major achievement in city defense. They have a higher Defense Factor and Hit Point rating than any of their predecessors, and they are able to successfully repel attacks by just about any less advanced unit. Though their role tends to be primarily defensive, Musketeers also make decent offensive units when matched against any less-advanced unit.

Note: Veterans of *Civilization* will note that both Musketeers and Riflemen in *Civilization II* have been significantly improved offensively over their original counterparts.

NUCLEAR MISSILE

Cost:	160
Movement Factor:	16
Attack Factor:	99
Defense Factor:	0
Hit Points:	1
Firepower:	1

Special Features:	Ignores enemy zones of control. Must hit its target at the end of its allotted movement or end its turn in a friendly city or on a friendly Carrier
Prerequisite:	Rocketry*
Obsolete:	Never

Nuclear Missiles are the ultimate offensive weapon. They can't be stopped by anything except for an SDI Defense, and they kill every unit in their target square and the eight surrounding squares instantly. They also cause a reduction in the civilian population of the target city. The drawbacks of Nuclear Missiles are their high cost and toxic side effects (massive pollution surrounding the target square). In spite of these problems, Nuclear Missiles are extremely popular among the more violent computer civilizations, who often let these weapons fly with wild abandon.

PARATROOPERS

Cost:	60
Movement Factor:	1
Attack Factor:	6
Defense Factor:	4
Hit Points:	2
Firepower:	1
Special Features:	Can make paradrops
Prerequisite:	Combined Arms
Obsolete:	Never

Paratroopers are similar to Marines with a slightly lower Defense Factor. The thing that makes Paratroopers unique is the ability to paradrop anywhere within a ten square range of the city or Air Base they occupy and attack one time from their new position. This leads to interesting and effective new strategies for taking over enemy cities. (See "The Art of Paradropping" later in this chapter for details.) Paratroopers are well worth their cost under the right circumstances.

---

*In addition, the Manhattan Project Wonder must have been built by one of the civilizations in the game.

PARTISANS

Cost:	50
Movement Factor:	1
Attack Factor:	4
Defense Factor:	4
Hit Points:	2
Firepower:	1
Special Features:	Ignores enemy zones of control. Treats all Terrain as roads (movement cost = $\frac{1}{3}$ point per square)
Prerequisite:	Guerrilla Warfare
Obsolete:	Never

Aside from their special movement abilities and their significantly higher cost, Partisans are identical to Fanatics. They are less powerful in both offensive and defensive capacity to Alpine Troops and Marines. Most players would never consider building Partisans. The fact is that you don't have to build Partisans in order to use them. If one of your cities is captured after the discovery of Guerrilla Warfare, a number of Partisan units appear near that city. These units are yours, free of charge, and they can be used (sometimes rather effectively) to recapture and defend the city. (See "Partisans and the Liberation of Cities" later in this chapter for details.)

PHALANX

Cost:	20
Movement Factor:	1
Attack Factor:	1
Defense Factor:	2
Hit Points:	1
Firepower:	1
Special Features:	None
Prerequisite:	Bronze Working
Obsolete:	Feudalism

Since Warriors are ineffective at defending cities against any serious attack, you should work towards better military technology fairly early in the game. While undeniably primitive, the Phalanx is one of the two early units that possesses a Defense Factor capable of withstanding an attack of any reasonable force. Archers, who possess the same Defense Factor but who are better offensive units, are a good choice for early defense as well, but the Phalanx is more cost-effective when you need a strictly defensive unit.

PIKEMEN

Cost:	20	
Movement Factor:	1	
Attack Factor:	1	
Defense Factor:	2	
Hit Points:	1	
Firepower:	1	
Special Features:	Defense Factor doubled against mounted units	
Prerequisite:	Feudalism	
Obsolete:	Gunpowder	

Pikemen appear as replacements for Phalanxes after the discovery of Feudalism. At first glance, it may seem that they are identical to Phalanx units; however, their Defense Factor versus mounted units makes them much more effective at city defense. If your opponents are gaining knowledge at the same speed you are, chances are that they are using mounted units more frequently by the time Pikemen become available to you. Their added defensive advantage and their low cost make it worth the effort to upgrade any existing Phalanxes to Pikemen as soon as you have the chance.

RIFLEMEN

Cost:	40	
Movement Factor:	1	
Attack Factor:	5	
Defense Factor:	4	
Hit Points:	2	

Firepower:	1
Special Features:	None
Prerequisite:	Conscription
Obsolete:	Never

After the discovery of Conscription but before the discovery of Tactics, Riflemen make the best city defenders. The Riflemen unit's defensive advantage makes it worth your while to upgrade any existing Musketeers who are defending your cities. Although Riflemen remain available through the end of the game, they should be discarded in favor of Alpine Troops or Mech. Infantry as soon as these more powerful units become available.

STEALTH BOMBER

Cost:	160	
Movement Factor:	12	
Attack Factor:	14	
Defense Factor:	3	
Hit Points:	2	
Firepower:	2	
Special Features:	Ignores enemy zones of control. Ignores the effects of City Walls. Must end every other turn in a friendly city, an Air Base, or a Carrier	
Prerequisite:	Stealth	
Obsolete:	Never	

After the discovery of Stealth, the Stealth Bomber replaces the standard Bomber unit. Its high price is offset by high offensive strength (the highest non-missile Attack Factor in the game), long movement range (50% better than the Bomber) and reasonably good defensive strength (a third better than the Bomber). Nevertheless, the Stealth Bomber suffers the same fuel limitation as other planes. Although both its single-turn range and attack strength are lower, the Helicopter is a good alternative to the Stealth Bomber.

STEALTH FIGHTER

Cost:	80
Movement Factor:	14
Attack Factor:	8
Defense Factor:	3
Hit Points:	2
Firepower:	2
Special Features:	Ignores enemy zones of control. Ignores the effects of City Walls. Can attack air units in flight
Prerequisite:	Stealth
Obsolete:	Never

Like the Bomber, the Fighter becomes obsolete when Stealth is discovered. Although the Stealth Fighter is more expensive than its predecessor, it has 40% more range, twice the attack strength, and a Defense Factor that is a third better. Replacing existing Fighter units with Stealth Fighters when they become available is a good move if your enemies are fond of using air units against you.

SUBMARINE

Cost:	60
Movement Factor:	3
Attack Factor:	10
Defense Factor:	2
Hit Points:	3
Firepower:	2
Special Features:	Invisible to most enemy ships. Can carry Cruise Missiles and Nuclear Missiles
Prerequisite:	Combustion
Obsolete:	Never

The unique capability of the Submarine to remain hidden from most enemy units until they attack, combined with an Attack Factor that is the second-highest among sea units and the ability to launch missile attacks, makes the Submarine a formidable unit. On the other hand, the relatively low defense factor of Submarines makes them a poor choice for frontal assaults and city sieges. This unit works best when used for the purpose for which it was designed: hit and run attacks on enemy ships, and launching offshore missile barrages. There is no better unit for attacking unit-laden enemy Transports.

TRANSPORT

Cost:	50
Movement Factor:	5
Attack Factor:	0
Defense Factor:	3
Hit Points:	3
Firepower:	1
Special Features:	Can transport up to eight friendly ground units
Prerequisite:	Industrialization
Obsolete:	Never

Although it seems strange to include the Transport (which has no attack capabilities) as a combat unit, the game treats it as such. The sole task of the Transport is to move ground units across the sea: it cannot initiate combat. If your purpose is to attack an enemy city from the sea and then occupy it, a sea unit capable of combat must accompany the Transport. If enemy activity is heavy, a Destroyer, Cruiser, or Helicopter escort is recommended to ensure that the Transport reaches its destination.

TRIREME

Cost:	40
Movement Factor:	3
Attack Factor:	1
Defense Factor:	1
Hit Points:	1
Firepower:	1
Special Features:	Can transport up to two friendly ground units. Must end its movement adjacent to land or risk being lost at sea

Prerequisite:	Map Making
Obsolete:	Navigation

Triremes are the first sea units available in the game. Although they suffer from a number of major weaknesses, the foremost being their tendency to become lost at sea when not adjacent to land at the end of their turn, Triremes are indispensable units for early exploration beyond the boundaries of your starting continent. Because of their offensive and defensive weaknesses, Triremes make poor combat units; but, as long as you are careful, Triremes can serve as adequate transports for ground units until the sturdier Caravel becomes available.

WARRIORS

Cost:	10
Movement Factor:	1
Attack Factor:	1
Defense Factor:	1
Hit Points:	1
Firepower:	1
Special Features:	None
Prerequisite:	None
Obsolete:	Feudalism

Under most circumstances, Warriors are the only units other than Settlers that you can produce at the start of the game. Because the statistics of this unit are the lowest for any ground combat unit in the game, Warriors should be used only until either Phalanxes or Archers become available. Warriors should be disbanded as soon as a replacement unit exists. The only purpose

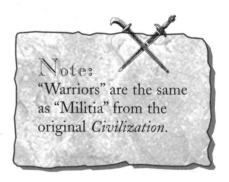

Note: "Warriors" are the same as "Militia" from the original *Civilization*.

Warriors serve after the discovery of Bronze Working and/or Warrior Code is as a cheap, temporary defense for newly-built cities when no better unit can be easily afforded.

Engaging in Combat

Even the most peace-loving players are forced to engage in combat, either defensively or offensively, at one time or another during an average game. Often, you are forced to conquer a nearby civilization in order to effectively expand your empire. Alternatively, you might become the victim of a rival civilization engaged in the same sort of expansion activity. Sometimes, the reason for combat is simply that one of your opponents is a bully, and you feel that it is your duty to teach him a lesson.

Whatever the reason for the war, you can fight it more intelligently if you understand the way the game handles combat. It also helps to learn a few useful tactics and techniques that might make the war a little easier to win.

THE COMBAT SYSTEM

When a combat unit attempts to move into any square occupied by an opposing unit, the result is a battle. When battles occur, the game uses a multi-step system to determine the results of the combat.

Battle Resolution

Civilization II handles combat in a slightly more complex manner than the original game; but at the heart of the new combat system is the same basic means of battle resolution that existed in Civilization. The following equation is used to decide the outcome of combat between two units:

$$\textit{attacker's Attack Factor} \div ((\textit{attacker's Attack Factor}) + (\textit{defender's Defense Factor}))^*$$

In the above equation, both the Attack and Defense Factors can be modified by several different factors including the Terrain the defending unit occupies, Veteran status, and a number of other situations. Table 8-2 lists the bonuses received by under various conditions.

---

*A random factor also exists to allow units with a Defense Factor of zero to occasionally survive an attack.

Sid Meier's Civilization II: The Official Stategy Guide

❖ Table 8-2. Attack and Defense Factor Bonuses

SITUATION	DEFENSE MULTIPLIER	ATTACK MULTIPLIER
Unit is a Veteran unit	50%	50%
Defending unit is behind City Walls	200%*	—
Defending unit is in a city with a Coastal Fortress	100%**	—
Defending unit is in a city with a SAM Missile Battery	100%***	—
Defending unit is in a Fortress	100%	—
Defending unit is Fortified	50%	—
Defending unit is on a Forest, Jungle, or Swamp square	50%	—
Defending unit is on a Hill square	100%	—
Defending unit is on a Mountain square	200%	—

* Does not apply versus Howitzers, air units, or sea units
** Applies only if the attacker is a sea unit
*** Applies only if the attacker is an air unit or a Cruise Missile

Note: Defense bonuses are cumulative. Each defensive bonus is calculated using the unit's base Defense Factor. For example, a fortified Veteran Phalanx in a city with City Walls has an effective Defense Factor of eight versus most attacks. This is calculated as follows:

Phalanx base Defense Factor = 2
Bonus for Veteran status = 1
Bonus for fortification = 1
Bonus for city walls = 4
Effective Defense Factor = (2 + 1 + 1 + 4) = 8
Fractional results are always rounded down.

One other modifier that applies to a unit's Attack Factor is fractional movement. When a ground unit moves along a road or a River, it uses only $\frac{1}{3}$ of a movement point for each square moved. If the amount of movement remaining for the attacking unit is either $\frac{1}{3}$ or $\frac{2}{3}$ of a point, the unit's Attack Factor is reduced appropri-

Note:
Although computer-controlled units might sometimes attack at $\frac{2}{3}$ strength, they seldom (if ever) attack at $\frac{1}{3}$ strength.

ately: if the unit has $\frac{1}{3}$ of a point remaining, its Attack Factor is reduced by $\frac{2}{3}$; if the unit has $\frac{2}{3}$ of a movement point remaining, its Attack Factor is reduced by $\frac{1}{3}$. For example, a non-Veteran Musketeers unit (whose Attack Factor is 3) moves two spaces along a road and then engages in combat. Because the number of movement points remaining is $\frac{1}{3}$, the Musketeer's effective Attack Factor is 1.

Firepower, Hit Points, and Damage

The new twist that makes the new combat system more complex than that of the original game is addition of the Firepower and Hit Point statistics to each unit. Hit Points represent the amount of damage the unit can take before it is destroyed (the actual number of Hit Points is determined by multiplying the Hit Points statistic by ten). Firepower represents the amount of damage a unit inflicts in each successful attack. In *Civilization*, the results of combat were absolute: the winner went on to fight another day and the loser was destroyed. This is no longer the case. In *Civilization II*, it is possible for the winning unit to sustain damage during combat.

When one unit attacks another in *Civilization II*, a series of individual battles is initiated. In each battle, the victor is determined using the system

Note: By selecting the "Simplified Combat" feature during game setup, you can utilize the combat resolution system from the original *Civilization*. If "Simplified Combat" is selected, Firepower, Hit Points, and unit damage are not utilized.

described in the previous section, "Battle Resolution." [The winner of each battle receives no damage, and the loser's Hit Points are reduced by the amount of the winner's Firepower. The units continue to battle back and forth until one of the two units is destroyed.

EXAMPLE: A Cannon (Attack Factor: 8, Defense Factor: 1, Hit Points: 2, Firepower: 1) attacks a Phalanx (Attack Factor: 1, Defense Factor: 2, Hit Points: 1, Firepower: 1). Neither unit currently receives any combat modifiers. The base chance for the Cannon to win each battle (as determined by the equation shown in "Battle Resolution") is 8 in 10, or 80%. The hypothetical battle takes the following course:

1. The Cannon wins the first battle, inflicting 1 point of damage (the Cannon's Firepower rating) on the Phalanx. The Phalanx is left with 9 Hit Points (remember—the unit's Hit Points rating is multiplied by 10 to get the actual number of Hit Points).

2. The Cannon gets unlucky and loses the second battle, receiving 1 point of damage (the Phalanx's Firepower rating). The Cannon is left with 19 Hit Points.

3. The Cannon wins the next 6 battles, leaving the Phalanx with 3 Hit Points.

4. The Phalanx wins another battle, leaving the Cannon with 18 Hit Points.

5. The Cannon wins 3 more battles, reducing the Phalanx to zero Hit Points.

After the battle is over, the Phalanx is destroyed and the Cannon is left with 18 of its original 20 Hit Points.

The addition of Hit Points and Firepower separates the abilities of early units and modern units by allowing more advanced units to both absorb and inflict more damage. This allows ancient units the possibility of inflicting damage on their modern counterparts, but reduces the possibility of the modern unit's destruction. The outcome of a battle between grossly mismatched units (a Battleship versus a Galleon, for example) can no longer end with the destruction of the superior unit based on a single lucky attack. The possibility of damaged units also adds a new level of realism, since it is unlikely that the victor of any military engagement would emerge undamaged.

✤ **Table 8-3.** Interpreting the Hit Points Bar Color

BAR COLOR	HIT POINTS % REMAINING
Green	67%–100%
Yellow	34%–66%
Red	33% or less

The Effects of Unit Damage

As a unit takes damage, the colored Hit Points bar at the top of its banner shrinks and changes color based on the amount of damage it has received. The color and length of the bar serve as a rough indicator of what percentage of the units Hit Points remain. The colors are interpreted as shown in Table 8-3.

The obvious effect of damage is that when a damaged unit enters combat, its chances of being destroyed are greater because it can take less damage before it is killed. The other effect is that the unit's movement is reduced in proportion to its damage. The percentage of movement lost is identical to the percentage of Hit Points lost. For example, if an Ironclad, whose normal Movement Factor is four, loses 50% of its Hit Points in combat, the unit's Movement Factor is reduced to two until it is repaired.

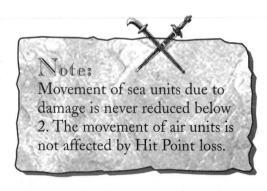

Note:
Movement of sea units due to damage is never reduced below 2. The movement of air units is not affected by Hit Point loss.

COMBAT TIPS AND TACTICS

The actual mechanics of combat in the game are pretty straightforward and, if you know how the combat system works, strategies like "don't attack Armor units with Legions" pretty much go without saying. There are, however, a number of combat strategies that tend to be very effective when used in the proper situation. The remainder of this chapter is dedicated to explaining some of these tips and techniques.

Total Victory Through World Conquest

It is important to note, especially for veterans of the original *Civilization*, that it is much harder to win a game of *Civilization II* through world conquest than it was in the original game. If conquest is your goal, your best bet is to conquer your immediate neighbors early, before they can come at you with advanced weapons. If you don't, you are positively guaranteed to be facing one or more very powerful enemies in the later stages of the game.

Keep Your Cities Well-Defended

Cities should never be left defenseless. One military unit should be fortified within the city at all times to protect it from attack. When enemy traffic in the area becomes particularly heavy, you should increase the defense force to at least two units per city.

It is equally important that all your defensive units be the best available for the job: the higher their Defense Factor and Hit Point rating, the more effectively they can defend the city. Make sure that your cities receive maximum protection; don't hesitate to build the best defensive unit you can produce, and upgrade to better units as they become available (see the next section for hints on upgrading units). If

Note: The units with the highest Defense Factors in the game are sea units, most notably the Battleship. Although these units can be placed in coastal cities to defend them from attack, there are two things you need to remember when doing so. First, sea units cannot be fortified and hence cannot receive the 50% fortification bonus. Second, the Firepower of all sea units is reduced to 1 in a city-defense situation, resulting in a reduction in the unit's effectiveness. This information also applies to air units.

you are tight on Shields and cash, and you can't afford the best available unit, remember that any defense you can afford is better than no defense at all.

Upgrade Outdated Units

Because the military forces built by the enemy are constantly changing, it is important that the units you have in the field and defending your cities be up-

> **Tip:** When you disband a unit inside one of your cities, half of the disbanded unit's value (in Shields) is contributed to the production of whatever item is currently being built. This is a great way to help finance unit upgrades. Old units can be disbanded inside the city to more quickly complete their upgraded replacements.

to-date. There is no quicker way to lose a battle than to have Phalanxes or Pikemen going toe-to-toe with Marines and Armor.

As soon as a significantly better military unit becomes available, make it a point to upgrade your defenses. Start with the cities closest to your opponents or closest to the coast, since these are the most likely candidates to be attacked first. Then work your way through the remainder of the cities until all defensive units have been upgraded. As new units are completed, disband the old city defenders to avoid paying high maintenance costs. Once your cities are adequately protected, begin replacing any units you have in the field.

Unit Stacking

"Unit Stacking" is a term that carries over from paper-based war games. When two or more game counters occupy a single square, they are considered to be "stacked".

Unit stacking is also possible in *Civilization II*. This practice is most common inside a fortress or in a city, where multiple units are massed for a defensive effort. In these situations, the strongest unit

> **Tip:** Keep an eye on enemy units as they approach your cities. The A.I. frequently stacks two or more units in a single square when it mounts a large offensive against you. When eliminating the offending units, go for the stacks first.

defends against the attack, and that unit is destroyed if it loses. The fact that defending units are destroyed one at a time makes it easier to mount an effective defense.

Tip: An exception to the normal rule of not stacking outside of cities and fortresses applies to the protection of sea units such as Transports. A stronger unit in the same square as the Transport acts as a shielding escort, giving the Transport a better chance of surviving an attack. If you lose, both units are still destroyed; but an escorted Transport has a much better chance of surviving an attack than one that is traveling alone.

Units can be stacked outside cities and fortresses as well, but this is a dangerous practice that is best avoided in most cases. When stacked units are attacked outside a city or fortress, the strongest unit in the stack once again defends for the entire stack; but in this situation, if the defending unit loses, all units in the stack are destroyed. When moving your units, especially when unloading them from a ship in preparation for an assault on an enemy city, avoid unit stacking at all costs.

The Art of Paradropping

After the discovery of Combined Arms, the Paratrooper unit becomes available. As described earlier in this chapter, the Paratrooper is strictly a middle-of-the-road unit as far as its statistics are concerned, inferior to both Alpine Troops and Marines. The thing that makes the Paratrooper so valuable is not its statistics but its mobility.

The capture of enemy cities is the Paratrooper's specialty. If you have a city or an Air Base within ten map squares of an opponent's city, that city is ripe for Paratrooper takeover (see Figure 8-2). There are a several ways you can use your Paratroopers in this manner.

Figure 8-2 Enemy cities within paradrop range of one another

One way is to stockpile a number of Paratroopers in your city or base, and paradrop all of them into the squares surrounding the enemy city. After performing a paradrop, each Paratrooper can move or initiate one attack. If you have a sufficient number of Paratroopers to overcome the city's defenses, the enemy city is yours. The problem with this plan is that the city might be heavily defended, forcing you to build lots of Paratroopers to make the plan successful.

Another way to handle the situation is to use powerful air units (or sea units, if the target is a coastal city) to destroy the units defending the city. Once the city's defenders have been destroyed, your Paratroopers can drop directly into the city and claim it in the name of your civilization.

The best, most certain method of making the Paratrooper attack successful is the "Nuke and Drop" strategy. This involves dropping a Nuclear Missile on the target city. Provided that the target city has no SDI Defense, the Nuclear Missile destroys all units in the city. Once the defending units are gone, your Paratrooper can drop right in and take over with no resistance at all.

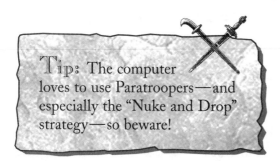

Tip: The computer loves to use Paratroopers—and especially the "Nuke and Drop" strategy—so beware!

The only drawback to this strategy is the possible appearance of enemy Partisans when the city is taken over (see the next section for details). Successfully holding the captured city depends on the quick installation of a strong defensive force and the quick elimination of enemy Partisans in the area.

Partisans and the Liberation of Cities

When one of your cities is captured, it could have significant impact on the economy and well-being of your civilization. If your situation permits you to do so, your priority should be to liberate the captured city as soon as possible, before the enemy has a chance to adequately protect it.

One of the features of the game that makes such a mission easier to mount is the role of the Partisan unit. As discussed earlier, Partisans are not particularly powerful units. However, they have the uncanny ability to be in the right place at the right time. After any civilization has discovered Guerrilla Warfare, and as long as you have discovered either Communism or Gunpowder and your government is either Communism or Democracy, Partisans units automatically appear in the area surrounding your city on the turn it is captured (see Figure 8-3). The number of Partisans that appears is based on a number of factors (random and otherwise), but the general rule is that the bigger the city, the more Partisans you receive at the time the city is captured. These free units can be used rather effectively to liberate the captured city if the conditions are right.

Figure 8-3 *Friendly Partisans surround a captured city*

Players new to the game might not realize that the Partisans that appear are theirs to use. The newly created Partisans are automatically fortified—that means that you have to activate them in order to use them.

When a city is captured, take note of the type of unit that defeated the city and is being used to defend it. Also, carefully watch the action during the remainder of the computer movement phase to see if any other units are moved into the city. If you feel that the number of Partisans surrounding the city can successfully defeat the enemy's defending units, activate all your Partisans at the start of the turn and move them in for the kill. Unless the units defending the city are extremely powerful, chances are that the combined assault of three or more Partisans has a fighting chance to recapture the city.

Two things to remember regarding Partisans: first, the sooner you attack, the better. Waiting even one turn can give the enemy a chance to further reinforce the captured city and to destroy some or all of your Partisans. Second, remember that the enemy also receives free Partisans as the result of your capturing their cities. Enemy Partisans behind your lines use their enhanced movement capabilities to do devastating economic damage by attacking the city, pillaging your Terrain, and destroying non-combat units. Eliminate them quickly, or you risk losing the city in the manner described above.

Note: No Partisans appear as the result of the liberation of a city. That is, if a city that belonged to an enemy is captured by you, then recaptured by the enemy, you receive no Partisans when the city is recaptured.

Using Fortresses

Fortresses, freestanding fortifications that can be built by Settlers and Engineers after the discovery of Masonry, are an often overlooked asset. Because of the defensive bonus they provide (unit Defense Factors are doubled inside the fortress), these structures can be used effectively for both city defense and for invasions of enemy cities.

To help protect your cities from attack, build several fortresses around the inside perimeter of the City Radius. In times of war, staff these fortresses with good defensive units, like Musketeers, and fortify the units. Manned fortresses act as an effective lure to the attacking units of your computer-controlled opponent; the attackers usually go after the fortresses and their occupants rather than pushing on to the city. This results in a high casualty rate for your attacker, while your city remains safe.

When planning a siege against an enemy city, risk using a Settler to build one or more fortresses within striking distance of the enemy city. The fortress gives your units a protected place to retreat to and from which to strike. Fortresses are particularly useful in coastal city raids. If built on the coast, ground units can be off-loaded from ships directly into the fortress. This provides the

Note: The perimeter fortress strategy works under any form of government. Units inside fortresses within three squares of their home city do not cause unhappiness under a Republic or a Democracy.

units with the defensive bonus of the fortress and prevents the stacked units from being killed simultaneously in a retaliatory attack.

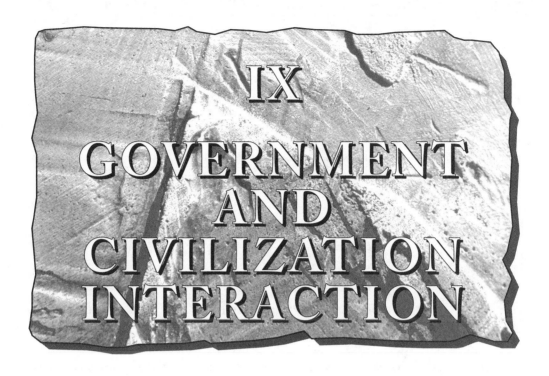

IX

GOVERNMENT AND CIVILIZATION INTERACTION

$\mathcal{B}$esides the turn-to-turn management of your cities, *Civilization II* has a broader, more political side. The politics of the game break down into two distinct segments: your system of government, and your interaction with other civilizations. This chapter is dedicated to examining the various aspects and strategies involved with each of these two areas.

Systems of Government

As you no doubt already know, there are seven systems of government available in the game: Anarchy, Despotism, Monarchy, Communism, Fundamentalism, Republic, and Democracy. At the start of the game, the only two types you have knowledge of are Anarchy and Despotism; the other systems of government are made available through the discovery of Civilization Advances.

The type of government you choose has a huge impact on many aspects of the game. Areas such as production of resources, corruption and waste, population happiness, and unit support vary drastically between advanced forms of government and their more primitive counterparts. Table 9-1 lists the systems of government from the least to the most sophisticated and shows each government's effect on certain vital aspects of the game.

The following sections analyze each type of government available.

ANARCHY

Anarchy is not actually a form of government—quite the opposite, actually. It is a state of confusion and chaos that exists between the fall of one ruling system and the installation of another. During this time, all scientific research and tax collection ceases, and corruption and waste become very high.

You cannot choose Anarchy as your governing system (not that you'd want to, anyway . . .). Anarchy only occurs when you declare a Revolution or when your Democracy falls as the result of Civil Disorder or an international incident. The period of Anarchy during a Revolution lasts from one to three turns. The number of turns is randomly generated. When Anarchy occurs as the result of the fall of a Democracy, it lasts from one to three turns (random) *plus* an additional three turns.

The period of Anarchy during a change of government lasts only one turn if you build or control the Statue of Liberty Wonder.

DESPOTISM

When the game begins, your government is automatically Despotism. Of all the government types in the game, Despotism is usually the absolute worst. Although unit support is inexpensive, and you can engage in unlimited expansion without penalty of unhappiness, you pay for this in other ways. Resource production is penalized and your levels of corruption and waste are extremely high, especially in cities far from your capital. Despotism also places a severe limit on how many cities you can control before your citizens start being unhappy due to the size of your empire.

✤ Table 9-1. Government Effects

Government Type	Food	Shields	Trade	Corruption & Waste	# Support-Free Units per City	Settler Support	Max. % for Tax/Luxury/ Science	Special Features
Anarchy	-1	-1	-1	Very High	All	None	60%	• No Taxes or Science are accumulated.
Despotism	-1	-1	-1	High	Up to city size	1 Food	60%	• Up to 3 units can be used to declare martial law
Monarchy	0	0	0	Moderate	3	1 Food	70%	• Up to 3 units can be used to declare martial law
Communism	0	0	0	None	3	1 Food	80%	• All Spies are Veterans • Up to 3 units can be used to declare martial law
Fundamentalism	0	0	0	Low	10*	1 Food	80%	• No citizens ever unhappy • Science output is halved • Happiness Improvements / Wonders produce money
Republic	0	0	+1	Low	None	2 Food	80%	• Every unit beyond the first away from its home city causes one unhappy citizen • Senate may force a peace treaty
Democracy	0	0	+1	None	None	2 Food	100%	• Every unit beyond the first away from its home city causes two unhappy citizens • Senate may force a peace treaty • The government collapses after two consecutive turns of civil disorder in any city

* Under Fundamentalism, Fanatics never require Shield support from their home city.

Note: The Food, Shields, and Trade columns reflect the change in the production of these resources in Terrain squares that normally produce three or more of the resource in question. Terrain that produces two or less of the given resource are not affected.

The institution of percentage limits on Taxes, Science, and Luxuries in *Civilization II* provides yet another reason to abandon Despotism as quickly as possible. Everyone's favorite tactic of setting their Science rate at 100% during the early stages of the game is no longer possible. The maximum percentage under Despotism is 60% for any of the three aspects of Trade. That means that, unless you change to a more advanced government, your research is greatly curtailed.

It is best to be rid of Despotism as soon as possible. In Chapter 6, the research path leading to Monarchy is illustrated. You are advised to follow this path quickly, and set your people free from the economic and social bonds of Despotism as soon as you can.

MONARCHY

When playing *Civilization*, many players tended to remain in Despotism until they could switch directly to Republic or Democracy. One reason for doing so was that it could easily be done by utilizing the original abilities imparted by the Pyramids Wonder. But the primary reason was that the old system of Monarchy saddled the player with unit support. This made sticking with Despotism for a long time more attractive than switching to Monarchy, especially for expansionist types.

The new definitions and characteristics of government types in *Civilization II* combine to make Monarchy a much more attractive ruling system. The unit support payments required under the old system have now been offset somewhat, allowing you to operate three units from each of your cities without having to pay any Shield support. Monarchy also has the advantage of allowing you to set your Tax/Science/Luxury rates as high as 70%. Although this is only ten percent higher than is possible under Despotism, that extra ten percent can make a significant difference in your rate of scientific discovery.

The main reason to choose Monarchy as your first step-up government from Despotism are the factors concerning population happiness. Monarchy charges no unhappiness penalties for having units away from their home cities as Republic and Democracy do. It is important to have this additional freedom of movement during the early stages of the game. Another aspect of happiness is that, in a Monarchy, you can use military units to impose martial law in your cities, forcing your citizens to be content. This is an important ability before the discovery of Monotheism (and the resulting ability to build Cathedrals), especially when you are playing on the higher levels of difficulty. It is advisable to stick with Monarchy until you have sufficient means to keep your citizens content.

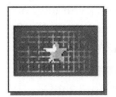

COMMUNISM

In terms of game effects, Communism is a mid-range compromise between Monarchy and Democracy. Unit support and population happiness, including the ability to impose martial law to keep your people content, are the same as under Monarchy. Communist governments don't receive a Trade bonus, but they do experience the same lack of corruption and waste enjoyed under a Democracy. Tax, Science, and Luxury levels can be set as high as 80%, the same level available under a Republic. Communism also has the unique ability to impart Veteran status to all the Spy units built under the Communist regime.

The major advantage of Communism is that it makes a good government during wartime. The lack of unhappiness penalties for units away from their home cities, as well as the lack of interference from your government concerning the making and breaking of peace treaties, makes it much easier to conduct a military campaign and to expand your empire. Expansion is also aided by a total lack of corruption and waste. The major downfall of this system is that Science and Tax collection tend to take a beating. Even with an 80% Science or Tax rate, Communism cannot compete with all the extra Trade that is produced by a Democracy. Communism is a true middle-ground government: Fundamentalism tends to be a better wartime government, while Democracy reigns supreme in times of peace. Communism is a good compromise between these two systems.

FUNDAMENTALISM

Fundamentalism is the new kid on the block government-wise. It offers a number of intriguing features that make it worth considering under certain situations.

The advantages provided by this system of government

are primarily military in nature. For example, you can operate as many as ten units out of each city support-free. Fundamentalism is also the only government that can produce Fanatics units which, as long as the government is not changed, never require Shield support—no matter how many you have. These two factors, plus the fact that no citizen is *ever* unhappy under this form of government, make Fundamentalism the best government to adopt if you are constantly at war.

Other positive aspects of Fundamentalism include the ability to set Taxes, Science, and Luxuries as high as 80% and lower diplomatic penalties for terrorist acts committed by Diplomats and Spies. Another critical advantage is the fact that all happiness-producing Improvements and Wonders produce money instead of happiness under Fundamentalism. Because of this, Fundamentalism has the potential to produce a tremendous amount of revenue.

Unfortunately, there are a number of negative aspects to consider as well. Not only does Fundamentalism not receive the Trade bonus provided by Republic and Democracy, but its Science output is also cut in half. So even though happiness and revenue problems are of little or no consequence, Fundamentalism causes you to fall seriously behind in the research of Civilization Advances. If you are determined to experiment with Fundamentalism, you need to discover all the Advances you think you'll need before you switch to this system. Otherwise, in order to keep up with your opponents, you might have to use Diplomats and Spies to steal the technologies you need to supplement your research effort.

In an all-out war situation, Fundamentalism is the way to go. If you find the lack of scientific achievement is too much to handle, consider Communism as an alternative.

REPUBLIC

The Republic is the most advanced of the three "ancient" forms of government, and is often useful well into the modern era.. There are a great many advantages associated with this system, including the ability to set the Tax, Science, and Luxury rate as high as 80%, and low levels of corruption and waste. The biggest advantage of the Republic, however, is the bonus of an additional unit of Trade in any Terrain square that is already generating Trade. The Trade bonus dramatically increases the prosperity, knowledge, and/or happiness of your civilization, depending on how you set your Trade percentages.

Figure 9-1 The Unit Roster of a city under a Republic. The "sad face" icons under the units each indicate a citizen who is unhappy due to the unit's absence from its home city.

There are several drawbacks associated with the Republic. The first consideration is the fact that every unit requires Shield support for its home city. That means that the more units a city controls, the slower its rate of unit, Improvement, and Wonder production.

Another problem, also associated with units, is that units away from their home city cause the population to become unhappy (see Figure 9-1). One unit can be away from the city without causing problems. Beyond that, every unit away from its home city (and every air and sea unit regardless of their location) causes one citizen to be unhappy. An exception to this rule is that any units inside a fortress within three squares of their home city do not cause unhappiness. This allows you to establish a realistic defensive perimeter. These penalties are much less severe than they were in the original *Civilization*, where every unit away from the city created one unhappy citizen under the Republic.

Tip: These additional sources of unhappiness, combined with the fact that you cannot declare martial law, means that the threat of Civil Disorder can present a serious problem in a Republic. Increasing the amount of Trade allocated to Luxuries to 20% or so and building Marketplaces and Banks in your cities to further enhance the effect of the additional Luxuries should offset the additional unhappiness. With all the extra Trade you earn under a Republic, your Science and Taxes should not experience much of a negative impact as a result of this strategy.

The other major drawback of the Republic is that you must answer to your Senate in matters of war and peace. If you refuse to talk when a rival civilization initiates contact while you are at war with them, there is a 50% chance that the Senate will sign a cease-fire agreement with the enemy behind your back. Likewise, if you agree to talk to your rival and they offer you peace, there is a 50% chance that the Senate will overrule your decision if you refuse

Note: The unhappiness penalty for units away from their home city under the Republic and the Democracy governments does not apply to any units with an Attack Factor of 0, such as Settlers, Explorers, Caravans, Diplomats, Spies, Galleons, Transports, and Freight units.

to sign. The final level of Senate intervention comes when you attempt to initiate hostilities with a civilization with whom you have signed a peace agreement of any sort. Once again, the Senate overrules you 50% of the time.

Despite the penalties involved, the Republic is an excellent peacetime government, and it can be used during wartime as well if proper precautions are taken to ensure your population's happiness. It is much easier to keep your people happy during wartime in a Republic than it is in a Democracy.

Note: The Senate intervention penalties for the Republic are now much less severe than they were in *Civilization*. In the original game, the Senate *always* accepted peace when offered and *never* allowed you to declare war on a civilization with whom you had a treaty. On the other hand, the Senate rules are now more strictly enforced. For instance, as the leader of a Republic, you could always refuse communication with your rival civilizations in the original game—an option that is no longer available to you. Similarly, you used to be able to circumvent the Senate by enraging your opponents with Diplomats. Now, if you intentionally provoke a war, your government has a chance of collapsing.

DEMOCRACY

Democracy is both the most advantageous and the most demanding form of government in the game. The advantages enjoyed under this system are many and varied. Democracies experience the same lucrative Trade bonus as Republics, as well as the total lack of corruption and waste enjoyed under Communism. This means that Democracies produce more Trade than any other form of government. This means that Democracies tend to be quite wealthy, and to zoom to the lead in the technology race. In addition, Democracy is the only system of government under which you can set Tax, Science, and Luxury rates at any level up to 100%. Democracy also protects your cities and units from being bribed by foreign Diplomats and Spies.

The demanding aspect of Democracy revolves around the attitude of your citizens and interference from your Senate. Citizens in a Democracy become unhappy as a result of units that are away from their home cities, just as they do under a Republic. However, under a Democracy, *two* citizens are made unhappy by every unit away from its home city. The Senate restrictions are also greater than those of a Republic. The Senate never allows you to refuse communication with another civilization, and it always requires that you sign a cease-fire agreement when you are offered one. The only exception to this rule is when you control the United Nations Wonder. If this is the case, you are permitted to refuse communication, or to refuse or break treaties 50% of the time.

Considering the many advantages of a Democracy, this system of government is more than worth the extra effort required to maintain it. The best way to handle the problems associated with a Democracy is to prepare ahead of time. Make sure that you have the ability to build Improvements and Wonders to keep your people happy, and allocate 20% or so of your Trade to Luxuries. If these are not in place when you are ready to switch governments, raise your Luxury rate or convert some of your citizens to Entertainers to compensate.

Note: If you find that your cities need more than one or two Entertainers in order to balance their unhappy populations, it might be a sign that Democracy is not the best government choice for you at that time.

Because of the military and treaty restrictions imposed on a Democracy, this form of government is not one for use in extended wartime situations. As a peacetime government, however, no other system comes close.

Tactical Revolutions

The reason you normally stage a revolution is to change your system of government. There is, however, a tactical use for revolutions as well.

As explained earlier, under Republic and Democracy your Senate might interfere if you want to break a peace treaty with one of your allies for any reason. The only way you can be certain that your attack is allowed is to temporarily switch to a non-representative government. When you want to break a treaty under Republic or Democracy, declare a revolution, and attack your enemy while you are in a state of Anarchy. This negates the treaty. Then, when you are offered a government choice, return to your former Republican or Democratic government. You are now at war with the offending civilization.

> **Tip:** If you are having trouble dealing peacefully with one of the civilizations with whom you have signed a peace treaty, and you can't break the treaty because your Senate won't let you, try to sign a treaty with an enemy of the offending civilization. If you break your treaty with the offending civilization at the request of another ally, the Senate cannot overrule your decision.

> **Tip:** Be careful when you declare a revolution for war purposes under a Republic or Democracy. When you are used to the heightened resource production under either of these systems of government, the results are often disastrous when you have to endure up to three turns of Anarchy. Settlers, Engineers, and population can be lost due to decreased Food output if no excess Food is available in their home city. Make sure that sufficient resource stores exist to carry you through Anarchy when you plan a revolution for any reason.

Diplomacy

Even if you are an isolationist, it is inevitable that you must deal with other civilizations sooner or later. The way you deal with rival leaders can be pivotal to the style of your game. If you treat your neighbors well, chances are that everyone can peacefully co-exist. If you treat your neighbors poorly or indifferently, however, you could very well be forced to abandon a peaceful game in favor of a long, costly war.

The following sections discuss the aspects of interaction between civilizations in the game and provide insights into how best to deal with your neighbors in a manner that is mutually beneficial.

THE DIPLOMATIC SYSTEM

The diplomatic system of *Civilization* was fairly straightforward. Although there were certain personality factors taken into account for different A.I. leaders, their behavior was based primarily upon the on the "map status" of the game. If you had a big empire, computer-controlled leaders with smaller empires tended to bend to your will in negotiations. If you had a small, struggling empire, your larger neighbors tended to bully you.

These factors are also taken into account in *Civilization II*, but they form only a small part of a much more complex diplomatic system. Each individual A.I. civilization "remembers" the way that you behave throughout the game, and you are treated according to how well you treat both one individual civilization and the other civilizations collectively. The two scales upon which you are rated are known as the Attitude Scale and the Reputation Scale.

The Attitude Scale

The Attitude Scale measures the attitude of enemy leaders toward your civilization. Since every leader may have a different opinion of your worth and power, the Attitude Scale is measured individually for each A.I. opponent. When you communicate with your opponents, their attitude is displayed at the top of the Diplomacy Screen (see Figure 9-2). Attitude is measured on a scale from zero (the opponent thinks you're wonderful) to 100 (the opponent thinks you're the most evil thing that ever walked the earth). The Attitude Scale is broken down as shown in Table 9-2.

✦ **Table 9-2.** The Attitude Scale

Attitude Score	Opponent Attitude
0	Worshipful
1–10	Enthusiastic
11–25	Cordial
26–38	Receptive
39–62	Neutral
63–75	Uncooperative
76–90	Icy
91–100	Hostile
100+	Enraged

The Attitude Scale is the portion of *Civilization II*'s diplomacy system that operates most like that of the original *Civilization*: an opponent's attitude is affected primarily by a comparison between their civilization and yours. The A.I. ruler's attitude is then combined with his/her personality, and actions are taken accordingly.

The actual numeric bonuses and penalties affecting the Attitude Scale depend on the prevailing game situa-

Figure 9-2 The Diplomacy Screen

tion, and therefore cannot be listed. However, the following actions and situations have an affect on an A.I. ruler's attitude toward you:

- ✦ A.I. leaders with peaceful personalities tend to like your more.
- ✦ Attitude improves if you consent to trade knowledge and if you agree to pay monetary tribute.
- ✦ A.I. leaders like you more if you are behind them technologically.
- ✦ A.I. leaders like you more if you are at peace with them.

- A.I. leaders like you more if you have less military units than they do.

- A.I. leaders respect your power (and, thereby, have a better attitude) if you have *significantly* more military units than they do.

- A.I. leaders respect your power (and, thereby, have a better attitude) if you have nuclear weapons—especially if they don't.

- Allied civilizations have a better attitude toward you if you are fighting one of their enemies.

- The farther you are ahead of a civilization technologically, the less that civilization likes you. This is especially true of allied civilizations.

- If you have a puny army (significantly less military units than the opposing civilization), the opponent has less respect for you and, therefore, a less favorable attitude toward you.

As you can see, the Attitude Scale is always in flux based on the prevailing game situation. When a civilization has a good attitude toward you, they are more receptive to your demands for tribute and technology exchanges. When an opposing civilization has a poor attitude, they are apt to demand money or a technology exchange in order to appease them. You can improve their attitude in these situations by giving in to their demands. This is usually only a temporary attitude-fix however; if the situation causing their bad attitude persists, so will their demands.

Tip: One way to tell what is causing the bad attitude of an opposing civilization is to examine their demands. Civilizations demanding money because of your civilization's "decadence," or demanding Advances because of their people's "jealousy" at your advanced culture, are suffering from envy of your superior position in the game. Those demanding tribute in exchange for not "crushing" you are making their demands because they don't respect your weak military position.

One of the fastest ways to improve the attitudes of opposing civilizations is to build the Eiffel Tower Wonder, which instantly subtracts 25 points from the attitudes of all opposing civilizations toward you.

The Reputation Scale

The Reputation Scale is the part of the diplomacy system that remembers your past actions and holds them against you. Whereas the Attitude Scale is calculated separately for each opposing civilization, the Reputation Scale is primarily universal. When you do something "bad," it is applied to your Reputation Scale for all your opponents to see.

Your reputation is based on the number of "black marks" you have. Black marks are penalty points you incur for doing underhanded and dishonorable things to your allies. The point breakdown of the Reputation Scale is shown in Table 9-3. Your reputation is shown near the top of the Foreign Minister's window, just above the list of rival civilizations.

At the start of the game, your reputation is "Spotless." Black marks are accrued when you break treaties. Each treaty you break results in two black marks with the following two exceptions:

✤ If you are incited to break a treaty by another civilization with whom you have a treaty, you receive only one black mark, and the civilization

✤ **Table 9-3.** The Reputation Scale

BLACK MARKS	REPUTATION
0	Spotless
1	Excellent
2	Honorable
3	Questionable
4	Dishonorable
5	Poor
6	Despicable
7 (or higher)	Atrocious

> Note: The effects of breaking treaties are cumulative. For example, you sign a cease-fire agreement with a civilization. This agreement lasts 16 turns. Within that time period, you sign a permanent peace treaty with the same civilization. Until 16 turns have passed from the signing of the first agreement, both the cease-fire *and* the treaty are in effect. (After the 16 turns, only the treaty remains.) If you attack the civilization within this time period, you receive a total of four black marks: two for breaking the cease-fire and two for breaking the permanent treaty.

who incited you to break the treaty doesn't count the black mark. This is the only situation that can cause your reputation to vary from one civilization to another.

* If you control the Eiffel Tower Wonder, you receive only one black mark when you break a treaty.

The effect of having a bad reputation is that your rivals are less likely to trust you when you negotiate treaties. The A.I. adheres to the following reputation parameters when negotiating peace with you:

* No alliances unless your reputation is Excellent or better.

* No permanent treaties unless your reputation is Questionable or better.

* If your reputation is Atrocious, the A.I. feels no compulsion to adhere to cease-fires or existing treaties with your civilization.

Reputation points can be regained, but it is a much more difficult process than improving your Attitude rating. Black marks are deleted one at a time, over a number of game turns. The actual number of turns it takes to erase one black mark is determined by the following formula:

(24 × Difficulty Level) Turns

where:

> *Difficulty Level* = 1 (Chieftain) or 2 (Warlord) or 3 (Prince) or 4 (King) or 5 (Emperor) or 6 (Deity)

> Reputation is regained at twice the normal rate, if you control the Eiffel Tower Wonder.

If you are able to behave yourself long enough, you can eventually return your reputation to "Excellent" status. You can only regain "Spotless" status if you control the Eiffel Tower Wonder.

The Patience Factor

Depending on their personality and attitude toward you, each leader has a varying degree of patience regarding negotiations. The more times you request an audience with a leader, and the more requests you make during each audience, the less patient the leader becomes. When the leader loses patience with you, he or she ends negotiations or refuses to meet with you.

When this situation occurs, the solution is simple: just leave the disgruntled leader alone. After several turns, the leader's patience returns, and he/she is once again willing to talk to you.

Making Treaties

In the original *Civilization*, there were two states of coexistence between your civilization and those controlled by the A.I.—peace or war. There was no middle ground; either you were fighting or you weren't. In *Civilization II*, there are several states of interaction, ranging from total peace to total war. These states are: alliance, treaty, cease-fire, and war.

An alliance is a state of total peace and productive coexistence between you and another civilization. As such, alliances are the rarest type of treaty and can only be initiated if your reputation is "Excellent" or better. Under an alliance, units belonging to either civilization can move freely in both in each others' territory, ignoring zones of control and causing no production penalties. In fact, wounded units can move into any allied city to undergo repairs. Allies are generally amenable to the exchange of Advances and map information, and will usually go to war with common enemies at your request. An alliance is the ultimate state of peace, but it requires that you be on your best behavior in order to establish and maintain it.

A peace treaty in *Civilization II* is a permanent agreement wherein you and an A.I. civilization agree to end hostilities and to maintain peace between your two societies. Under the terms of a peace treaty, each party must withdraw their troops from the territory of the other. Units still obey the normal rules for zones of control, and any rival unit within a City Radius prevents the square it occupies from producing any resources. Any of your units remaining inside the territory of a civilization with whom you have a treaty might cause the A.I. opponent to break the treaty if the units are not removed within a few turns. If enemy units encroach on your territory, you have the option to contact the rival leader and insist that they withdraw their troops.

Like alliances, treaties require that you possess a certain reputation level in order to initiate them; however, treaties can be initiated even if your reputation is "Questionable."

The lowest level of peace is the cease-fire. Cease-fires are not permanent—they last only 16 turns. At the end of this time, a new cease-fire or a treaty must be signed, or hostilities recommence. Besides their short duration, the conditions of a cease-fire are identical to those of peace treaties in the original *Civilization*. During the cease-fire, the only requirement of the two parties is that no hostilities be initiated. Enemy units are free to enter and leave your City Radii, and they may fortify their positions inside your territory, as long as they don't pick a fight. Cease-fires can be initiated no matter what your current reputation might be. However, the worse your reputation, the more likely it is that your opponents might break the cease-fire agreement.

The final state of coexistence is all-out war, a state of affairs that requires no explanation. At any time during a war, you may be offered the opportunity to sign a cease-fire agreement by your enemy, or you can offer such an agreement by contacting the enemy leader yourself.

Other Types of Interaction

All interaction in *Civilization II* doesn't take place on a purely diplomatic level: it also takes place through trade and espionage, both of which can be conducted in conditions of either peace or war. The following sections examine these alternative forms of civilization interaction.

TRADE ROUTES

Trade routes are one of the most important aspects of *Civilization II*, just as they were in *Civilization*. As soon as you discover the Trade Civilization Advance, you gain the ability to build Caravan units. Caravans (and, later in the game, Freight units) can be used to establish trade routes between your own cities or between one of your cities and the city of a rival civilization. On the turn the route is established, you receive an immediate cash payment which is added to your treasury, and an equivalent number of Science icons which are added to your current research project. Afterwards, you receive a fixed amount of bonus Trade each turn. Each city can operate up to three trade routes. If more than three are established, the three most profitable routes are maintained while the remainder are dropped. The amount of Trade received by a city each turn as a result of its

> **Note:** Unlike the original game, *Civilization II* gives you the Trade benefits generated by any trade routes established with your cities by rival civilizations.

trade routes is shown in the Info Display of the City Display (see Figure 9-3).

Figure 9-3 The City Display of a city, showing the Trade generated by its trade routes

Determining Trade Route Income

Both the amount of Trade generated each turn by a trade route and initial cash and Science bonus are determined based on a number of factors. The following sections give details on how both are calculated.

TRADE ICONS GENERATED

The number of additional Trade icons generated by the trade route in the source and the destination cities is determined by the following equation:

$$Trade\ Icons = (source\ Trade + destination\ Trade + 4) \div 8$$

source Trade = the amount of Trade generated by the Caravan/Freight unit's home city

destination Trade = the amount of Trade generated by the Caravan/Freight unit's destination city

(Source and destination Trade *excludes* Trade icons generated by other trade routes.)

The total number of Trade icons generated by the trade route is modified depending on certain situations. These modifiers are listed in Table 9-4. All modifiers are cumulative.

INITIAL TRADE ROUTE BONUS

In *Civilization*, the initial trade route bonus was determined strictly based on the amount of Trade generated in both the source and destination cities, and the distance between the two cities. *Civilization II* adds the new dimension of

✤ **Table 9-4.** Basic Trade Route Income Modifiers

SITUATION	MODIFIER
Source and destination cities are both your cities	– 50%
Establishing unit is a Freight unit	+ 50%
Cities are connected by a road *	+ 50 %
Cities are connected by a railroad *	+ 50%
Both cities have Airports *	+ 50%
Cities are on different continents	+ 100%
Source city has Superhighway Improvement	+ 50%

*Applies only to cities on the same continent

supply and demand to the game, so that trade routes are more profitable if you are transporting goods required by the destination city. The trade route formula for determining the initial bonus for establishing the trade route is as follows:

$$\textit{Base Initial Bonus} = ((\textit{distance} + 10) \times$$
$$(\textit{source Trade} + \textit{destination Trade})) \div 24$$

distance = the number of squares between the source and destination cities (diagonal squares count as 1.5 squares when figuring distance)

source Trade = the amount of Trade generated by the Caravan/Freight unit's home city

destination Trade = the amount of Trade generated by the Caravan/Freight unit's destination city

The Initial Bonus for the trade route, like the number of Trade icons generated, is modified by the factors listed in Table 9-4.

The addition of supply and demand factors can potentially increase a trade route's initial bonus, provided the demand is met. Table 9-5 shows the bonus gained if the trade route successfully fulfills a trade demand in the destination city.

Once both the Base Initial Bonus and the Demand Bonus have

> **Tip:** As implied by the Base Initial Bonus equation, the greater the distance between the source and destination cities, the greater the initial bonus.

✤ **Table 9-5.** Bonuses for Fulfilling Demand

ITEM(S) DEMANDED	BONUS FOR FULFILLING DEMAND
Uranium	(Base Initial Bonus × 2)
Oil	(Base Initial Bonus × 1.5)
Silk, Spice, Gems, Gold	(Base Initial Bonus)
Silver, Cloth, Wine	(Base Initial Bonus ÷ 2)
All other commodities	No Bonus

> **Note:** Supply and demand changes over time. If you send a Caravan or Freight unit on a particularly long run, re-check the destination city's demands before you establish the trade route. Otherwise, you might be unpleasantly surprised at the results.

been figured, the final equations come into play to determine the Modified Trade Route Bonus. If the destination city belongs to your civilization, the following equation is used:

Modified Trade Route Bonus = (Base Initial Bonus × 2) + Demand Bonus

If the destination city of the trade route belongs to another civilization, the following equation is used:

Modified Trade Route Bonus = (Base Initial Bonus + Demand Bonus) × 2

After the Modified Trade Route Bonus is calculated, there remains one more set of modifiers to apply in order to determine the Final Trade Route Bonus. These modifiers are shown in Table 9-6.

As you can see, once you get past all the calculations, trade routes can be extremely useful. They are especially helpful when your research needs an extra infusion of Science in order to make discoveries more quickly. Establish trade routes early and often to maximize the generation of Trade in each city.

✦ **Table 9-6.** Equations to Determine Final Trade Route Bonus

SITUATION	FINAL TRADE ROUTE BONUS
During the first 200 game turns *	(Modified Trade Route Bonus × 2)
After the discovery of Railroad	(Modified Trade Route Bonus × .67)
After the discovery of Flight	(Modified Trade Route Bonus × .33)

*Or until Navigation *and* Invention have been discovered.

> **Tip:** As implied by the Modified Trade Route equation, it is much more profitable to establish trade routes with foreign cities than it is to establish trade routes between your own cities.

> **Note:** The game sets an upper limit on the amount of the bonus that can be generated through trade routes. The limit is $\frac{2}{3}$ of the number of Science icons required to complete the research of a Civilization Advance.

TRADE ROUTE CALCULATION EXAMPLE: A Freight unit from the American city of Washington establishes a trade route with the French city of Paris, which is 12 squares away. The Freight unit delivers Uranium, which is demanded by Paris. It is past turn 200 of the game, and the Americans have discovered Railroad but not Flight. The cities are on the same continent, but they are not connected by roads or railroads. Washington is currently generating 8 Trade, and Paris is generating 5. The value of the trade route is calculated as follows (all fractions are rounded down):

$$\text{Trade Icons} = ((8 + 5 + 4) \div 8) \times 1.5 = 3$$
$$\text{Base Initial Bonus} = ((12 + 10) \times (8 + 5)) \div 24 = 11$$
$$\text{Demand Modifier} = (11 \times 2) = 22$$
$$\text{Modified Initial Bonus} = (11 + 22) \times 2 = 66$$
$$\text{Final Initial Bonus} = (66 \times .67)$$
$$\text{Final Initial Bonus} = 44$$

So, in the above example, Washington receives a bonus of 44 coins and 44 Science icons when the trade route is first established, and both cities receive 3 additional Trade icons each turn as a result of the trade route.

DIPLOMATS AND SPIES

Although the activities of both Diplomats and Spies are often considered to be anti-social and subversive, both of these units are still a means by which you interact with your rivals. Diplomats are capable of the same basic functions as they were in *Civilization*. Spies are, essentially, updated Diplomats who have additional commands and abilities and are much more effective at most tasks. Spies function 50% more efficiently if they are Veteran units.

The following sections describe the ways in which Diplomats and Spies can "interact" with your rivals—both constructively and subversively. Some basic information on mission types, for both Diplomats and Spies, is found in Table 9-7.

♣ **Table 9-7.** Information Concerning Diplomat/Spy Missions

MISSION TYPE	MONETARY COST	FATE OF DIPLOMAT	FATE OF SPY
Establish Embassy	—	Removed from game	Removed from game
Investigate City	—	Removed from game	Remains in position
Steal Technology	—	Removed from game	May survive and be removed to nearby friendly city
Industrial Sabotage	—	Removed from game	May survive and be removed to nearby friendly city
Poison Water Supply	—	N/A	May survive and be removed to nearby friendly city
Plant Nuclear Device	—	N/A	May survive and be removed to nearby friendly city
Incite A Revolt	Yes	Removed from game	May survive and be removed to nearby friendly city
Bribe Unit	Yes	Survives	Survives

Establish Embassy

This is one of the peaceful, non-subversive functions of a Diplomat or Spy. When an embassy is established in an enemy city, you have access to a great deal of vital information concerning that civilization. This information includes the amount of money in their treasury, the civilization's war or peace status with other civilizations in the game, a list of their cities, and the Civilization

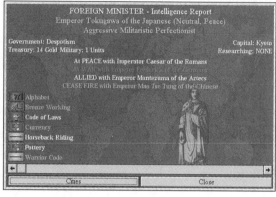

Figure 9-4 The information provided by an embassy

Tip: Before you go to the trouble of establishing embassies with everyone in the game, consider building Marco Polo's Embassy or the United Nations. Both of these Wonders of the World give you an automatic embassy with every civilization in the game.

Advances they have discovered (see Figure 9-4). Once the embassy is established, the Diplomat or Spy is removed from the game.

Embassies are useful tools for determining how far rival civilizations are ahead of you (and vice versa). Embassies also give you a good indication of how well they might withstand an attack from your forces.

Investigate City

Investigate City is also considered a peaceful, non-subversive act. This function allows you to look at the City Display of a rival civilization's city (see Figure 9-5). When a Diplomat investigates a city, the Diplomat is removed from the game. If the investigating unit is a Spy, the Spy remains active.

The Investigate City option is an excellent tool for use in planning an attack on an enemy city. The investigation allows you to assess the strength of the city's defenses and the overall worth of the city based on the Improvements and Wonders constructed there. While somewhat costly when using a Diplomat (because the Diplomat is lost), Investigate City is very cost-effective when using a Spy.

Steal Technology

Steal Technology is the first of the antisocial activities available to Diplomats and

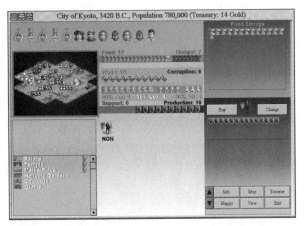

Figure 9-5 Investigating an enemy city

Spies. This option allows you to steal an Advance that you do not currently possess from your rival. In the case of Diplomats, the Advance stolen is randomly selected. Once an Advance is stolen by a Diplomat, the Diplomat is removed from the game. Only one Advance per enemy city can be stolen by a Diplomat over the course of a game.

When a Spy attempts to Steal Technology, you can either steal a random Advance, or you can select the option to choose a specific Advance for the Spy to steal. When you chose a specific Advance, there is a greater risk of the Spy being captured. When a Spy successfully steals an Advance, there is a chance that she can escape capture. Escaped Spies are promoted to Veteran status and instantly returned to one of your cities for "recuperation." If the Spy is captured, she is removed from the game. Unlike Diplomats, Spies can steal more than one technology from a single enemy city. On subsequent attempts, you cannot choose a specific technology and the risk of capture is much higher.

Stealing Civilization Advances from your neighbors is considered to be an act of war in most cases, so you shouldn't use this ability recklessly. This is especially important if you attempt to steal Advances from civilizations with whom you are allied. When you do this, you are warned that the action might cause an incident. It often does. If you are considering such a course of action, make sure you look at the situation from all angles. You must decide whether the theft of a single Advance is worth the possible collapse of the peace treaty, the fall of your government, a loss of reputation, and a war. It is best to steal technology only from your enemies.

Industrial Sabotage

Industrial Sabotage works in much the same way as Steal Technology, except that it is not limited to one attempt per city for Diplomats. When successful, Industrial Sabotage destroys either the item currently under construction in the enemy city or an existing City Improvement. The item destroyed is random for Diplomats. Spies are allowed to select the item to be destroyed, but this increases their risk of being caught. Diplomats are removed from the game after committing an act of Industrial Sabotage. Spies have a chance of surviving their mission and being returned to a nearby friendly city.

Industrial Sabotage is a much riskier proposition in *Civilization II* than it was in the original game. In *Civilization*, a Diplomat could commit an act of sabotage against an allied civilization without fear of reprisal. This is no longer true. If a Diplomat or Spy is caught in an act of Industrial Sabotage against an ally, it is considered a treaty violation. This gives you two black marks against your reputation, starts a war, and, possibly, precipitates the collapse of your government. Like Steal Technology, Industrial Sabotage should only be performed against your enemies.

Poison Water Supply

Poison Water Supply is one of the new "Spy-only" missions. Its one and only purpose is to reduce the population of an enemy city by one. This is an obvious act of war, and, if the Spy is caught in the act, she is removed from the game and the victim civilization is out to get you. If the victim was an allied civilization, the Spy's capture results in the dissolution of the treaty, a war, and, possibly, the collapse of your government. If, on the other hand, the Spy is not captured, she is safely returned to a nearby friendly city and you are none the worse for your dastardly deed.

As a general rule, Poisoning the water supply is not a very effective strategy, since it does nothing to reduce the city's defensive capability. If you were persistent enough, you *could* conceivably destroy the city after many repeated poisonings, but considering the risks and the possible cost in lost Spies, a conventional war usually works just as well.

Plant Nuclear Device

After you have discovered both Nuclear Fission and Rocketry, and someone in the world has built the Manhattan Project, the "Plant Nuclear Device" option appears on the Spy's options menu. This option allows you to move the Spy into an enemy city and set off a nuclear explosion with the same effects as that of a Nuclear Missile. The advantage to nuking a city in this manner is that an SDI Defense has no effect. There is a possibility that this action might cause an international incident; but, if your Spy isn't caught, its a great way to attack an allied civilization without interference under a Republic or Democracy. The Spy is always destroyed as a result of planting a nuclear device.

Bribe Unit

An extremely useful function of Diplomats and Spies is their ability to convince enemy units to join your civilization through bribery. The amount of money required to successfully bribe a unit is determined as follows:

$$Bribe\ Cost = ((enemy\ treasury + 750) \div (distance + 2)) \\ \times (Enemy\ Unit\ Cost \div 10)$$

where:

> *distance* = the distance from the enemy unit's Palace (diagonal squares count as 1.5 squares when figuring distance)
>
> *distance* = 32, if the enemy has no Palace
>
> *distance* = 16, if the enemy is a Barbarian
>
> *maximum value of distance* = 10, if the enemy government is Communism
>
> *Bribe Cost* = *Bribe Cost* ÷ 2, if the enemy unit is a Settler

There is no risk involved when bribing enemy units. Diplomats and Spies alike survive this mission whether they are successful or not (unless, of course, they are killed by the unit they fail to bribe on the following turn . . .). The only reason *not* to bribe an enemy unit is if you are low on cash or the unit is to weak to be worth your time and attention.

Civilization II does add two twists over the original *Civilization* when it comes to bribery. First is that it is impossible to bribe the units of a civilization that is ruled by Democracy. This is an important factor to consider, especially

> **Tip:** Bribed units follow the same rules as mercenary units found in villages with regards to support. In other words, when a unit is successfully bribed, it's home city is the city closest to the unit at the time it is bribed. If the closest city is one of your cities, the unit requires support from that city. However, if the closest city is an enemy city, the home city of the unit is listed as NONE, and the unit requires no support! If you don't want to pay support for newly bribed units, make sure you bribe them while they are close to an enemy city.

since the second twist added is that enemy Diplomats and Spies frequently use bribery against *you*. If you rule through Democracy, your units remain safe from the temptations of the enemy.

Incite A Revolt

The final option available is a costly but extremely powerful Diplomat/Spy function. Incite A Revolt is, essentially, paying a bribe to incite an entire enemy city to join your civilization. The amount of money required to "buy" an enemy city is determined using the following formula:

Revolt Cost = ((enemy treasury + 1000) ÷ (distance + 3)) × city size

where:

distance = the distance from the enemy unit's Palace (diagonal squares count as 1.5 squares when figuring distance)

distance = 32, if the enemy has no Palace

distance = *distance* ÷ 2, if the city has a Courthouse

maximum value of distance = 10, if the enemy government is Communism

✤ **Table 9-8.** Modifiers Applied to the Revolt Cost for an Enemy City

SITUATION	AFFECT ON REVOLT COST*
City is in Civil Disorder	Revolt Cost = Revolt Cost ÷ 2
No units inside city	Revolt Cost = Revolt Cost ÷ 2
The city originally belonged to you	Revolt Cost = Revolt Cost ÷ 2
Unit inciting the revolt is a Spy	Revolt Cost = Revolt Cost × .84
Unit inciting the revolt is a Veteran Spy	Revolt Cost = Revolt Cost × .67

*These modifiers are cumulative.

A number of other factors also affect the cost of inciting a city to revolt. These are shown in Table 9-8.

    If you have enough money to pull it off, inciting a revolt is an excellent way to expand your empire. Of course, inciting a revolt also causes an international incident, and all the normal problems that go along with it. As usual, if the victim civilization is an ally, treaties are broken, your reputation is tarnished, and your government might fall.

    If you can afford to pay double the normal cost, you are offered the opportunity to subvert the rival city rather than inciting a revolt. What you get for all that extra money is a revolt without incident. Subversion gives you the city without arousing the anger of the city's owner or breaking any treaties. When either incitement to revolt or subversion is successful, the city in question and all its dependent units become a part of your civilization. In addition, you get to steal one Civilization Advance of your choice from the other civilization, just as you do when you capture a city by force (provided the opposing civilization possess technology that you have not yet discovered).

> **Note:** Regardless of their government type, a civilization's capital city can never be incited to revolt or subverted.

Like the Bribe Unit option, be aware that A.I. opponents frequently engage in the subversion of your cities (especially at higher levels of difficulty) and that Diplomatic governments are not affected by this action. If a Spy resides inside a city, that city is protected from bribery by the enemy regardless of government type.

Expulsion of Diplomats and Spies

At King Level or above, while a peace agreement of any kind is in effect, your opponents have the option of expelling your Diplomats or Spies from their territory at will. (You have this option regarding their Diplomats and Spies as well, regardless of difficulty level.) When expelled, the Diplomat or Spy is instantly returned to the nearest friendly city.

You can prevent the expulsion of your Diplomats and Spies by having them travel in pairs. When two Diplomats or Spies occupy the same square, neither can be expelled.

The Diplomat-Perimeter Strategy

If your peaceful neighbors have a tendency to wander around in your territory and you want to put a stop to it, here is an interesting strategy to try.

Set up national borders using Diplomats (or Spies). Place two in each square along a narrow part of the border between your two civilizations and fortify them. Because Diplomats and Spies cost no upkeep and do not cause unhappiness under the Republic and Democracy, this serves as an adequate barrier between you and your nosy neighbor, keeping your wandering visitors to a minimum.

X
GAME CUSTOMIZATION AND MODIFICATION

*T*he original *Civilization* had a quality that many computer games on the market today consistently lack: replay value. After three years, players are still hooked on Sid Meier's classic strategy game. *Civilization II* has the same addictive quality as the original, perhaps even more so. But *Civilization II* goes one step further, by providing easily accessible ways for players to make their own custom modifications to the game. This chapter discusses some of the ways you can modify the game.

The Map Editor

Like *CivNet*, the multiplayer version of *Civilization*, *Civilization II* includes a utility for creating and editing game maps (see Figure 10-1). The map editor is accessible by double-clicking its icon in the *Civilization II* Program Group in Windows.

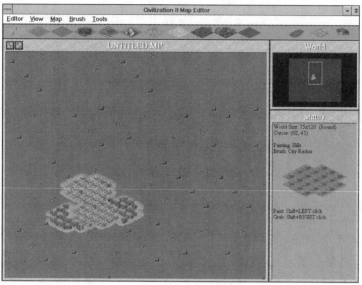

Figure 10-1 The Civilization II Map Editor

The map editor is the easiest way to customize the game. It is capable of generating entire worlds, randomly or to your specification. It also contains a variety of "brushes" allowing you to modify the maps it generates or to create a world from scratch starting with a blank ocean map. It functions like a paint program that uses terrain types, as opposed to colors and textures, to build a picture of the world. It even allows you to choose the starting locations for civilizations. (Complete instructions on the controls and functions of the map editor can be found in the game manual.)

Maps created with the map editor can be saved. Saved maps use the ".MP" file extension, and can be used in any game of *Civilization II*. Map files from existing saved games can also be loaded into the map editor and saved as .MP files. To play on a customized map, choose "Start on Premade World" from the Main Menu when setting up a game. A file menu appears, displaying all the available map files.

The map editor can be used to create truly unique worlds. One of the most popular uses of the editor is to create "ultimate" maps, where perfect city sites can be found just about anywhere. Another popular type of map is the "hostile world" map, which makes the game much more challenging by creating a world with very few good city sites. This type of world forces massive terrain modification by Settlers and Engineers in order to make it hospitable.

It is important to note that it is possible to create an "illegal" map that could cause the game to malfunction. The rules for what constitutes a legal map are extremely flexible, but certain factors like too much land or too much water could affect the way that the A.I. opponents respond to and interact with their surroundings. (They are more likely to do "dumb" things.) Additionally, a map with insufficient land might cause problems when the computer attempts to position the civilizations when the game begins. If there isn't enough land for everyone, unpredictable results could occur.

Most map problems can be detected in the map editor by selecting the "Analyze Map" command from the Map menu. This command checks the map and reports any errors that might cause the game to malfunction if the map is used.

The analyze utility can also detect "impossible" maps. Impossible maps are the "hostile world" map (described earlier) taken to extremes. For example it is possible to create a map that consists entirely of Mountains and Oceans. Such a map can be perfectly legal according to the map rules. However, this type of map would make it impossible to create even one city that would survive and grow. It also makes movement and exploration extremely slow due to the movement cost. A game played on this type of world would not be much fun—nor would it last for long.

The map editor adds an interesting dimension to the game, and should prove to be quite a popular tool among devout players. Undoubtedly, customized map files will be appearing on BBSs and on-line services almost immediately after the game is released.

THE "RESOURCE SEED"

One of the options available in the map editor is the ability to change the "Resource Seed." This option changes the distribution and types of Special Resources on your map. The best way to see the effects produced by changing this number is by using the map editor to generate maps with various Resource Seed values and taking note of the resource distribution pattern. When you find a pattern you like, remember the Resource Seed value you used for future reference.

Customizing Game Rules, Statistics, and Components

Nearly every game on the market, from strategy games to flight simulators, has some sort of tool available that allows players to customize certain aspects of the game. While these utilities are sometimes provided by the manufacturers of the games themselves, they are more often produced by players and hackers and uploaded to BBSs and other on-line services. Game modification utilities are usually hex editors that allow certain portions of the game code to be altered in order to make the desired changes to gameplay. Although hex editors sometimes cause crashes or unexpected game results, they often work quite well and become popular among diehard players (and players with a tendency to bend the rules in their favor). Unfortunately, most people lack the programming knowledge to create editors of their own.

Civilization II bypasses this problem by providing easy access to many key data elements of the game. Rather than encoding all vital game information within the compiled program, *Civilization II* retrieves much of its gameplay data from standard ASCII text files. As a result, modifications to the game can be made by anyone, using a word processor or any other program capable of reading and storing ASCII text files. Once changes have been made to the files, they must be saved as "Text Only" in ASCII format.

Note: Prior to making any of the modifications described in this chapter make a backup copy of the text file you are changing. Go to File Manager in Windows and switch to the directory where you installed *Civilization II*. Highlight the RULES.TXT file by clicking on it. From the File menu, choose "Copy." When the dialog box appears, type **RULES.BAK** (or any file name, as long as you can remember what it means at a later date). This makes a copy of the original file, which you can use to restore the original game data in case you make a mistake or want to go back to the original game rules and statistics.

> **Warning:** Keep in mind that any alterations you make to the data files are being made "at your own risk." Nothing you change can harm or damage your computer in any way; however, certain alterations can cause the game to malfunction. This is especially true if lines are deleted from the text files, the new data you enter is faulty, or the values are out of the expected range for the altered game statistic. If you notice problems with the game, change the values again or restore the default values from the file backup you created.

The following sections explain how to modify many key aspects of the game. All of the alterations described in this chapter involve changes to the text file entitled "RULES.TXT." You should read this entire section before attempting to change any statistics. The easiest way to comprehend the information presented here is to print out a copy of the RULES.TXT file and examine the information in it while reading this chapter. That way you can get an idea of how the game data is formatted and what needs be changed.

This chapter assumes that you are familiar with how to load, edit and save ASCII text files. If you do not, consult the manual for your word processor or text editor for details.

If you fail to make a backup copy of the file and you want to restore the default data, you must re-install the game from the original CD.

NEVER set any value below zero. This can precipitate extremely weird results and cause major gameplay problems.

Finally, PLEASE don't complain to MicroProse if game variables and constants that you have altered cause the game to behave badly (or worse). If you produce such a problem, reverse it by replacing the original RULES.TXT file. You have been warned . . .

MODIFYING THE GAME RULES

Many of the calculations and principles of the game are based on constant values. The very heart of the game can be modified by changing some or all of these constants. These basic game principles can be found in the file entitled RULES.TXT. The game constants are located under the header "@COSMIC" on the first page of the file.

Each of the constants listed in this section are simply a single, integer value. To change the value, simply delete the old value and enter a new one. The following sections explain each of the constants and the effect of any changes you may wish to make. The default value for each constant is provided for reference.

> **N**ote: When changing these values to your benefit, keep in mind that the rules you are changing also benefit your computer opponents.

Road Movement Multiplier

Default = 3

This is the number used to determine how many movement points are expended to move one space when traveling along road and River squares. The unit's Movement Factor is multiplied by this number in order to determine how far it can move while traveling on a road or River.

For example, using the default value, a unit with a Movement Factor of one can move three spaces along a road. Increasing the Road Movement Modifier decreases the amount of movement expended by a unit, thereby increasing the distance it can travel on a road or River in a given turn. Decreasing the number causes the unit to expend more movement and, therefore, travel less distance each turn.

Trireme "Lost at Sea" Modifier

Default = 2

When a Trireme is not adjacent to land at the end of its turn, there is a 1 in x chance that it will be lost at sea. The Trireme "lost at sea" modifier provides the value for x.

Using the default value, a Trireme has a 1 in 2 (50%) chance of being lost at sea. Increasing this value decreases the chance of the Trireme being lost. Decreasing the value makes the Trireme's loss more likely.

Citizen Food Consumption

Default = 2

This constant determines the number of Food units each of your citizens consume per turn. Increasing this number reduces the amount of surplus Food available each turn, slowing city growth. Decreasing this number increases the amount of surplus Food, making city growth more rapid.

Number of Rows in Food Box

Default = 10

This constant controls the number of Rows it takes to fill the Food Storage Box. At the default value, there are 10 Rows to fill. Once all the rows have been filled (plus one additional food icon), the city's population increases by one, the Food Storage Box is emptied, and the process begins again. The number of icons required to fill the Food Storage box is determined by the equation:

$$rows \times (city\ size + 1)$$

Like the Citizen Food Consumption constant, this constant affects the speed of city growth. By decreasing the number of Rows in the Food Storage Box, you effectively increase the growth rate of your cities. For example, by changing this value to 5, a city with a size of one needs to accumulate only 6 units of Food in the Food Storage Box in order to grow to size 2 rather than the normal 11. If the constant is increased, the city growth rate decreases proportionally.

Number of Rows in Shield Box

Default = 10

This value performs a function similar to that of the Number of Rows in Food Box constant, with the exception that it affects the number of Shields needed to complete the production of units, Improvements, and Wonders. The name is somewhat misleading, since this number actually refers to the number of Shields that constitute a "complete row" of shields in the Production Box.

The speed of production is based on how quickly the requisite number of Shield-rows can be filled in the Production Box. The cost stated for each unit, Improvement, and Wonder is based on the assumption that each row contains

Improvement, and Wonder is based on the assumption that each row contains ten shields. By decreasing the Number of Rows in Shield Box constant, you effectively speed up production by making each row contain less Shields.

For example, a Battleship's cost is 160 Shields. In order to complete construction of this unit at the default value, 16 rows of 10 Shields each must be filled in the Production box. By lowering this constant to five, the Battleship is completed after filling 16 rows of 5 shields each, for a total Shield cost of 80. Reducing the constant by half, halves the price of production and the unit is produced twice as fast.

The opposite is true as well: if the value of this constant is increased, cost and production time are increased as well.

Settler Food Consumption (Govt. ≦ Monarchy)

Default = 1

This constant controls the amount of Food consumed by Settlers and Engineers under Anarchy, Despotism, and Monarchy. Raising this value causes Settlers and Engineers to consume more Food each turn. If the value is set to zero, Settlers and Engineers do not consume Food under these systems of government.

Settler Food Consumption (Govt. ≧ Communism)

Default = 2

This constant controls the amount of Food consumed by Settlers and Engineers under Communism, Fundamentalism, Republic, and Democracy. Raising this value causes Settlers and Engineers to consume more Food each turn. Lowering the value causes Settlers and Engineers to consume less Food under these systems of government.

City Size for First Unhappiness at Chieftain Level

Default = 7

This constant determines the size to which a city must grow before its citizens are "born" unhappy.

For example, using the default value, once a city in a Chieftain Level game grows to the size of six, every citizen added to the population thereafter (citizen number seven and up) is automatically unhappy. In other words, all citizens are born content up to the value of this constant minus one. Increasing this constant allows cities to grow larger without the citizens automatically becoming unhappy. By lowering the constant, automatically unhappy citizens show up earlier.

The label for this constant is somewhat misleading, as it is actually the basis for determining the level of automatic unhappiness in *every* difficulty level. If this constant is "x," the first automatically unhappy citizen on Warlord Level is $x-1$; on Prince Level the first unhappy citizen is $x-2$, and so on.

Riot Factor Based on Number of Cities

Default = 14
Riot Factor is used to determine the maximum number of cities you can control before the size of your empire starts to cause unhappiness. The higher the Riot Factor, the more cities you can control without experiencing additional unhappiness.

Aqueduct Needed To Exceed Size

Default = 8
This constant determines the size to which a city can grow before it must build an Aqueduct. If no Aqueduct is constructed, population growth stops at this population size. Decreasing this constant forces you and your opponents to build Aqueducts earlier in the game; increasing this constant allows Aqueducts to be ignored in favor of other production.

Sewer System Needed to Exceed Size

Default = 12
This constant determines the size to which a city can grow before it must build an Sewer System. If no Sewer System is constructed, population growth stops at this population size. Decreasing this constant forces you and your opponents to build Sewer Systems earlier in the game; increasing this constant allows Sewer Systems to be ignored in favor of other production.

Tech Paradigm

Default = 10
This constant is the percentage "cost" to research Civilization Advances divided by ten. In other words, at the default value, the research of Civilization

Advances is 100%, requiring the expenditure of the "normal" number of Science light bulbs.

Decreasing this value decreases the light bulb cost of research. For example, if this constant were changed to 5, each Advance would require only 50% of its normal research expenditure, decreasing the amount of time required to make new discoveries. Increasing this value slows research: if the constant were set to 15, each Advance would require 150% of its normal research expenditure.

Base Time for Engineers to Transform Terrain

Default = 20

This is double the number of turns required for an Engineer unit to perform a Terrain transformation using the "Transform Terrain" command. This should not be confused with the number of turns it takes to change Terrain through mining or irrigation, which is individual to each type of Terrain.

A lower value makes the transformation faster and a higher value makes the transformation slower.

Monarchy Pays Support Past This

Default = 3

This constant represents the number of units requiring no Shield support from their home city under a Monarchy. By default, your first three units in each city do not require Shield support. From the fourth unit on, each unit requires one Shield per turn for support.

Increasing this constant allows you more support-free units under a Monarchy. Lowering the number increases military costs by requiring that more units pay Shield support.

Communism Pays Support Past This

Default = 3

This constant represents the number of units requiring no Shield support from their home city under Communism. By default, the first three units in each city do not require Shield support. From the fourth unit on, each unit requires one Shield per turn for support.

Increasing this constant allows you more support-free units under Com-units pay Shield support.

Fundamentalism Pays Support Past This
Default = 10
This constant represents the number of units requiring no Shield support from their home city under Fundamentalism. By default, the first ten units do not require support in the amount of one Shield per turn. The exceptions to this rule are Fanatics, which never require support under a Fundamentalist government, regardless of the value of this constant.

By lowering this constant, you can make the support structure for Fundamentalism more like that of the other governments. You could virtually eliminate unit support under Fundamentalism by raising this value to an extremely high number. (How often would you build more than, say, 50 units in one city?)

Communism is Equivalent to This Palace Distance
Default = 0
This constant is the value used to determine the level of corruption and waste in your cities under Communism. In most government types, the amounts of corruption and waste that exist in a city are based on that city's distance from the civilization's capital. By default, there is no corruption or waste under Communism, because all your cities are considered to be a distance of zero squares from your capital.

By increasing this constant, you are, effectively increasing each city's distance from the capital, thus increasing the level of corruption and waste in all cities. No matter what value this constant contains, the level of corruption experienced in each city is "flat." In other words, this constant ensures that all cities are considered to be equidistant from the capital. Thus, every city experiences the same level of corruption and waste no matter what its true map-distance from the capital happens to be.

Fundamentalism Loses This % of Science
Default = 50
This constant controls the amount of Scientific research lost under a Fundamentalist government. By default, the number of Science light bulbs generated each turn is multiplied by 50% (in other words, halved) before they are applied

to the Civilization Advance research currently in progress.

Lowering this number makes Fundamentalism a much more attractive form of government, by taking away its one true penalty: reduced scientific research. By the same token, raising this value makes Fundamentalism even less effective in the area of research and advancement than it already is.

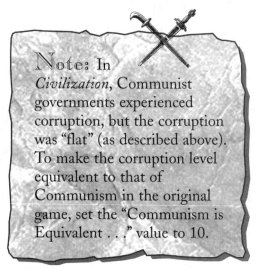

Note: In *Civilization*, Communist governments experienced corruption, but the corruption was "flat" (as described above). To make the corruption level equivalent to that of Communism in the original game, set the "Communism is Equivalent . . ." value to 10.

Percent Shield Penalty for Production Type Change

Default = 50

This constant represents the percentage penalty for changing production from one type to another in mid-production on any level except for Chieftain. By lowering this value, you lose less of your accumulated Shields each time a change of production type is made. By increasing the value, you lose more Shields when such a change is made.

Max Paradrop Range

Default = 10

This constant sets the maximum distance over which Paratroopers can make paradrops. (Paradrops are described in Chapter 8.)

Max Paradrop Range simply represents a number of map squares. Increasing the value increases the effective range of paradrops, while decreasing the value decreases the range.

Mass/Thrust Paradigm

Default = 75

The Mass/Thrust Paradigm is the equation that controls the amount of time it takes for a spaceship to reach Alpha Centauri. The factors affecting this equation are numerous. They include: the number of Thrust Components; the number of Spaceship Structural, the number of Modules, and a whole slew of less

> **Note:** Changing the rules is fun and can significantly change the "feel" of the game. Please remember, however, that the game was tested and balanced using the default values. Changing the rules alters the balance of the game and might result in a decided advantage for the player (making the game too easy) or for the computer (making the game too difficult). Be prepared for the consequences if you choose to "bend the rules."

ber of Spaceship Structural, the number of Modules, and a whole slew of less definable concepts.

I have been assured that the equation is much too complicated to be easily explained, but the effects of changing the Mass/Thrust Paradigm constant are fairly straightforward. By increasing this number, you increase the number of turns between the launch of the spaceship and its arrival at Alpha Centauri. By decreasing the number, you reduce the number of turns you have to spend waiting for your spaceship to complete its journey.

CHANGING THE RESEARCH TREE

Like the constant values used to determine many of the game's basic features and formulae, the flow of the research tree affecting the discovery of Civilization Advances is controlled from the RULES.TXT file. Civilization Advances and their accompanying data are listed under the heading "@CIVILIZE" in the text file.

By manipulating the information listed for each Advance, you can completely re-work the research tree for the game. The following sections explain how this can be accomplished.

Deciphering the Civilization Advance Data

Each Civilization Advance is listed by its name, followed by a line of somewhat cryptic information. An example appears below:

Advanced Flight,4,-2, Rad, Too,3,4;AFl

Before setting out to alter this information, it is important to know what each part of the line means. Each Civilization Advance line in RULES.TXT contains eight distinct pieces of information separated by commas or semicolons. Each line can be interpreted as follows:

Advance Name, A.I. Value, Modifier, preqA, preqB,Epoch, Category;
Abbreviation

Each piece of information, from left to right, is described below:

- ✤ **Advance Name**—The full name of the Civilization Advance
- ✤ **A.I. Value**—The value computer civilizations place on the Advance. This determines the order in which Advances are pursued (through research and exchange/theft of knowledge) by computer-controlled civilizations.
- ✤ **Modifier**—A modification to the base A.I. Value of an Advance based on the personality of rival leaders. A positive Modifier increases the value of an Advance for civilized leaders, while decreasing the value for militaristic leaders. Negative values vice-versa.
- ✤ **Prerequisite 1 (preq1)**—The abbreviated name for the Advance's prerequisite Advances. An entry of *nil* indicates that there is no prerequisite Advance.
- ✤ **Prerequisite 2 (preq2)**—The abbreviated name for the Advance's prerequisite Advances. An entry of *nil* indicates that there is no prerequisite Advance. Note that some Advances have only one prerequisite. If this is the case, Prerequisite A contains a value, while Prerequisite B is *nil*.
- ✤ **Epoch**—The historical era with which the Advance is typically associated: 0 = Ancient; 1 = Renaissance; 2 = Industrial Revolution; 3 = Modern.
- ✤ **Category**—The area of knowledge into which the Advance falls: 0 = Military; 1 = Economic; 2 = Social; 3 = Academic; 4 = Applied. The Category more or less predicts the types of units, Improvements, and Wonders to which this line of research leads.

✤ **Abbreviation**—The abbreviated name used to reference the Advance (for the purposes of prerequisites).

Altering Existing Advances

Using the information provided in the previous section, it is possible to alter the flow of research in the game by changing certain aspects of the Civilization Advances. Depending on what changes you choose to make, the effects on gameplay can be rather significant.

Altering the prerequisites of an Advance can greatly impact gameplay. You can alter the prerequisites in such a way that it is more difficult, if not impossible, to achieve a given Advance. Or, by making both prerequisites *nil*, you make it possible to research any Advance from the start of the game. However, if your goal is to handicap your computer opponents or to give yourself an advantage they do not possess, this won't help. Such changes benefit both you *and* the opposing civilizations.

The real power available when altering Advances lies in the A.I. Value and the Modifier statistics. By making adjustments to these values, you affect the choices made by your computer opponents when researching new Advances, while experiencing no ill effects to your own gameplay.

As explained earlier, the A.I. Value determines the "value" computer-controlled rulers place on each Civilization Advance. By lowering the A.I. Value of an Advance, you make that Advance less attractive to your opponents. This effect can be further enhanced by placing a negative value in the Advance's Modifier statistic. By changing the Modifier, you can fool the computer into believing that an Advance is of low military significance. This keeps the armies of war-loving enemies technologically inferior to your own for longer than normal.

All the effects described above can be further enhanced by increasing the A.I. Values and Modifiers for non-military Advances.

Also, improper alteration of prerequisites can cause an Advance to "disappear" from the research tree. If the prerequisite abbreviations entered for an

Warning:
Keep in mind that alteration of existing research statistics can cause problems in the balance of gameplay.

Advance do not match Advances that exist in the game, it becomes impossible to ever research that Advance.

Creating Your Own Civilization Advances

At the bottom of the Advances list are three inactive Advances called "User Def Tech A, B, & C". These three positions are included to allow you to create your own Civilization Advances and include them in the game. By creating new Advances, you can personally customize the research tree and experiment with new game permutations. User-defined Advances can be seamlessly integrated into the game; they can be used as prerequisites for existing Advances, units, Improvements, and Wonders, or for custom units and Advances you create yourself.

Creating a user-defined Advances are created through the following procedure:

1. Enter a new name for the Advance by overwriting the generic name.
2. Enter an A.I. Value for the Advance. When doing so, keep in mind the effects produced by the values entered in this field (described earlier in this chapter).
3. Enter a Modifier for the Advance. Again, keep in mind the effects produced by this value.
4. Enter the prerequisites required for the Advance. Use the abbreviations listed at the end of the prerequisite Advance's statistics line, not the full name of the Advance. If you choose not to require prerequisite Advances, type **nil** in place of an Advance abbreviation. If you choose to require only one Advance as a prerequisite, enter its abbreviation in the "preqA" position, and enter *nil* in the "preqB" position.
5. Enter the Epoch (historical period) with which the Advance is associated (0-3).
6. Enter the Category of the Advance (0-4).

An example and analysis of modifications to "User Def Tech A" to create an Advance is shown below:

Self-Aware Computers, 3, -2, Cmp, Sup, 3, 4;U1

- The generic title ("User Def Tech A") has been replaced with the new title.
- The A.I. Value and Modifier have be set in such a way as to give this Advance fairly high military value (the same as that of the "Stealth" Advance).
- "Self-Aware Computers" requires two prerequisite Advances: "Computers" and "Superconductor" (Cmp and Sup).
- The Advance is associated with the modern age.
- The Advance is an "applied" Advance, meaning that it leads to primarily technological benefits.
- The abbreviation "U1" remains the same.

Note that in modifying the Advance, all punctuation and spacing are maintained, and the abbreviation was not altered.

As long as the modifications to the three user-defined Advances are made as described above, the Advances are automatically linked into the game as specified by the availability flag, and they appear as research options when the appropriate prerequisites (if any) have been discovered.

MODIFICATION OF CITY IMPROVEMENTS AND WONDERS OF THE WORLD

Following the data that controls Civilization Advances, RULES.TXT contains data that defines the attributes of City Improvements and Wonders of the World. This information is found in the text file under the heading "@IMPROVE."

Deciphering Improvement and Wonder Information

Like the data presented for Civilization Advances, the information listed for Improvements and Wonders must be understood before alterations are attempted. The following is a sample listing from the Improvements/Wonders section of RULES.TXT:

Factory,   20, 4, Ind,

This information is broken down as follows:

Improvement/Wonder Name, cost, Upkeep, prerequisite

- **Improvement/Wonder Name**—The name of the Improvement or Wonder
- **Cost**—The number of Shields required in order to build the Improvement/Wonder. This number is multiplied by the "Number of Rows in Shield Box" constant (explained earlier in this chapter) in order to arrive at the actual cost.
- **Upkeep**—The amount of money that must be paid each turn in order to maintain the Improvement.
- **Prerequisite**—The Civilization Advance that must be discovered in order to build the Improvement/Wonder. If no prerequisite is required, *nil* is listed this position.

Altering Improvement/Wonder Statistics

Although there are no provisions for user-defined Improvements or Wonders, any information concerning existing Improvements and Wonders can be altered to suit your purposes:

- Cost can be altered to make the item more or less expensive. (Remember: the cost is also affected by a constant listed in the @COSMIC section of RULES.TXT.)
- Upkeep costs can be increased, reduced, or eliminated. Wonders of the World, which normally have no Upkeep, can be altered so that they do.
- Prerequisites can be changed. They can also be set to *nil*, allowing you to build Improvements and Wonders from the start of the game.

As always, keep in mind that what helps you also helps your opponents: if you can build the Manhattan Project in 3000 BC, so can they!

ALTERING THE EXPIRATION DATES OF WONDERS OF THE WORLD

Following the statistics for the City Improvements and Wonders of the World is a section headed "@ENDWONDER". This section contains information on the expiration of Wonders of the World. The following is a sample line from this section of the file:

> Cmn,   ;Marco Polo's Embassy

As you can see, each line contains only two pieces of information:

> expiration Advance, ;Wonder name

Once the expiration Advance is discovered by any civilization in the game, the effects produced by the listed Wonder expire. Wonders whose effects do not expire have *nil* listed in the first column.

Unlike previous sections, where there were several alterations possible on every line, only one item per line can be changed to produce an effect on the game: the Advance that causes each Wonder to become obsolete. This single change, however, can produce significant results.

Many Wonders of the World produce powerful effects that influence various aspects of your civilization. For example, Sun Tzu's War Academy essentially acts as a Barracks in each of your cities, allowing them to produce units that are automatically Veterans. Normally, the effects of this Wonder expire when Mobile Warfare is discovered. However, if the expiration Advance is changed to *nil*, the effects of the Wonder *never* expire.

> **Tip:** Arguably the single greatest change you can make to the RULES.TXT file is to set the expiration of Leonardo's Workshop to *nil*. With no expiration, this extraordinary Wonder continues to upgrade obsolete units for free throughout the entire game. For example, Cavalry are upgraded to Armor upon the discovery of Mobile Warfare, Cannons are upgraded to Artillery upon the discovery of Machine Tools, and so on. This one small alteration to the rules takes a Wonder that is already pretty incredible and turns it into the end-all, beat-all Wonder of the game. Just make sure that your civilization remains in control of it.

As usual, the only down-side to changing the statistics is that your opponents also benefit from the changes if they happen to control the Wonders in question.

MODIFYING AND ADDING UNITS

Statistics for all the units of the game are found under the header "@UNITS". By making alterations to the information in this area you can fine-tune units to your own specifications. You also have the option of creating up to three custom units of your own design.

Interpreting Unit Information

The statistics controlling the characteristics and operations of the units are the most complex in the RULES.TXT file. An example of a unit and its statistics is listed below:

Marines, nil, 0, 1.,0, 8a,5d, 2h,1f, 6,0, 0, Amp, 000000000000100

This complex mass of information is interpreted as follows:

unit name, until, domain, move, rng, att, def, hit, fire, cost,
hold, role, preq, flags

* **Unit Name**—The name of the unit.
* **Until**—The abbreviation for the Civilization Advance that makes the unit obsolete (obsolete units are removed from the Change Production menu). An entry of *nil* indicates that the unit does not expire.
* **Domain**—The movement domain of the unit: 0 = ground, 1 = air, 2 = sea.
* **Move**—The number of movement points available to the unit at the start of each turn.
* **Range (rng)**—The fuel supply carried by air units. This number indicates the turn on which the unit must return to a friendly city, Carrier, or air field to refuel. For example, a Bomber (whose range is 2) must refuel at the end of the second turn or be destroyed. Range is always "0" for non-air units.

* **Attack Factor (att)**—The attack factor of the unit. This number is used to determine the unit's chance to score a hit in an attack.

* **Defense Factor (def)**—The defensive strength of the unit. This number determines a defending unit's chance of fending off an attack when factored in with the attacking unit's attack statistics (see Chapter 8 for details).

* **Hit Points (hit)**—The amount of damage a unit can sustain before it is destroyed. This number is multiplied by 10 to determine the actual number of hit points the unit has (see Chapter 8 for details).

* **Firepower (fire)**—The amount of damage a unit causes to its target as the result of a successful attack (see Chapter 8 for details).

* **Cost**—The cost (in Shields) to produce the unit. This number is multiplied by the "Number of Rows in Shield Box" constant (described earlier in this chapter) in order to arrive at the actual unit cost.

* **Hold**—The number of cargo holds on board a sea unit. This statistic indicates the number of ground units that can be transported aboard the ship. For air and ground units, this number is "0."

* **A.I. Role (role)**—This characteristic defines the way a unit is utilized by computer-controlled civilizations. The values are shown in Table 10-1.

* Table 10-1. The effects of unit A.I. Role values

A.I. ROLE VALUE	EFFECT
0	Unit is used for attack
1	Unit is used for defense
2	Unit is used to achieve naval superiority
3	Unit is used to achieve air superiority
4	Unit is used as a means of sea transport
5	Unit performs Settler functions
6	Unit performs Diplomat functions
7	Unit performs trade functions

As shown in Table 10-1, values of 0 through 4 affect only the role the unit serves in computer-controlled civilizations. An A.I. Role value of 5, 6, or 7, however, actually affects the abilities of the unit in general. For example, any unit with an A.I. Role of 5 can perform all the functions normally associated with Settlers and Engineers. Assigning a 5 to an Armor unit allows the Armor unit to build cities, build roads, irrigate land, and so forth. Likewise, assigning a 6 to a unit's A.I. Role allows a unit to perform all the functions associated with Diplomats and Spies, and assigning a 7 to A.I. Role allows a unit to perform the trade functions of Caravans and Freight units.

* **Prerequisite (preq)**—The abbreviation for the Civilization Advance that must be discovered in order to build the unit. If *nil* appears in this category, no prerequisite Advance is required.

* **Flags**—These values determine the unit's special characteristics, if any. The system used to specify the unit's special characteristics is shown in Table 10-2.

* **Table 10-2.** The Effects of Unit Flag Values

Unit Flag Value	Effect
000000000000001	Unit has two-spaces of visibility
000000000000010	Unit ignores enemy zones of control
000000000000100	Unit can attack directly from a ship
000000000001000	Unit has Submarine advantages/disadvantages
000000000010000	Unit can attack air units
000000000100000	Unit can be lost at sea (like a Trireme)
000000001000000	Unit's attacks ignore the effects of City Walls
000000010000000	Unit can transport air units
000000100000000	Unit can make paradrops
000001000000000	Unit uses only ⅓ movement point in any Terrain
000010000000000	Defense Factor doubled versus mounted units
000100000000000	Unit requires no support under Fundamentalism
001000000000000	Unit is destroyed after attacking (like missiles)
010000000000000	Defense Factor doubled versus air units
100000000000000	Unit can spot Submarines

The characteristics defined in the unit Flags are combined to form a composite of each unit's abilities. For example, consider the Flags for the Helicopter unit shown below:

100000000000001

The Helicopter's Flags indicate the following:

- The unit has a visibility of two squares.
- The unit can spot Submarines.

Altering Existing Units

As with Advances, Improvements, and Wonders, it is possible to alter the characteristics of any unit in the game by manipulating its statistics. Movement factors can be increased or decreased. Attack, Defense, Hit Points, and Firepower can be adjusted to create ultimate fighting machines. Just about any modification can be made to make units more unique or more effective. As always, keep in mind that these changes, for better or worse, also affect the enemy.

Extra caution should be exercised when adjusting the unit's Flags. Because the Flags have been designed to handle so many different unit types and situations it is possible to produce odd (or even catastrophic) game effects by mixing nonsensical values. For example, by setting the Flags in a certain way, you could create a Carrier that can be paradropped. Care must be taken not to create such combinations.

Creating Custom Units

Civilization II provides three customizable unit types. The user-definable units appear at the end of the list and are labeled "Extra Land," "Extra Ship," and "Extra Air.

To create a custom unit type, follow these steps:

1. Enter a new name for the unit by overwriting the generic name.
2. Enter the name of the Advance that makes the unit obsolete. Use the abbreviated name for the Advance (described earlier in this chapter). If the unit doesn't become obsolete, enter *nil*.

3. Specify the unit's domain (0 = land, 1 = sea, 2 = air).

4. Enter the unit's Movement Factor.

5. Enter the unit's Range. If the unit is not an air unit, enter "0" for this statistic.

6. Enter the unit's Attack Factor.

7. Enter the unit's Defense Factor.

8. Enter the number of Hit Points the unit possesses. (Remember—this number is multiplied by 10 to get the unit's actual number of Hit Points.)

9. Enter the unit's Firepower rating.

10. Enter the Cost of the unit. (Remember—this number is multiplied by the "Number of Rows in Shield Box" constant to get the actual price of the unit.)

11. If the unit is a sea unit, decide how many cargo Hold spaces are available to carry ground units. If the unit is not a sea unit, enter "0" for the Hold value.

12. Decide the type of A.I. Role you want the unit to perform and enter a value of 0 to 7.

13. Enter the name of the Advance required in order to build the unit. Use the abbreviated name for the Advance. If the unit doesn't require a prerequisite Advance, enter *nil*.

14. Finally, set the unit's Flags. (Remember—to avoid bizarre and unforeseen circumstances, avoid mixing nonsensical Flag values.)

An example and analysis of a custom unit appears below. Note that all punctuation remains the same as presented in the text file:

Hovercraft, nil, 2, 8., 0, 0a,1d, 2h,2f, 7,8, 4, MP, 100000000000001

✤ The generic name has been replaced with the new unit name.

✤ The Obsolete value indicates that the unit does not become obsolete.

✤ The unit has a Domain of "2" (it is a sea unit).

✤ The unit has 8 movement points each turn.

✤ The unit has a range of "0" (it is not an air unit).

✤ The unit has an Attack Factor of "0" (it cannot attack) and a Defense Factor of "1".

- The unit has a Hit Point rating of "2" (which is multiplied by 10, for a total of 20 Hit Points).

- The unit has a Firepower rating of "2". (A unit must have a Firepower rating even if it cannot attack.)

- The unit has a Cost of 70 Shields. (The cost factor (7) multiplied by the default "Number of Rows in Shield Box" constant (10).)

- A total of 8 ground units can be carried in the Hovercraft's Hold.

- The Hovercraft has an A.I. Role of 4, indicating that it is used by computer civilizations as a sea transport.

- The Prerequisite value indicates that the unit requires the discovery of Mass Production (MP).

- The unit Flags have been set so that the Hovercraft has a visibility range of 2 and is able to spot Submarines.

Although the three user-definable units included in the text file are specifically labeled as one land, one sea, and one air unit, it is not necessary to use them as such. You can mix and match the three unit types in any combination; simply change the Domain of each custom unit to the desired value.

Once again, it is important to remember that when you make a "super-unit" capable of wiping out your enemies, just remember that the enemy has access to that unit as well. You might find yourself up against an ultimate weapon of your own design.

Tip: Let's say you REALLY want to cheat. If you want to create an ultimate combat unit, but you don't want it used against you, set its A.I. Role to 7. This essentially defines the computer's use of the unit as a trade unit, which is never used for attack. At the very worst, your computer-controlled enemy might establish a nasty trade route with one of your cities—but you'll never have to fight your ultimate fighting machine. Note that such a unit cannot be used to attack a city (it can only establish a trade route when you try!), but it can be used to defend a city and to attack units.

Icons for Custom Images

Although it is easy to define custom units in the game, the image used for the custom unit's icon cannot be easily customized. The artwork for unit icons are stored in a file called UNITS.GIF. It is inadvisable to tamper with this file. To accommodate the use of the three custom units, generic icons have been provided for each. The generic icons are automatically accessed when the custom units become active.

MODIFICATION OF TERRAIN TYPES

As described in Chapter 4, each Terrain type in *Civilization II* produces a certain amount of Food, Shields, and Trade. These values, like so many other game data values, are contained in RULES.TXT. The Terrain statistics appear beneath the header "@TERRAIN." This section also contains the statistics for each Special Resource type (Buffalo, Gold, Gems, and so on). By modifying the Terrain and Special Resource statistics, you can make the game world a better and more profitable place for your civilization.

Interpreting the Terrain Statistics

The statistics for Terrain and Special Resources appear in a format similar to that of the other game statistics found in the text file. An example of a Terrain type and its statistics appears below:

Desert, 1,2, 0,1,0, yes, 1, 5, 5, yes, 1, 5, 3, Pla, ;Drt

These statistics are interpreted as follows:

Name, move, def, fd, shd, trd, irr, i bns, i turns,
ai irr, mne, m bns, m turns, ai mne, trans, ;abbr

The first six pieces of data appear for both Terrain types and Special Resources:

* **Name**—The name of the Terrain or Special Resource type.
* **Movement Cost (move)**—The number of unit movement points that must be expended to move through the Terrain type.
* **Defensive Bonus (def)**—The bonus added to a unit's Defense Factor

when the unit occupies the Terrain type. This number is multiplied by 50 to get the percentage of the unit's normal Defense Factor with which it can defend in that Terrain type.

EXAMPLE: A Terrain type with a Defensive Bonus of "3" means that a unit defends with 150% of its normal Defense Factor; so a unit with a Defense Factor of 2 defends as if it had a Defense Factor of 3 while occupying that Terrain type.

* **Food (fd)**—The number of Food units produced by the Terrain/Resource.

* **Shields (shd)**—The number of Shields produced by the Terrain/Resource.

* **Trade (trd)**—The number of units of Trade produced by the Terrain/Resource.

The following statistics appear only for the eleven Terrain Types:

* **Irrigation (irr)**—This piece of data indicates whether or not a Terrain type can be irrigated by Settlers/Engineers. "Yes" indicates that irrigation is possible, "no" indicates that it is not. When a Terrain Abbreviation appears in this category, it indicates that the Terrain is converted to the Terrain type listed in this category when irrigated.

    EXAMPLE: The Irrigation statistic for the "Forest" Terrain type is *Pln.* This indicates that, when irrigated, a Forest square is converted to a Plains square.

* **Irrigation Bonus (i bns)**—Indicates the number of additional Food units produced by the Terrain type as a result of irrigation.

* **Turns to Irrigate (i turns)**—The base number of turns required for a Settler unit to irrigate the Terrain type.

* **A.I. Irrigation (ai irr)**—The minimum system of government a computer-controlled civilization must achieve before it "wants" to irrigate the Terrain type. This is a value from 0 to 6. The effects of each value are shown in Table 10-4.

* **Mining (mne)**—This indicates whether or not a Terrain type can be mined by Settlers/Engineers. "Yes" indicates that mining is possible, "no" indicates that it is not. When a Terrain Abbreviation appears in

✤ **Table 10-4.** The Effects of A.I. Irrigate and A.I. Mining Values of Terrain Types on Computer Civilizations

A.I. VALUE	EFFECT
0	Never irrigated/mined by computer civilizations.
1	Computer civilization can always irrigate/mine (Despotism).
2	Not irrigated/mined by computer civs until the discovery of Monarchy.
3	Not irrigated/mined by computer civs until the discovery of Communism.
4	Not irrigated/mined by computer civs until the discovery of Fundamentalism.
5	Not irrigated/mined by computer civs until the discovery of the Republic.
6	Not irrigated/mined by computer civs until the discovery of Democracy.

this category, it indicates that the Terrain is converted to the Terrain type listed in this category when mined.

EXAMPLE: The Mining statistic for the "Swamp" Terrain type is *For*. This indicates that, when mined, a Swamp square is converted to a Forest square.

> **Warning:** Do not change the Abbreviation for any Terrain type. This value is used to reference each type of Terrain for the purposes of Terrain improvements and transformation.

✤ **Mining Bonus (m bns)**—Indicates the number of additional Shields produced by the Terrain as a result of mining.

✤ **Turns to Mine (m turns)**—The base number of turns required for a Settler unit to mine the Terrain.

✤ **A.I. Mining (ai mne)**—The minimum system of government a computer-controlled civilization must achieve before it "wants" to mine the Terrain type. This is a value from 0 to 6. The effects of each value, which are the same as the values for "A.I. Irrigation", are shown in Table 10-4.

Note: Upon examining the statistics listed for Grasslands in RULES.TXT, you might have noticed that this type of Terrain appears to generate one Shield, while in the game it actually generates none. The reason for this is that some Grassland squares actually do produce one Shield. These squares, which are referred to as the Special Resource "Grassland (Shield)" are actually the default form of Grasslands. When the map is generated, approximately 50% of the Grassland squares are Grassland (Shield), and the rest produce no Shields.

- **Transform**—This indicates the type of Terrain that results from ordering an Engineer to transform the Terrain type. This statistic contains the abbreviation of the resulting Terrain type.

  EXAMPLE: The "Transform" statistic for the "Tundra" terrain type is "Des," indicating that a Tundra square is converted to Desert square through Engineer transformation.

- **Abbreviation (abbr)**—The abbreviated name of the Terrain type

Altering Terrain and Special Resource Statistics—Some Suggestions

No provision is made for creating custom Terrain or Special Resource types; however, existing Terrain and Resources can be improved or made less effective if desired.

Certainly, there are great advantages to improving the characteristics of the Terrain. By increasing the amount of Food, Shields, and Trade produced, the Terrain becomes more valuable which, in turn, allows your cites to be more prosperous and to grow more quickly.

In the same vein, you could alter the Irrigation and Mining statistics themselves so that the Terrain can be transformed to different Terrain types through these processes. For example, Deserts can be both irrigated and mined for bonus

Food and Shields respectively. By changing the Desert's Irrigation statistic from "yes" to "Gra," you give Settlers and Engineers the ability to change Deserts to Grasslands through irrigation. The result is a much more useful Terrain type rather than the meager Food bonus provided by normal irrigation of a Desert.

If you don't want to make such blatant changes to resource production, you can make it easier for your Settlers/Engineers to improve the Terrain by decreasing the Irrigate and Mine Turns statistics. This allows irrigation and mines to be built more quickly. You could also increase the Irrigation and Mine Bonus statistics so that these Terrain improvements lead to even more valuable results.

A subtle, yet powerful change that can be made is to increase the Defensive Bonus for certain Terrain types. The Defensive Bonus is gained not only by units in the field, but by units defending cities as well. Unfortunately, by default, the Terrain types with the highest Defensive Bonus values are unsuitable as city sites due to their low resource production. By increasing the Defensive Bonus of productive Terrain (such as Plains, which normally has no Defensive Bonus), you create a Terrain type that is not only resource-rich, but highly defensible.

As always, feel free to experiment with different changes of your own. Just remember—what helps you, helps your opponents (and vice-versa).

MODIFICATION OF LEADER PERSONALITIES

Certain behavior patterns of the leaders of computer-controlled civilizations are based on values set in the RULES.TXT file. The information concerning each leader can be found under the heading "@LEADERS." By altering certain data in this section of the file, you can assume some control over the attitudes and actions of your computer opponents.

Interpreting Leader Information

An example of a leader's statistics appears below. (Note that due to the length of some of the information fields, the statistics for a given leader might span two lines in the file.)

Ramesses, Cleopatra, 1, 4, 0, Egyptians, Egyptian, 0, 0, 1, 1, Pharaoh, Pharaoh, 2, Great Pharaoh, Great Pharaoh

The leader data is interpreted as follows:

m name, f name, m/f, color, style, plural, adjective, attack,
expand, civilized, govt, m title, f title

✤ **Male/Female Name (m name, f name)**—The name of the civilization's leader. The first field contains a name for a male leader, the second field contains the name for a female leader.

✤ **Male or Female (m/f)**—Identifies the leader of the civilization as either male (0) or female (1).

✤ **Color**—The color used to identify the units and cities of the leader's civilization. The color codes range from 1 to 7, as shown in Table 10-5.

✤ **City Style (style)**—The architectural style of the leader's cities. Style values range from 0 to 3, as shown in Table 10-6. Note that these are the same styles from which you select your own city style during game setup.

✤ **Plural**—The plural version of the civilization's name (example: Egyptians).

✤ **Adjective**—The adjective used when describing achievements of the civilization. (EXAMPLE: "*Egyptian* wise men discover. . . .")

✤ **Attack**—The personality trait of the leader that determines whether he/she is likely to initiate an attack in any given situation. Aggressive

✤ **Table 10-5**. Color Code Values for Computer-Controlled Leaders

CODE	COLOR
1	White
2	Green
3	Blue
4	Yellow
5	Light Blue
6	Orange
7	Violet

Sid Meier's Civilization II: The Official Stategy Guide

✤ **Table 10-6.** City Style Values for Computer-Controlled Civilizations

VALUE	CITY STYLE
0	Bronze Age Monolith
1	Classical Forum
2	Far East Pavilion
3	Medieval Castle

leaders (leaders likely to attack) have an Attack value of "1." Rational leaders (more prone to negotiation than attack) have an Attack value of "–1." Leaders whose actions fall in between these attitudes have an Attack value of "0."

✤ **Expand**—The personality trait of the leader that determines how quickly he/she expands his/her empire. Expansionists (leaders who aggressively expand the boundaries of their civilizations) have an Expand value of "1." Perfectionists (leaders who prefer a smaller number of prosperous cities to a large number of mediocre cities) have an Expand value of "-1." Leaders whose actions fall in between these attitudes have an Expand value of "0."

✤ **Civilized**—The personality trait that determines whether or not the leader is "civilized". Civilized leaders (those more likely to pursue knowledge than to build large military forces) have a Civilized value of "1." Militaristic leaders (those who prefer military might over knowledge) have a Civilized value of "-1." Leaders whose actions fall in between these attitudes have a Civilized value of "0."

✤ **Government Type (govt)**—This number represents one of the seven forms of government available in the game, as shown in Table 10-7.

✤ **Male/Female Title (m title, f title)**—The titles used for male leaders (m title) and female leaders (f title) under the form of government specified in "Government Type" (govt).

For each form of government, there are default honorifics, or titles, used to refer to the ruler of a civilization using that particular government type. These titles are listed in RULES.TXT under the heading "@GOVERNMENTS." If no

✤ Table 10-7. Government Values Used for Title Replacement

VALUE	FORM OF GOVERNMENT
0	Anarchy
1	Despotism
2	Monarchy
3	Communism
4	Fundamentalism
5	Republic
6	Democracy

"Government Type" and "Male/Female Title" are provided in the data line for a ruler, the default honorifics are used. If you want a leader to be addressed by a specific title under one particular form of government, specify the value corresponding to the government in the "Government Type" position, and the custom titles you wish to use in the "Male/Female Title" positions.

Note: The "Government Type" and "Male/Female Title" statistics might be a bit confusing. These values are used to customize the titles used for the leader of a particular race under specific forms of government.

This process can be repeated for as many government types as you want by simply adding them on to the end of the leader's data line. Upon examination of the leader data listed in the text file, you will note that many of the leaders have customized titles listed for one or more government types.

For example, examine the information for the Egyptian leader listed earlier in this section. You can see that for Government Type "1" (Despotism) the game is instructed to use the Male/Female Titles "Pharaoh" and "Pharaoh." These replace the default titles of "Emperor" and "Empress" normally used for Despotic leaders. Also, for Government Type "2" (Monarchy), the Egyptians substitute "Great Pharaoh" for both the Male and Female Titles normally used in a Monarchy ("King" and "Queen"). The titles used for Government Types "0" and "3" through "6" are not specified in the data line, and therefore use the default titles in the "@GOVERNMENTS" section of the file.

The title substitution provided by these two pieces of data for computer-controlled leaders is exactly the same as changing your own titles for each form of government during game setup.

Changing Leadership Characteristics — Some Suggestions

Much of the information contained in the "@LEADERS" section of the text file is superficial. You can change the names and titles used by the computer-controlled leaders, as well as the color and style of city they use. You can also change the default sex of the leader by changing the "Male/Female" attribute.

The meaningful changes that you can make involve the "Attack," "Expand," and "Civilized" categories. As noted earlier, each of these statistics has only three possible values: "1," "0," and "-1" (any other value entered is meaningless). By changing any or all of these statistics to their opposite value, you can drastically alter the personality and attitude of the leader. Normally aggressive leaders, like Louis XIV of the French and Lenin of the Russians, can be made rational. Perfectionists like Gandhi of India can be turned into territory-grubbing expansionists. And normally neutral leaders like Sitting Bull of the Sioux can be turned into militaristic warmongers.

Tinkering with the personalities of the computer-controlled leaders can add variety to the game. Do some experimentation, and find out what types of leaders you can produce through different combinations of Attack, Expand, and Civilized statistics.

MISCELLANEOUS CUSTOMIZATIONS AND CHANGES

All of the meaningful changes that can be made to gameplay have been addressed in previous sections of this chapter. However, the RULES.TXT file contains several other pieces of information that can be altered. While these remaining changes are strictly superficial, they can be fun and (in some ways) mildly useful.

Permanent Changes to Leader Titles

As mentioned earlier, a list of default male and female honorifics, or titles, used for leaders is maintained in the section of the text file headed "@GOVERNMENTS."

When you choose a custom tribe during game setup, you are given the opportunity to change the titles by which the game addresses you under each form of government. If you find that you are constantly using the same custom titles for each type of government, you can save yourself a few seconds at the start of the game by permanently changing the titles for each government type in the text file. Once changed and saved, the titles you entered in the file now appear as the default titles for each government type. Of course, if you so desire, the titles can still be changed in the normal manner during game setup.

Changing the Names of Trade Commodities

Under the heading "@CARAVAN" appears a list of 16 items. These are the trade commodities that appear in each city's supply and demand list in the City Display Info section and on the list of supplies that can be carried by Caravans and Freight units. The names of these trade goods can be changed to anything you want, although this has no effect whatsoever on gameplay (other than to display different names for trade commodities, of course).

Changing Unit Order Banners

Under the heading "@ORDERS" is a list of orders describing actions that last for more than one turn (Build Road, Clean Pollution, and so on). Next to the order itself is a single letter. This is the label displayed in a unit's banner (the little shield that shows the unit's color, damage, and so forth) while that unit is carrying out the order given. For example, when a Settler is building a road, an "R" appears in its banner until the current section of road has been completed.

By changing the letter listed next to the order, you can change the label that appears in the unit's banner while the order is being executed. If the single letter is replaced with a label consisting of multiple characters, only the first character is displayed in the unit banner.

Such changes have no effect on gameplay.

Changing the Difficulty Labels

Under the heading "@DIFFICULTY," is a list of the six difficulty levels of the game. This list merely acts as a source of labels used to refer to difficulty levels in the game; you can change them to whatever names you want. This has no effect on gameplay.

Changing Attitude Descriptions

The last section of the RULES.TXT file, headed "@ATTITUDES," lists the nine possible moods that are experienced by opposing civilizations. One of these mood descriptions appears in the King Screen when you make contact with another civilization.

The descriptions can be changed to whatever descriptive terms you feel best convey the moods presented. Once changed, the new descriptions appear in King Screens during contact with other civilizations. Such changes have no effect on gameplay.

What SHOULDN'T Be Changed

As you have gathered from the information presented in this chapter, you can make alterations to nearly every section of RULES.TXT without causing problems other than gameplay abnormalities related to altered statistics.

Problems arise if any of the header lines ("@COSMIC," for example) are deleted or altered. Without a section header, the program cannot find the data for that section. This causes a catastrophic malfunction of the game. Less serious (but very troublesome) problems also arise if any item (Advance, Improvement, Unit, etc.) is deleted completely from the file. If this occurs, the program might retrieve information improperly, fouling up statistics in the Civilopedia and certain aspects of gameplay.

As long as these two scenarios are avoided, you should have no problems.

Changing Text Files Other Than "RULES.TXT"

A great deal of data not dealing directly with the statistics of gameplay is stored in text files. Among other things, this facilitates the easy translation of the game to other languages. The descriptive text for the Civilopedia, item names listed in game menus, and many other text-oriented data items are stored and installed as text files, and can be edited in the same manner as RULES.TXT.

Don't do it.

RULES.TXT was designed to be edited by players. The other text files are not. Alteration of other text files can cause the game to malfunction. There is nothing that needs to be changed in any of the other text files, so leave them alone!

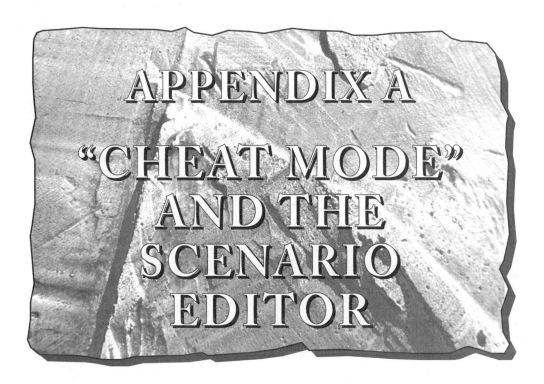

APPENDIX A
"CHEAT MODE" AND THE SCENARIO EDITOR

*A*nd now, for those of you who *really* want to cheat, with no subtlety involved, you have finally reached the section of the book you have been waiting for.

During the testing phase of *Civilization II*, a "cheat mode" was included to allow for the testing of changes made to units normally available only late in the game and other subtle aspects of the game. During Beta testing, the "cheat mode" was always active. The "cheat mode" is still available in the released version of the game, but it must be activated by choosing "Toggle Cheat Mode" from the Cheat menu.

Near the end of the development cycle, a number of pre-generated scenarios were added to the game. The Cheat Mode incorporates several functions which allow you to modify the existing scenarios and to create scenarios of your own.

The following sections explain the options on the Cheat menu. The keyboard command for each cheat is listed next to the name of the feature.

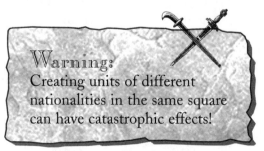

Note: When you choose to activate the cheat mode, your score for the rest of that game is marked to indicate that you cheated to attain the score.

Create Unit (Shift F1)

This feature allows you to instantly create any unit in the game. When this feature is selected, a menu appears showing all the units you can build at your current level of technology. You can create any of these units by simply clicking the desired unit and then clicking OK.

The buttons along the bottom of the menu enhance the abilities of the Create Unit feature:

* **Foreign**—Allows you to create a unit and assign it to any computer opponent's civilization

* **Veteran**—Automatically assigns Veteran status to any unit created with the Create Unit feature

* **Obs**—Allows you to create units that have become obsolete in the current game

* **Adv**—Allows you to create any unit available in the game regardless of whether you have discovered the necessary Advance to allow the unit.

Units created through this cheat are subject to normal Shield support rules. They are assigned to the friendly city nearest the unit's point of origin (if the unit created is a foreign unit, it is assigned to the nearest city belonging to that civilization). Create Unit places the new unit at the current cursor or active unit location. This forces you to be careful about where the cursor is when you create a unit. Land units created in Ocean squares are unable to move. Sea units created on land suffer the same fate.

Warning: Creating units of different nationalities in the same square can have catastrophic effects!

Reveal Map (Shift F2)

This cheat allows you to see as little or as much of the world map as you want by revealing black sections of the world that you have not yet explored. You have the option to reveal only the portion of the map visible to specific opponents or to reveal the entire world map. Once the map is revealed, you can click on any civilization's city and manipulate it as if it were your own.

Set Human Player (Shift F3)

Don't particularly like the way your game is going? Jealous of all the Advances and cool units an opponent has? Well, the Set Human Player feature lets you do something about this situation.

With this cheat, a menu appears allowing you to trade places with any computer-controlled civilization by simply clicking the button next to their name. When you do so, you instantly take over all their cities, units, and technology. In turn, the computer player you replace takes over and plays your original civilization. Set Human Player also provides an option to set the game for "No Human Player," allowing the computer to play against itself.

Set Game Year (Shift F4)

This cheat option allows you to reset the number of turns that have elapsed since the beginning of the game. With this cheat, you can effectively lengthen or shorten the game.

Kill Civilization (Shift F5)

Nuclear Missiles not powerful enough for you? Try the Kill Civilization cheat instead. This option brings up a menu of all civilizations in the game. Click the button next to an opposing civilization's name and then click OK. The selected civilization ceases to exist: all their cities and units are instantly destroyed. Only terrain improvements remain to show that there was once a thriving culture in the area. You can, if you so desire, destroy your own civilization in this manner as well!

Technology Advance ([Shift][F6]); Edit Technologies ([Ctrl][Shift][F5])

Tired of that long waiting period between the discovery of new Civilization Advances? The Technology Advance cheat instantly grants you the Advance you are currently researching.

If you want even more control over the discovery of Advances by both your own civilization and your opponents, select "Edit Technologies". When this option is chosen, pick a civilization from the list provided. This opens a menu that lists all the Civilization Advances in the game. Advances marked with a dash (-) have not yet been researched because the chosen civilization has not yet researched the required prerequisite Advances. Advances without a notation are ones which have not yet been researched, but for which the chosen civilization possesses the prerequisites. Advances marked with an asterisk (*) have already been discovered by the selected civilization.

By clicking the Advance name, you can toggle the Advance on and off; that is, you can give the Advance to or take the Advance away from the chosen civilization. If you want to give (or take away) *all* of the Civilization Advances, click the "Give/Take All" button.

Force Government ([Shift][F7])

This cheat allows you, at any time during the game, to switch to any of the six government types regardless of whether you have discovered them. This change of government works just like a Revolution, except that the change is instantaneous and there is no period of Anarchy.

Change Terrain At Cursor ([Shift][F8])

This useful cheat function brings up a dialog box listing all the possible Terrain improvements (roads, irrigation, etc.) for the square currently occupied by the cursor or the currently active unit. By choosing items from the menu, you can instantly improve the Terrain square to its maximum potential by building any Terrain improvement you want to build there.

In addition, you can use this function to instantly change a selected Terrain square to any Terrain type in the game. When you click the "Terrain" button, a

> **Tip:** The ability to change Terrain types during the game is a great cheat. You can use it to isolate an enemy (surround his cities with Oceans, for instance), or to create a land bridge between continents for colonization and exploration purposes.

list of Terrain types appears. Simply click the type of Terrain you want and then click "OK".

Destroy All Units At Cursor (Ctrl Shift D)

The Destroy All Units cheat does just what its name suggests. All units occupying the Terrain square at the cursor's position are instantly destroyed.

Change Money (Shift F9)

This cheat allows you to choose the amount of money you want in your treasury. Any amount from 0 to 30,000 can be entered. When the treasury exceeds 30,000, odd things start happening to your money supply, so *do not exceed this amount.*

Edit Unit (Ctrl Shift U)

The Edit Unit cheat allows you to make certain changes to the currently active unit or to the unit that occupies the cursor position. The following options are available:

- ❖ **Toggle Veteran Status:** Switches the unit from normal to Veteran status (and vice-versa)
- ❖ **Clear Movement Allowance:** Resets the unit to its full movement allowance. For example, say a unit with a Movement Factor of three has only one space of movement remaining. Selecting this option would reset the unit's movement to three, allowing the unit to move farther.

> **Tip:** The Set Home City option is great for Caravans and Freight units. For example, if you have two cities that are close to one another, you can build a Caravan in one city and send it to the other. Just before the Caravan enters the city, set the Caravan's home city to the city that is most distant from the Caravan's destination. This gets you the benefits of a long-distance trade route without having to actually move the Caravan unit over the intervening Terrain. Using this same strategy, you could establish all of your trade routes with Caravan and Freight units built in a single city.

✤ **Set Hit Points:** Allows you to raise or lower a unit's level of sustained damage (0 = no damage, 20 = all but dead)

✤ **Set Home City:** Lets you choose a new home city for the unit from a list of all of your cities. If you don't want the unit to have a home city (in other words, you want the unit to be support-free), click the "None" button.

✤ **Fortify/Unfortify:** Instantly fortifies or unfortifies the unit in its current position

✤ **Change Caravan Commodity:** Allows you to change the trade goods carried by a Caravan or Freight unit at any time. You choose the new cargo from a list of all the trade goods available in the game.

Edit City (Ctrl Shift C)

This feature, which is half cheat and half scenario editor, allows you to change many of the vital features of a city. To use this feature, you must place the cursor on the city you want to alter. The following options are available:

✤ **Change Size:** Let's you to choose the number of citizens you want in the city

✤ **Delete All Wonders:** Removes all the Wonders of the World from the chosen city. Once removed, these Wonders once again become available for construction by any civilization in the game.

❧ **Clear Disorder and We Love King:** Instantly cancels the effects of Civil Disorder or We Love the King Day in the chosen city for the current turn. Note that this does *not* remove the factors that caused the Disorder or We Love the King Day celebration. Assuming that these conditions are not changed in some way, the Disorder or the celebration will occur again on the following turn.

Warning: There are two things to watch out for when altering city size. First, as far as the game is concerned, you have to consider the happiness of the population: remember, happiness is affected by city size. You must also make sure that Food supplies are adequate to support the population size chosen.

The other precaution has to do with the number of citizens you choose. The chosen population must be between 1 and 127. Values outside this range cause unpredictable and undesirable results.

❧ **Copy Another City's Improvements:** This option presents a list of all the cities (friendly and otherwise) in the game. When you select a city from the list, all of the Improvements (but *not* the Wonders) in that city are instantly added to the city you are editing.

❧ **Set Shield Progress:** Allows you to set the number of Shields that have been allocated to the item currently being built in the city.

Edit King (Ctrl Shift K)

Like Edit City, this option is half cheat and half scenario editor. It allows you to control a wide variety of factors that affect both research progress and interaction and attitudes amongst the civilizations in the game.

When you activate this option, you must first choose one of the civilizations in the current game. For reference purposes, we'll call this "*civilization A*". All the changes you make afterwards pertain to civilization A. For example, if you choose the Romans, and you then Edit Treaties, you are editing treaties between the Romans and other civilizations.

The following choices are available:

* **Edit Treaties:** Allows you to edit the treaty status between *civilization A* and another civilization (*civilization B*). All of the options on the Edit Treaties menu are simply check boxes: if the box is checked, the option is active. The following options are available:

* **Contact:** When chosen, it means contact has been madebetween *civilizations A* and *B*.

* **Cease Fire:** A cease fire situation exists between *civilizations A* and *B*.

* **Peace:** A peace treaty exists between *civilizations A* and *B*.

* **Allied:** A military alliance exists between *civilizations A* and *B*.

* **War:** *Civilizations A* and *B* are at war.

* **Vendetta:** A long-lasting state of war exists between*civilizations A* and *B*. This is basically a scenario option, allowing you to set up pre-existing conditions of war between civilizations in the scenario.

* **Embassy:** *Civilization A* has an embassy with *civilization B*.

* **Set Last Contact:** Allows you to set the number of the last turn *civilization A* made contact with *civilization B*

* **Set Attitude:** Sets *civilization A*'s current attitude toward *civilization B* (see Table 9-2 for the effects of attitude values)

* **Set Reputation:** Sets *civilization A*'s reputation level (see Table 9-3 for the effects of reputation values)

* **Clear Patience:** Clears *civilization A*'s patience level with *civilization B* (patience is explained in Chapter 9)

* **Clear All Embassies:** Removes all of *civilization A*'s embassies with other civilizations

* **Set Research Goal:** Allows you to choose a Civilization Advance for civilization A to research. If civilization A was already researching a topic, that topic is replaced by the new choice when you choose Set Research Goal. Any Science icons already accumulated are applied to the new research topic.

* **Set Research Progress:** Allows you to enter the number of Science icons that *civilization A* has accumulated toward its current research project (from one to the maximum number of Science icons required to discover the Advance).

* **Clear Research Goal:** Sets *civilization A's* current research goal to nothing. A new research goal for civilization A is chosen on the following turn. Any Science icons already accumulated are applied to the new research topic when one is chosen.

* **Edit Name:** Allows you to change the king and tribe name for civilization A

* **Copy Another King's Tech:** Gives *civilization A* all of the Advances currently possessed by *civilization B* (the ones that *civilization A* doesn't already have)

Scenario Parameters (Ctrl Shift P)

This option's primary function is to set up the conditions for a new scenario, or to modify an existing scenario. There are, however, some parameters that can be used as cheats as well. The following options are available:

* **Tech Paradigm:** Increases or decreases the base number of Science icons required for the discovery of new Civilization Advances. Lower numbers make research faster; higher numbers make research slower. (The default value is 10.)

* **Turn Year Increment:** Sets the amount of time that passes each turn. Positive values indicate the number of years that pass each turn (example: a value of 10 means that 10 years pass each turn). If a negative value is entered, it changes the time system from years to months (example: a value of -6 means that 6 months pass each game turn). The default value, 0, means that time passes normally for the selected difficulty level (see Table 2-1 for details).

* **Starting Year:** Sets the starting year for the scenario. Negative values are BC; positive values are AD (example: a value of -1701 is the year 1701 BC). If you have set the Turn Year Increment to months instead

of years, multiply the starting year by 12 to get the desired starting date (example: if you want to start in early 100 AD, you would have to enter 1200 for the Starting Year).

- **Maximum Turns:** Sets the maximum number of turns that can be played before the scenario ends
- **Toggle Scenario Flag:** Turns a normal game into a scenario (subject to the currently selected Scenario Parameters) and vice-versa
- **Wipe All Goody Boxes:** Removes all unexplored villages (huts) from the map (For more information on villages, see Chapter 4.)
- **Restore All Goody Boxes:** Restores all villages (huts) to the map; even the ones that have already been explored
- **Reveal Whole Map:** Removes all unexplored (black) territory from the map
- **Cover Whole Map:** Blacks out the entire map except for your civilization's existing cities
- **Set Scenario Name:** Allows you to name your scenario

Save As Scenario (Ctrl Shift S)

Saves the current game as a scenario (.SCN) file.

The Production Menu Cheat

In addition to the cheats available from the Cheat menu, there is a "Cheat!" button located at the bottom of the City Screen Production Menu. Clicking this button instantly completes the unit, Improvement, or Wonder currently under construction in the city. As an added bonus, any Shields you have already allocated to that item are not lost—they are applied to the next item you choose to build (subject, of course, to the normal production-switching penalty where applicable).

INDEX

Index

Production. *See also* Bonuses; Penalties
  phase of game, 29-30
Production Box, 28
  "Buy" button, 28
Pyramids, 209, 224
  food production and, 83
  Granaries and, 191, 224

R

Radio, 125, 164
Raging Hordes Barbarian activity, 44
Railroads, 125, 164
  Civilization Advance, 77
  Navigation and, 160
  resource production and, 81
Raw materials. *See* Shields
Reassigning units for Shield production, 95-96
Recycling, 125, 165
Recycling Centers, 184, 199
Refining, 125, 165
Refrigeration, 125, 166
Renaissance, 8
Republic, 11, 282, 286-288
  bypassing Monarchy for, 177
  Civil Disorder threat in, 287
  Civilization Advance, 125, 166-167
  drawbacks of, 287
  finances in, 111
  gray face icon, 25
  in peaceful game, 180
  revolution in, 290
  Senate in, 288
  Shakespeare's Theatre and, 225
Reputation Scale, 294-296
Research. *See also* Science
  indicator, 17
  paths, 6
  strategies for, 176-177
  Wine square, building on, 73
Research Labs, 9, 184, 199
  Science output, 84
Research Tree, changing the, 323-327
Resource Map, 21-22
Resources, 48. *See also* Food; Raw materials;
    Shields; Trade
  governments and, 84

increasing production of, 80-84
opposing units and nearby cities, effect of, 96-98
Pollution, 98
in Production phase of game, 29
Resources Chart information, 22-24
We Love the Leader Day, 94
Work Force distribution, 82-83
Resources Chart, 22-24
  Shields Chart, 24
Resource Seed, 313
Restless Tribes Barbarian activity, 44
Revolt, Incite A, 303, 308-309
Reynolds, Brian, 2, 219
Riflemen, 237, 264-265
  Metallurgy and, 156
Riot Factor, 88
  modifying factor based on number of cities, 319
Rivers, 60-61
  movement along, 12, 19
  Trade and, 116
Road Movement Modifier, 316
Roads
  corruption and waste, reduction of, 106
  resource production and, 81
  Terrain and, 52
  Trade income and, 116
Robotics, 125, 167
Rocketry, 125, 167-168
Roving Bands Barbarian activity, 44
Rows in Food Storage Box feature, 41
Rows in Shield Box feature, 41
Rules of game, modification of, 315-323
RULES.TXT file, 314-315

S

Sabotage, Industrial, 303, 306
SAM Missile Battery, 9, 184, 200
Sanitation, 126, 168. *See also* Sewer Systems
  Invention and, 178
Saving maps, 312
Science, 51, 114-119. *See also* Civilization
    Advances; Research
  Fundamentalism and, 91, 321-322
  government affecting, 11, 118-119
  Improvements and, 117, 118

Computer Game Books

1942: The Pacific Air War—The Official Strategy Guide	$19.95
The 11th Hour: The Official Strategy Guide	$19.95
The 7th Guest: The Official Strategy Guide	$19.95
Aces Over Europe: The Official Strategy Guide	$19.95
Across the Rhine: The Official Strategy Guide	$19.95
Alone in the Dark 3: The Official Strategy Guide	$19.95
Armored Fist: The Official Strategy Guide	$19.95
Ascendancy: The Official Strategy Guide	$19.95
Buried in Time: The Journeyman Project 2—The Official Strategy Guide	$19.95
CD-ROM Games Secrets, Volume 1	$19.95
Caesar II: The Official Strategy Guide	$19.95
Celtic Tales: Balor of the Evil Eye—The Official Strategy Guide	$19.95
Cyberia: The Official Strategy Guide	$19.95
Computer Adventure Games Secrets	$19.95
Dark Seed II: The Official Strategy Guide	$19.95
Descent: The Official Strategy Guide	$19.95
DOOM Battlebook	$19.95
DOOM II: The Official Strategy Guide	$19.95
Dracula Unleashed: The Official Strategy Guide & Novel	$19.95
Dragon Lore: The Official Strategy Guide	$19.95
Dungeon Master II: The Legend of Skullkeep—The Official Strategy Guide	$19.95
Fleet Defender: The Official Strategy Guide	$19.95
Frankenstein: Through the Eyes of the Monster—The Official Strategy Guide	$19.95
Front Page Sports Football Pro '95: The Official Playbook	$19.95
Fury3: The Official Strategy Guide	$19.95
Hell: A Cyberpunk Thriller—The Official Strategy Guide	$19.95
Heretic: The Official Strategy Guide	$19.95
I Have No Mouth, and I Must Scream: The Official Strategy Guide	$19.95
In The 1st Degree: The Official Strategy Guide	$19.95
Kingdom: The Far Reaches—The Official Strategy Guide	$14.95
King's Quest VII: The Unauthorized Strategy Guide	$19.95
The Legend of Kyrandia: The Official Strategy Guide	$19.95
Lords of Midnight: The Official Strategy Guide	$19.95
Machiavelli the Prince: Official Secrets & Solutions	$12.95
Marathon: The Official Strategy Guide	$19.95
Master of Orion: The Official Strategy Guide	$19.95
Master of Magic: The Official Strategy Guide	$19.95
Microsoft Arcade: The Official Strategy Guide	$12.95
Microsoft Flight Simulator 5.1: The Official Strategy Guide	$19.95
Microsoft Golf: The Official Strategy Guide	$19.95
Microsoft Space Simulator: The Official Strategy Guide	$19.95
Might and Magic Compendium: The Authorized Strategy Guide for Games I, II, III, and IV	$19.95
Myst: The Official Strategy Guide	$19.95
Online Games: In-Depth Strategies and Secrets	$19.95
Oregon Trail II: The Official Strategy Guide	$19.95
The Pagemaster: Official CD-ROM Strategy Guide	$14.95
Panzer General: The Official Strategy Guide	$19.95
Perfect General II: The Official Strategy Guide	$19.95
Prince of Persia: The Official Strategy Guide	$19.95
Prisoner of Ice: The Official Strategy Guide	$19.95
Rebel Assault: The Official Insider's Guide	$19.95
The Residents: Bad Day on the Midway— The Official Strategy Guide	$19.95
Return to Zork Adventurer's Guide	$14.95
Romance of the Three Kingdoms IV: Wall of Fire—The Official Strategy Guide	$19.95
Shadow of the Comet: The Official Strategy Guide	$19.95
Shannara: The Official Strategy Guide	$19.95
Sid Meier's Civilization, or Rome on 640K a Day	$19.95
Sid Meier's Colonization: The Official Strategy Guide	$19.95
SimCity 2000: Power, Politics, and Planning	$19.95
SimEarth: The Official Strategy Guide	$19.95
SimFarm Almanac: The Official Guide to SimFarm	$19.95

SimLife: The Official Strategy Guide	$19.95
SimTower: The Official Strategy Guide	$19.95
Stonekeep: The Official Strategy Guide	$19.95
SubWar 2050: The Official Strategy Guide	$19.95
Terry Pratchett's Discworld: The Official Strategy Guide	$19.95
TIE Fighter: The Official Strategy Guide	$19.95
TIE Fighter: Defender of the Empire—Official Secrets & Solutions	$12.95
Thunderscape: The Official Strategy Guide	$19.95
Ultima: The Avatar Adventures	$19.95
Ultima VII and Underworld: More Avatar Adventures	$19.95
Under a Killing Moon: The Official Strategy Guide	$19.95
WarCraft: Orcs & Humans Official Secrets & Solutions	$9.95
Warlords II Deluxe: The Official Strategy Guide	$19.95
Werewolf Vs. Commanche: The Official Strategy Guide	$19.95
Wing Commander I, II, and III: The Ultimate Strategy Guide	$19.95
X-COM Terror From The Deep: The Official Strategy Guide	$19.95
X-COM UFO Defense: The Official Strategy Guide	$19.95
X-Wing: Collector's CD-ROM—The Official Strategy Guide	$19.95

Video Game Books

3DO Game Guide	$16.95
Battle Arena Toshinden Game Secrets: The Unauthorized Edition	$12.95
Behind the Scenes at Sega: The Making of a Video Game	$14.95
Boogerman Official Game Secrets	$12.95
Breath of Fire Authorized Game Secrets	$14.95
Complete Final Fantasy III Forbidden Game Secrets	$14.95
Donkey Kong Country Game Secrets the Unauthorized Edition	$9.95
EA SPORTS Official Power Play Guide	$12.95
Earthworm Jim Official Game Secrets	$12.95
Earthworm Jim 2 Official Game Secrets	$14.95
GEX: The Official Power Play Guide	$14.95
Killer Instinct Game Secrets: The Unauthorized Edition	$9.95
The Legend of Zelda: A Link to the Past—Game Secrets	$12.95
Lord of the Rings Official Game Secrets	$12.95
Maximum Carnage Official Game Secrets	$9.95
Mega Man X Official Game Secrets	$14.95
Mortal Kombat II Official Power Play Guide	$9.95
NBA JAM: The Official Power Play Guide	$12.95
GamePro Presents: Nintendo Games Secrets Greatest Tips	$11.95
Nintendo Games Secrets, Volumes 1, 2, 3, and 4	$11.95 each
Ogre Battle: The March of the Black Queen—The Official Power Play Guide	$14.95
Parent's Guide to Video Games	$12.95
Secret of Evermore: Authorized Power Play Guide	$12.95
Secret of Mana Official Game Secrets	$14.95
Sega CD Official Game Secrets	$12.95
GamePro Presents: Sega Genesis Games Secrets Greatest Tips, Second Edition	$12.95
Official Sega Genesis Power Tips Book, Volumes 2, and 3	$14.95 each
Sega Genesis Secrets, Volume 4	$12.95
Sega Genesis and Sega CD Secrets, Volume 5	$12.95
Sega Genesis Secrets, Volume 6	$12.95
Sonic 3 Official Play Guide	$12.95
Super Empire Strikes Back Official Game Secrets	$12.95
Super Mario World Game Secrets	$12.95
Super Metroid Unauthorized Game Secrets	$14.95
Super NES Games Secrets, Volumes 2, and 3	$11.95 each
Super NES Games Secrets, Volumes 4 and 5	$12.95 each
GamePro Presents: Super NES Games Secrets Greatest Tips	$11.95
Super NES Games Unauthorized Power Tips Guide, Volumes 1 and 2	$14.95 each
Super Star Wars Official Game Secrets	$12.95
Urban Strike Official Power Play Guide, with Desert Strike & Jungle Strike	$12.95

TO ORDER BOOKS

Please send me the following items:

Quantity	Title	Unit Price	Total
_____	_____	$_____	$_____
_____	_____	$_____	$_____
_____	_____	$_____	$_____
_____	_____	$_____	$_____
_____	_____	$_____	$_____
_____	_____	$_____	$_____
		Subtotal	$_____
		7.25% Sales Tax (CA only)	$_____
		8.25% Sales Tax (TN only)	$_____
		5.0% Sales Tax (MD only)	$_____
		7.0% G.S.T. Canadian Orders	$_____
		Shipping and Handling*	$_____
		TOTAL ORDER	$_____

*$4.00 shipping and handling charge for the first book, and $1.00 for each additional book.

By telephone: With Visa or MC, call 1-916-632-4400. Mon.–Fri. 9–4 PST. **By mail:** Just fill out the information below and send with your remittance to:

PRIMA PUBLISHING
P.O. Box 1260BK
Rocklin, CA 95677-1260

Satisfaction unconditionally guaranteed

Name_____

Address_____

City_____ State_____ Zip_____

Visa /MC#_____Exp._____

Signature_____

UP IN THE HEAVENS, ALL HELL'S ABOUT TO BREAK LOOSE.

From the creators of Master of Orion,™ **Computer Gaming World's** 1994 Premier Award winner, comes the sequel you've been waiting for.

Banished from Orion, a xenophobic race lurks in the darkness. You prayed they would never return. But now, in the deepest reaches of outer space they plan their revenge. Introducing MASTER OF ORION™ II. Discover new technology. Command detailed tactical combat. Come face to face with new alien creatures. Use the multi-player feature to challenge friends over a local area network, go head-to-head via modem, or compete in a hot seat game. Whatever you do, lead your team cautiously. Because you must master the ultimate evil before it masters you.

MASTER OF ORION II
BATTLE AT ANTARES™

MICRO PROSE

For IBM®-PC & Compatibles on CD-ROM.   1-800-879-PLAY.   http://www.microprose.com